BRUTAL
BARGAIN

Hot Alphas. Smart Women. Sexy Stories.

BRUTAL BARGAIN

NEW YORK TIMES BESTSELLING AUTHOR
LAURELIN PAIGE

ALSO BY LAURELIN PAIGE

WONDERING WHAT TO READ NEXT? I CAN HELP!

Visit www.laurelinpaige.com for content warnings and a more detailed reading order.

Brutal Billionaires

Brutal Billionaire - a standalone (Holt Sebastian)

Dirty Filthy Billionaire - a novella (Steele Sebastian)

Brutal Secret - a standalone (Reid Sebastian)

Brutal Arrangement - a standalone (Alex Sebastian)

Brutal Bargain - a standalone (Ax Morgan)

Brutal Bastard - a standalone (Hunter Sebastian)

The Dirty Universe

Dirty Duet (Donovan Kincaid)

Dirty Filthy Rich Men | Dirty Filthy Rich Love

Kincaid

Dirty Games Duet (Weston King)

Dirty Sexy Player | Dirty Sexy Games

Dirty Sweet Duet (Dylan Locke)

Sweet Liar | Sweet Fate

(Nate Sinclair) Dirty Filthy Fix (a spinoff novella)

Dirty Wild Trilogy (Cade Warren)

Wild Rebel | Wild War | Wild Heart

Men in Charge

Man in Charge

Man for Me (a spinoff novella)

The Fixed Universe

Fixed Series (Hudson & Alayna)

Fixed on You | Found in You | Forever with You | Hudson | Fixed Forever

Found Duet (Gwen & JC) Free Me | Find Me

(Chandler & Genevieve) Chandler (a spinoff novel)

(Norma & Boyd) Falling Under You (a spinoff novella)

(Nate & Trish) Dirty Filthy Fix (a spinoff novella)

Slay Series (Celia & Edward)

Rivalry | Ruin | Revenge | Rising

(Gwen & JC) The Open Door (a spinoff novella)

(Camilla & Hendrix) Slash (a spinoff novella)

First and Last

First Touch | Last Kiss

Be sure to **sign up for my newsletter** where you'll receive **a FREE book every month** from bestselling authors, only available to my subscribers, as well as up-to-date information on my latest releases.

PRO TIP: Add laurelin@laurelinpaige.com to your contacts before signing up to be sure the list comes right to your inbox.

DID YOU KNOW...
This book is available in both paperback and audiobook editions at all major online retailers! Links are on my website.
If you'd like to order a signed paperback, my online store is open several times a year here.

I am an only child, but my mother came from a big family like the Sebastians. All those members can be confusing.

To help sort that out, you can find a family tree on my website.

*For every girl who fears that love
only exists in romance books.*

*And for our smut peddlers—ahem, I mean bookstore owners.
Thank you for doing the Lord's work.*

PROLOGUE
ADLY

Eighteen months ago

The thing I hate most about Axel Morgan is his mouth.

Which is saying something, because I hate so much about the thirty-nine-year-old pompous asshat (I feel uniquely qualified to call him such because I've known him for all of my life, since our fathers are friends).

He used to taunt me at family gatherings—pull on my braids and hide my stuff-stuffs and do his damnedest to make me cry. And he was six years older than me. I mean, I was a precocious kid who tried to tag along with the teens, but what kind of thirteen-year-old douchebag torments a seven-year-old for fun?

The asshat kind, that's who.

Even back then, his mouth was the worst of him, calling me names like "spoiled doll" and "little girl" and "princess." Words that maybe shouldn't have hit so hard, but the world we live in is full of glass ceilings and boundaries and barriers for the "fairer sex"—an ironic term for the gender that is decidedly always getting the short end of the stick—and Ax very cruelly liked to remind me of the fact.

Still does, actually.

Then he got older and perfected a seductive curl of his lips. The corners tug up so unpredictably that it can be extremely disarming when it happens. Along with his perfectly chiseled jaw, he hides that mouth behind the scruff he's maintained since he could grow facial hair, it's impossible to tell if it's not really a sneer. If he's charming his audience or mocking them.

It's frustratingly alluring.

Not to me, obviously, but I wouldn't be surprised to find he has a god tier panty collection considering how many women have fallen prey to that wicked mouth of his.

And that's just counting the ones that I know about.

The most tragic thing about that mouth of his, though, is how goddamn full and inviting it is. It should be a criminal offense to have lips that belong to the hero of a romance novel and a personality that's so...Ax. They're the kind of lips that can be distracting at the most inopportune times, like during exec meetings when he's rattling off the new season's programming lineup that will inevitably lead to having to fire someone (or someones), or a reshuffling of staff that will have to be dealt with by HR.

That's me—I'm HR.

Or when we're at a work retreat and he's trading spars

with the CEO of the news company we work for, who just so happens to be my brother, which means that when I step in to mediate, I'm accused of nepotism.

Or when Ax and I both happen to be at my cousin's night club, and I'm with a boring man who probably only wants me for my hundred-million-dollar trust fund, but I should give him a fair shot so I have to pretend I'm not curious about Ax at the bar trying to pick up some girl who looks way too young to have even been let in the door.

Or when he's smirking like he has something on me or is about to one-up me. Kind of like the smirk he's giving right now when—after I snuck out of the corporate Christmas party to raid the top-shelf booze my brother keeps hidden in his office, despite already being buzzed from champagne—I put my stolen code into the keypad, open the door, and find Ax sitting in the moonlight with his feet kicked up on Holt's desk, drinking straight from a bottle of Macallan 30-year double cask scotch.

A *five-thousand-dollar* bottle of scotch.

He holds it up when he sees me standing in the door-frame. "Looking for this?"

"Not now that it has your dirty lips all over it." Just one more reason to hate that stupid mouth.

"Afraid I have cooties?" He gives me that smile/sneer, and I unwittingly scowl.

"You know Holt will have your job if he catches you in his office."

"You gonna run and tell him?"

I consider it for all of five seconds. Truth is that Holt won't do shit. Ax's job is protected by his father, who's on the board, and you'll never hear me say it, but Ax is actually good at what he does. It would take a pretty major infraction for him to get canned.

Pretty much the same boat I'm in, except that, unlike me, that extra appendage between his legs means he's not stuck in Human Resources. The board is stuffed with traditionalist men who have capital "I" Ideas about where women belong, and it's not in any positions of real power.

The few times I've dared challenge my father about it, he's merely said, *Be glad we let you have a job at all.*

Needless to say, Sebastian News Corp is not the most female-friendly environment.

When I don't move to "run and tell" my brother, Ax seems to take it as a win. His sneer turns into a grin as he holds the bottle out in my direction. "You're only punishing yourself."

With a roll of my eyes, I let the door shut behind me and cross the room with quick strides. "Give me that."

I swipe the bottle from his hands and make a show of rubbing off his "germs" before taking a swig.

Damn, my brother has good taste.

The liquid is smooth and hot down my throat. A brief moment of would-be bliss if it weren't poisoned by the presence of the asshat.

"How did you get in here anyway?" I ask. "There's no way Holt gave you the code."

He didn't give the code to me either.

But I'm close to Holt. We share trauma, and I know a good deal of his deep dark secrets. Holt is smart and strategic as fuck, but his office password wasn't too hard to crack once I thought about it a bit. Pretty astute for Ax to just guess.

"Hmm," he says, watching me take another swallow. "For me to know and you to find out, I suppose."

"Hmm," I say, mimicking him. "Are you twelve?"

"Thirteen next week." The moonlight catches on the white of his teeth, and even in the mostly dark room, that mouth of his is captivating.

So irritating.

I shove his feet off the desk in annoyance. "Get out of Holt's chair."

"Aw. Wook at the wittle sister wooking out for her big brover." Even though he mocks me with a little kid voice, he relinquishes the seat. "Worried I'll somehow take the position from him just by sitting behind his desk?"

"More concerned you'll leave fleas. Seriously. I don't trust what goes on in those pants of yours." I realize what I've walked into as soon as the words are out.

He tugs suggestively at his belt. "Now Adly, if you're really interested, I'm happy to give—"

"Fuck off, and find someone who cares. Micro-peen is not on my holiday bingo card."

He bends his six-foot frame—not too far since I'm a good five eight—positioning his mouth by my ear. "Macro, is the word you're looking for. But don't worry, baby. It only hurts the first time."

Goosebumps run down my arms, and my nipples bead.

The fan must be on or something. Weird for the middle of December, but I refuse to entertain any other possible explanation.

"You wish. You couldn't find your way into a vagina if you had GPS tracking."

He guffaws, snatching the bottle from my grasp, and

circles around the desk to sit on the arm of the sofa. "I'm so good with pussies, they start purring as soon as I enter the room."

I glance toward my lady parts before looking back at him. "I assure you, this pussy isn't purring."

I mean, said lady parts might have tingled a bit when he mentioned the word, but only because I've been drinking, and it's been a minute since they've had interest from anyone other than me, so it doesn't take much to catch their attention.

"That's because your vagina is full of cobwebs. The 'out of order' sign has been there so long, it's a permanent fixture."

The accuracy of his statements is vexing, but I vow not to let it show. "You seem awfully preoccupied with the status of my cooter, Ax Morgan."

"What can I say? I'm not immune to the thrill of a first-rate challenge."

I toss my brown hair back and laugh outright. "To dream the impossible dream."

He winks like he's about to hand someone his beer...er, scotch. "I'm just saying—I happen to be quite skilled in a clean-out."

I shiver.

No, no. It's a shudder. Definitely a shudder. "Delighted to hear that the sex workers you hire know how to put on a convincing show. Nice to know you can still pay for value."

"Whatever you need to believe, darling." He throws back the scotch, and I'm annoyed all over again that he's drinking straight from the bottle.

"For the love of anything you find holy, there's a

tumbler on the cart. Could you please treat that liquor with respect?" I click a button on the desk remote, turning on the drop pendant over the mini bar, which lights the room well enough that now I can see the rims of brown in Ax's dark eyes.

"Ah, but I am respecting. A thirty-year-old whiskey like this should be savored in its original oak cask. It would be disrespectful to drink it any other way."

Unfortunately, I think I remember hearing that before. *Goddammit.*

I hate it when he's right. "Thank you for the mansplaining. I'm sure Holt will appreciate the addition of your saliva to his prized liquor when he drinks out of that bottle next."

"You assume there will be any scotch left when we're through."

Well, touché.

Because as unsatisfying as the idea of drinking with Ax is, I have zero intention of going back down to the company party. There was a limbo game starting when I left, and I try not to bend in any form....except during yoga and sex.

I suppose I could always go home.

Usually, the promise of a quiet apartment and a new book on my kindle would have me calling my driver for a pickup as soon as I'd put in a party appearance.

But this dumbass, yours truly, chose tonight's event to poke at my father about the possibility of adding "Vice President" to my Chief Human Resource Officer title. It was a long shot, but since Daddy's recent heart attack forced him to relinquish his CEO position to Holt, I thought he might consider securing more of the top roles at the company with the rest of his children.

To say I was wrong was an understatement.

Let's just say Daddy has not been visited by any Christmas spirits inspiring him to change his ways. Or if he has, like a typical hard-headed Sebastian, he told that spirit to fuck directly off.

Hence what led me to search for spirits of a different kind.

...and just my luck, Ax Morgan had to beat me to the punch.

It's fine. I'm committed to not leaving the Sebastian Center tonight until I'm thoroughly plastered, and if I have to suffer in Ax's company whilst I get to that state, I'm sure I'll soon be too drunk to care.

"Then if we're drinking together, could you stop hogging the damn thing and pass it over?"

He gets up and takes the couple steps to hand the bottle to me over the desk, since I'm still standing behind it.

My fingers brush his when I take it from him, and I jolt when a shock of electricity passes between us. "You did that on purpose."

"Now who's twelve." He watches me while I take a swallow, and when he opens his mouth to speak, I'm sure he's about to say something about me forgetting to wipe off the rim first. "You're not going to sit?"

Surprised he missed an opportunity to tease me, it takes a second to realize he's suggesting I take the desk chair.

I stare at the empty spot. Holt's throne, so to say. He hasn't had the top position long enough to feel like this is *his* office—all my life this space belonged to my father, and I was never allowed anywhere near the desk then.

Then when Holt took over, he got all new furniture,

including this chair. I don't think I've been in this space since then without him sitting in it, and I can't deny the pull to try it out.

But the barriers that keep me from ever being able to occupy the seat for real feel all too present. "I'm not sitting anywhere you put your smelly ass."

It's actually a very tight ass, not that I've looked or anything.

"Suit yourself." He says it like he understands what's going through my head. Like he knows what it would mean for me to be behind that desk.

More likely I'm tipsy enough to interpret his tone as such because there's no way he really understands.

Bottle in hand, I loop around to the front of the desk wondering what it would feel like if the office actually was mine. I lean my backside against the solid mahogany, which swallows my slight frame, and imagine the dimly lit room full of men in suits, all heads turned toward me to hear what I have to say.

It's such a good fantasy, I top it off with another swallow of scotch.

"You're bogarting." He doesn't make a move to take the bottle, though. Instead, he leans back against the sofa in an aloof way that would be sexy if he were a book boyfriend.

I clutch the bottle closer. "My last name on the door, not yours." It's not like that's not true. "I think I have more right to it than you."

Ax chuckles. "God, I can't..."

He trails off, and my head snaps toward him, alert and ready to arm. "You can't...what? Picture me here? You don't think I could do this job?"

"I think a lot of balls would be busted if you had this job."

It almost sounds like a compliment.

Close enough so that it feels like permission to let my mind run wild. I set the scotch down on the desk and then hoist myself up so I'm sitting on the edge. Crossing my legs, I brace my hands on either side of me, lean forward, and….pretend. "Mr. Morgan, I'll assume that you have the fourth quarter projections ready, as well as the new lineup proposal for January?"

Man, that felt good.

Powerful. Arousing.

Ax doesn't blink a brown eye. "I put the new lineup on your desk yesterday, Ms. Sebastian. The fourth quarter projections will need some more time."

"They're already a week late," I say, getting into the role. "You think this is acceptable from the President of Programming?"

His eyes flash. "I apologize, sincerely. As you know, we're still adjusting to the change in management. The workload has increased significantly since you've taken the helm, and—"

I cut him off. "This is shaping up to sound like an over-inflated excuse."

"No ma'am. Just the facts."

"The *fact* is that I've made my wishes clear, and I'm quite unhappy with having to repeat myself. When I give you a deadline, I expect that you'll meet it. Do I need to put a woman in your job instead?" I retrieve the scotch and bring it to my mouth to hide the giggle bubbling under my fake stern tone.

Ax, on the other hand, keeps a perfectly straight, chiseled face. "I'm sure the right woman would excel in the position, but I sincerely hope that you would give me another chance before such a drastic move."

"Drastic? I don't see how holding people accountable for their responsibilities is drastic." We could stand to see a lot more of that in the corporate world, if anyone asks me, and if I was really in charge, my first act of disruption would be to make all the execs reapply for their jobs.

"You're right. It's not ridiculous to expect me to perform my job. But please...it's almost Christmas."

"Oh, God. The 'poor me' routine." I roll my eyes and take another swig from the bottle. I'm feeling the liquor everywhere now. It didn't help that I was already pretty buzzed when I arrived.

Ax pushes off the couch arm, taking a step toward me. His dark brown hair, tousled just so, frames his rugged face. In this lighting and with that imploring expression, he's wickedly handsome. "Please, Ms. Sebastian. I'll do anything."

Right. As if Ax Morgan would ever beg, let alone beg a female superior. He's not even respectful to Holt.

But it's sort of exciting to believe that he might. That anyone might react to my authority by falling all over themselves to make me happy. The thought makes me giddy, and it takes everything in me not to laugh as I lift my leg off the chair and press the heel of my shoe into his chest. "Anything?"

"Anything. Just name it." His eyes meet mine, and my breath catches to find his expression so earnest.

It shakes my game. "Uh...kiss my foot," I say, attempting to regain control in this game.

I'm not sure what I think he'll do with that, but I'm definitely not expecting him to slip off my heel and kiss the tip of my holiday-red painted big toe. Tingles run up my leg. "Oh."

"Where else should I kiss you?"

My pulse skitters, and a giggle escapes. "My ass." I try to pull my foot away, but he keeps a firm grip.

"Would you like that with tongue?" His voice is deep. Gravelly.

It gives me butterflies, but instead of feeling them in my belly, they flutter lower—in my pussy region—and I'm starting to feel like Ax is teasing me again. Trying to prove I could never actually have control over a man. Over him.

But it's like a game of chicken—I can't be the one to end it now. "If you think it's their ass that a woman wants—"

He cuts me off, "Oh, I know where a woman wants my tongue." His fingers move up my calf, and he places his lips on the inside of my ankle, his eyes never leaving mine. "Though I should add, if you don't like your ass kissed, it's because it's never been kissed by the right man."

"And that would be you?" I don't know why my voice pitches higher.

"Best man for the job." He kisses the middle of my shin. "*Only* man for the job." Another kiss on the inside of my knee.

He's still playing pretend.

And I'm suddenly very aware that he will pretend this all the way to...well, all the way. If I wanted him to.

Do I want to?

His lips are on the top of my thigh before I've come to a conclusion. "I really believe I could make it up to you, Ms. Sebastian. If you let me try."

The intoxicating thing about pretend is how real it can feel. And this little game I'm playing with Ax right now is the only way I'll ever have this kind of control over a man, real or pretend. As long as my father's generation has control of the board, I won't be given any position of real authority at this company.

And I want it.

And I'm drunk.

And Ax is an asshat, but he's not really *Ax* when we're playing pretend.

And his mouth—*that mouth*—is hot on the inside of my bare thigh. Hotter, somehow, when he slides my dress up to my belly, spreads my legs apart, and presses his lips over the crotch panel of my thong, applying just enough pressure to send my nervous system into overdrive.

Oh, fuck. He does know where the clit is.

"I suppose you could attempt to make it right, Mr. Morgan," I pant. "Just this one time."

"Just this one time," he repeats before that damn mouth of his gets busy.

CHAPTER **ONE**
ADLY

Present

"This is the last time. The absolute last time."

My words sound choppy and breathless, a side effect of being bent over a pool table and railed like it's my occupation. It doesn't help that I'm minutes away from what I predict will be an especially explosive climax.

Admittedly, my statement probably lacks conviction.

"Does that mean you're finally going to make an offer, Ms. Sebastian?" While Ax is also winded, he sounds a whole lot more put together than I feel.

If that wasn't ego-shattering enough, he's just pointed out that I've dropped character. Which means he wins this match.

In the year and a half we've been fucking around like this, we've never specifically stated that this is a game or that there are rules, but it goes without saying that the goal is to get off while simultaneously acting like I didn't.

Yes, I'm aware that it's a paradoxical state of being, and yet I've become somewhat of a master, perfecting the ability to release without letting on. I'm like the opposite of the women who fake their O—I fake a not-O. When Ax makes me come—and he always makes me come—I swallow my cries and tense my body so he doesn't see the pleasure trembling in my limbs.

While it does take some of the physical pleasure out of the climax, it's worth it to make Ax feel like these rendezvous benefit him more than me. I'm generally good at keeping up the pretense, but he's currently hitting a spot inside my pussy that I didn't know existed. A spot that makes me see the entire universe, not just stars. How am I supposed to remember that I walked into this apartment today pretending to be shopping for real estate when my mind has gone to pure mush?

Ax, on the other hand, never drops character. "If you close this week and in cash, I think I can get the table included in the price."

That had been what I'd been bargaining for when I'd dropped my panties. *I won't make an offer if the pool table isn't part of the deal,* I'd said.

It's custom-made. I don't think the owner will part with it. Frankly, I don't feel comfortable asking.

I'm sure there's something I could throw in that would change your mind…

Thirty minutes later, I'm biting my tongue, trying to keep quiet, while Ax pummels into me from behind.

"You think you can convince your client to part with it?" I pace my words so they don't sound so belabored.

"I think that—" He interrupts himself to instruct me. "Close your legs together."

I do as he says, tightening my pussy around him. His next thrusts are slower—jab, pause, jab, pause. Jab—and then he's grunting out a "Fuck" as he climaxes.

Not for the first time, his release triggers my own. It's the best way to hide my O because he's too distracted to notice me burying my face in my arm, gnawing at the material of my blouse sleeve while pleasure ripples through my nervous system.

I've seriously become so good at simultaneous orgasm, I should teach classes. Sure, I might not be using the technique the way most people might, but I'm a motherfucking pro.

It's fucked up. I know. I'm aware.

Why else would I be saying this needs to end?

As soon as I can breathe without gasping, I shove my elbow back into Ax's side and force him off of me before standing and straightening my skirt. "I've changed my mind about the pool table. It didn't bring me as much...joy as I'd assumed it would."

Ax runs a hand through his dark hair—so dark it's practically black—and tries to catch his breath. His sweats are still down around his ankles, pussy juice dripping from the tip of his condom, and he looks so wrecked that I can't help but think maybe I actually was the winner of the round.

"You know, joy is in the eye of the beholder, Ms. Sebastian."

"Sounds like something someone says when they routinely don't provide joy." Considering how much I needed this orgasm today, and how much I enjoyed it, I feel a little guilty about the dig.

Not that guilty, though.

"Shame. You're the only customer who ever complains."

For whatever reason, I prickle at the mention of other "customers." It's not like I don't know that Ax is a horndog. That he's got a different woman in his bed every night. It's not like I have any right to fuss over that. We never said this was an exclusive thing. We never said this was a thing at all. Except for when it's happening, we try to pretend it doesn't.

So very fucked up.

This has to be the last time.

I pick up my purse from where I dropped it on the floor and grab my phone so I can use the camera as a mirror to check my lipstick. I don't expect it to be too smeared—we never kiss, but after muffling my mouth as much as I did, I'm not surprised to see I need to freshen my gloss.

In my periphery, I watch Ax remove the condom, tie it off, and pull up his pants. "Does that mean you aren't interested in the apartment? I could ask my client to show you around personally, if that would help you reevaluate the assets of the space."

He's setting up the next roleplay. This is often how we do it—on the heels of the last. Later this week, he'll call me up and say he's the client and ask if he could help assuage any of my doubts about the place.

There must be something truly wrong with me because I'm two minutes post-orgasm, and my pussy is already fluttering in anticipation of a next time.

No, no, no, pussycat. We have to be strong.

I bring my phone down so I can level a stare in his direction. "I meant what I said, Mr. Morgan."

"About this being the last time you see the place?" He chuckles. "Sure, you did."

Okay, I might have said it before—or several times before—but I mean it this time. If all goes as planned, soon enough I'll be too busy for this situationship of ours. Too busy to even think of Ax Morgan, and since we won't be sharing the same workspace, I doubt he'll ever cross my mind again.

I'm hoping, anyway.

This time my pussy twitches in disappointment.

I'll buy you a new vibrator. You'll be fine.

"I know you were looking forward to that commission." I put my phone and gloss away and pull the strap of my purse onto my shoulder, all the while realizing that if I really wanted to get through to him, I wouldn't still be playing this customer-in-search-of-an-apartment character.

When I turn to look at him again, I catch him throwing away the condom in the trash can hidden in the shelving.

"Hey, you can't put that there!" I rush over to him before he can shut the compartment door and search in the waste for the discarded rubber.

"Where am I supposed to put it? The desk drawer?" He doesn't wait for me to answer. "Are you fucking kidding me right now? Do you know how many condoms are disposed of in this apartment?"

I'm sure it's a lot considering who owns the place—my half-cousin who is also my half-brother and also Ax's best friend. For a myriad of reasons—many having to do with the complicated half-cousin/half-sibling thing, which we tend to simplify by referring to each other as the former— Hunter and I do not get along. Even if we were as close as a pair of Reese's peanut butter cups, I wouldn't want Hunter to know about this thing with Ax.

I don't want *anyone* to know about this thing with Ax.

So far, no one does, except Riah Watson, a pop star who's dating my cousin Alex. I trust her since she seems to have her own messy situationship she's been dealing with, but that's neither here nor there. The point is, there can be no proof that Ax and I have *ever* happened, let alone that we've happened here.

I pull the evidence out and hold it up and away from me like it's going to bite me. "Are you telling me you've thrown our condoms away here before?"

Because the stupid thing is that this isn't even the first time we've banged in Hunter's place. I don't pretend to understand their relationship, but apparently he lets Ax have free rein of the apartment, and I'll be honest—there is a bit of a kinky thrill involved when we do the deed in places we shouldn't be doing it. So sometimes when Ax texts me with the start of a new scenario, I don't ask questions. I just come.

Literally and cliterally.

Not that I'd ever let on to him.

Ax's expression says all I need to know.

With a groan, I scan the library for a box of tissues. Then I wrap the dripping condom up and stuff it in my purse to dispose of later. "If you want something done, you have to do it yourself."

"I hope you're taking that advice and diddling that doodad of yours on your own. Since this encounter was so unfulfilling and all." Ax says it like he knows I've been faking it—or faking not it—but he always acts like he has something on me, and I've rarely seen it turn out to be the case.

"How about you worry about your own doodad, and leave mine to the experts." My eyes catch the pair of panties dangling from the desk lamp.

My pair of panties.

They were discarded rather hastily earlier when I was bargaining with my "realtor."

I cross to grab them, only to have them instantly yanked out of my hands.

"You know the drill. These are mine to deal with." Ax shoves them into the pocket of his sweats.

For half a beat, I consider arguing with him about it, but that would be a major change in precedent. When he'd said he was keeping them that first night in Holt's office—when it was still Holt's office and not once again my father's—I was grateful to have Ax deal with what I considered evidence of the crime.

My mistake was telling him so.

After that, he's taken them every time. It's lost me several really stellar pieces of lingerie. Thankfully, I'm a Sebastian and can afford an unlimited line of credit at La Perla. I wish I could say I haven't thought about what becomes of them after Ax takes ownership, but of course I have. I've decided he either actually disposes of them like he pretends he's going to, or he adds them to a giant collection of women's underwear he keeps so he can count his conquests any time he gets the urge.

My bet's on the latter.

Probably keeps them in a safe. What else would Ax Morgan consider a prized possession?

If I ever find myself in his bedroom, I might get curious enough to look for them.

Except I have no plans of ever being in his bedroom. And after I get the fuck out of Sebastian News Corp, I'll have no reason to bump into Ax, and this fooling around will come to an end, once and for all.

In the end, I decide it isn't worth the battle. "Just...make sure you don't leave them anywhere they can be found."

Ax smirks. "Is there a reason your...*cousin* would be able to identify these panties as yours?"

"I think finding anyone's panties would make your client realize he's hired an unprofessional tool to sell his property." *Now who's maintained character?*

"Ah, looking out for me. Who knew you cared?" He checks his phone, whether looking at the time or a text, I'm not sure, and I tell myself I don't care. "Speaking of clients, I have another showing lined up, so if you don't want this to turn into a threesome, you might want to make your exit right about now."

It's possible that's his way of saying Hunter's on his way home, but there's a good chance he actually has someone lined up for a fuck after me.

The thought makes my stomach knot.

Not because I care what Ax does with other women,

exactly. He can fuck the entire zip code if he wants. It's not my business.

And if sometimes I might long for an all-night thing instead of just a penciled-in affair—a night spent in (heaven forbid) a bed—I wouldn't choose to spend it with Ax Morgan.

"Maybe you'll have better luck with this next one," I say, already heading toward the front door. "I mean, I doubt it, but what do I know?"

I manage to throw him a smug smile over my shoulder. It disappears as soon as I'm facing front again.

This has to be the last time. The very last time.

CHAPTER
TWO
ADLY

Not twenty-four hours after my last time with Ax, I'm already itching for another last time.

I blame it on the book that kept me and my vibrator up until too-late o'clock last night. It was a mafia romance with an arranged marriage and a hero who said things like, *"Don't make me have to tie you to the headboard on the first night."*

I'm a sucker for a bully with a cinnamon roll heart. Doesn't take a psych degree to work that one out. I've been surrounded by alphaholes my entire life—my father included—all of them claiming their misogynistic words and actions were demonstrations of love. I've been groomed to find that behavior attractive. The meaner they are, the harder I fall.

Or I did, until I learned that life isn't a romance book, and what you see on the outside is what you get on the inside. If a guy's a douche, then he's a douche. There is no hidden teddy bear inside his personality who will sacrifice or protect or show vulnerability, or even just be a halfway decent human.

Now, at the ripe old age of thirty-three, I'll bang around, but I reserve my heart for fictional men only. It's saved me a lot of pain and bullshit. And led to some pretty hot one-nighters. Nights that rival the spicy scenarios I've often read about.

Though, I can't really remember the last guy I fucked around with who wasn't Ax, which is probably why he's the man who comes to mind when I'm feeling unsatisfied.

Like last night.

Which has carried over into today.

I had my toy fully charged, and I still didn't get to a happy ending before it died. Either it's karma for all the Os I've faked not getting or else my body has grown partial to the seduction techniques of one Mr. Morgan.

Excuse me while I vomit in my mouth.

Fortunately, though it's a Saturday, I have business to conduct. Business that I'm not only interested in, but excited about, and while that fact isn't entertaining to the girl boss between my legs, my head is the one in charge of my agenda, and she is focused.

Mostly.

As I walk down the hall at SHE Network, on my way to the exec offices, I type out a text to Zuleika Amari. Mainly because I'm convinced our collective dreams are about to come true, and I want to share the moment, but also because I need to distract my fingers from texting anyone I shouldn't be thinking about at present.

> Walking into Holt's office to discuss our official offer!

My phone buzzes immediately with Zully's response, reminding me to put it on silent before my meeting.

> AGHH! I'm freaking out. Tell Holt not to fuck this up, and keep me posted!

I reread her text several times, my face beaming. The mentality around wealth in my disgustingly rich family has always been *the more there is for me, the more there is for me.* I've never understood how my relatives don't see the joy of sharing with others. If we can pull off this buyout my brother and I are planning, Zully is only the first of many that I hope to share the opportunity with.

I'm still staring at my phone when Holt opens his office door to me. "What's that on your face? Are you...grinning?"

"I smile, assHolt." I heard his fiancée call him that once and now it's my brother's official name, as far as I'm concerned.

I hand him my phone so he can see the reason. So that he can remember what the real reward is for this project of ours.

He studies the screen, then furrows his brow. "Who's *He Who Shall Not Be Named*?"

"Hm?" I panic as I grab for my phone. There's a reason He Who Shall Not Be Named is saved in my contacts that way, and it's not because I'm a Harry Potter fan.

Always the teasing big brother, Holt holds my cell out of

my reach. "Apparently he thinks you might be able to help him with a bump on the top of his dick—"

"Give that to me, you fucker!"

"—and wants to know if he should make an appointment with the good doctor. Should I ask for a pic?" He's thoroughly amused.

Of all the times Ax could choose to play doctor...

I'm hiding my mortification under rage. "Give me my GD phone, Holt."

In the scuffle that follows, several emojis get accidentally pushed so that when I finally have the device back in my hand, I see that Ax has been sent a message consisting of three fire emojis, a magnifying glass, a rain cloud, a ninja, two fingers giving the peace sign, an eye, and no less than seven thumbs pointing up.

How the hell did I get lucky enough to have his text come in just as I was trying to show Holt what Zully had sent?

I literally growl, as I type and retype several messages before giving up. There's no way in hell Ax won't take this as an invitation to start sexting. Anything I try to say now will only dig myself deeper.

Deciding this is a later problem, I shove my phone into the pocket of my romper and try to put it out of my mind for the time being.

Meanwhile, Holt is planning never to let me live this down. "So you're a doctor now? Do you work out of a clinic or make house calls?"

Holt's mocking tone says he knows whatever that message was, it was of a kinky nature.

Kill me now.

He covers his hand with his heart. "Dad will be so proud."

I give him my famous death glare, which only makes him double down. "Do you focus just on male anatomy, or are all forms of genitalia in your area of specialty?"

My pocket vibrates with an incoming text, undoubtedly from Ax.

That ass will have to wait while I deal with the ass in front of me. "Are you asking because you need something checked out for yourself?" Hopefully, the thought of his little sister anywhere near his dick is enough to nip this in the bud.

Victory is accomplished when he says, "Ew," shuddering as he takes a perch on the edge of his desk. "In all seriousness…"

With a sigh of relief, I sit down in one of his guest chairs, ready to get down to business.

But then Holt frowns.

"What is it?" Shoulders tense, I brace for bad news. *Oh, please, oh please, don't say the deal is off.*

"Would that be an oral exam you conduct for that or…?"

I've never wished so hard that I was adopted.

"Fuck off, Holt, can you please forget the whole thing?" Stupid question, because I know from experience that the more riled up I get, the more interested he is in taunting me.

Sure enough…

"I don't know, Ad. It seems really inconsiderate to

ignore that you obviously have a core competency in penises that has not been fully appreciated. I kind of think it's my brotherly duty to make more of our friends and family aware of this talent of yours."

I lean back, my stare challenging. "So you're saying that you want to hear all the details about your little sister's sex life? How about I start with the time—?"

Picking up the receiver on his desk phone, Holt cuts me off. "Let me just get Alex on speaker, and I can give you both the deets at the same time."

Ten points for me.

That should be the end of that.

While Holt dials our cousin, I reflexively grab for my phone. An awful habit, though I'm proud to say that most of the time I'm opening up an e-book, rather than scrolling social media.

Of course what I'm met with this time is Ax's text.

> Thank you, Doc. I appreciate your eager response. Fairly certain you won't be needing the 🔍.

It's too easy.

> We are talking about your dick, right?

> Ah. I see your previous patients have set a standard that I'm about to shatter.

I'm in the process of thinking of a stellar reply, when I hear Holt telling Alex, "She's here, but she's busy sexting at the moment. Some unknown individual. Listed in her phone as He Who Shall Not Be Named."

Alex's voice comes over the speaker. "You know, I'm pretty sure I saw her yesterday in the lobby of Hunter's building."

I pray my face isn't as red as I think it is. "For fuck's sake…"

Holt chokes out a laugh. "Are you suggesting that Adly is hooking up with our brother?"

"And I thought all the best Sebastian scandals ended with our parents' generation."

"I don't know why I ever thought I wanted to go into business with the two of you." I stand up, phone in hand, and make a big show of stomping out.

The one good thing about Holt and his brotherly taunting is that he knows when to stop. "Truce, truce. I'm done. I promise."

This will finish it, no doubt, but I remain with my back to him, my hand on the doorknob. Just to really hammer home the point that, while I'll begrudgingly accept this shit from my family, I won't tolerate it with my business partners.

"Wait, Adly, I swear. Don't go. She's leaving, Alex."

"Sorry, Adly," my cousin says over the line. "Holt's a prick. I've always known it."

I glance over my shoulder at my brother. "He's not wrong."

"He's not, and I'm done. Strictly business from here on out." He puts his hand over his heart. "Mea culpa, mea culpa."

I turn around, but don't return to my chair. "This is supposed to be a female-first environment, remember? I will not allow a boys' club culture if I'm going to be in charge."

"Understood," Alex says.

"And respected," Holt adds, sincerely. "Thank you for reminding me of the bar we want to set."

"Anytime." I'm smug as I walk back to my chair, and not because I won another round.

Well, not *just* because I won another round.

Even though this investing in SHE was Holt's idea, it's become everything to me. It's like one of those romance storylines where he fell first and she fell harder. This is my baby. I want it more. I need it.

The plan evolved when Holt came to work for the small women-focused news network after he left SNC. He was acting in an advisory capacity and it occurred to him that a company that promoted women should be owned and run by a woman. Unfortunately, the current owner—Bob Peterson—is a jerkface that will only sell to a team led by men.

Holt could have let the matter go or found some other men to invest with, but I guess falling in love ushered in my brother's feminist ally era because a couple of months ago, the same day he proposed to his fiancée, Brystin, he suggested we pool our resources and buy it together. He'll be the face of the deal, and after the sale goes through, I'll take over as CEO.

Instantly, I saw the opportunity for what it is—my escape plan. A chance to spread my wings and make an impact and really lead. At a place where I will not only have a voice, but *be* the voice.

I said yes faster than my father's ever told me no, which is pretty damn speedy.

We began putting the deal together immediately. Pretty soon, we discovered that Holt's abundant trust fund wasn't quite enough collateral for the loan we needed for a complete buyout. I'm still three years away from inheriting mine—unless I get married, because as progressive as my Grandpa Irving has become over his lifetime, he still had a traditionalist mindset when he set up the funds for us—so when we found out our cousin Alex was looking to invest his recently inherited wealth, Holt thought we should bring him in on the deal. He was a branding specialist for another Sebastian-owned company, and has a lot to offer.

I was a little leery, only because one Sebastian male is already a lot of alpha to contend with, let alone two. But both Holt and Alex are pretty busy with other projects (and their girlfriends) and since I don't quite have the experience needed for a leadership role—thank you, Dad, for keeping me from learning what the boys have—I could really use their knowledge and guidance.

Better believe I made them swear fealty on their knees as well as on paper.

Well, Holt was on his knees, anyway. Alex only officially joined yesterday morning, and I haven't seen him since he left to go on tour with his pop star situationship, but when he's back, I'll expect the same promises from him.

And while the teasing about my sex life is minor as far as harassment can go, I am so very dedicated to the vision of creating a work environment that pays, promotes, and protects women. Alex and Holt are good men, but they have built their careers in corporations that were steeped in misogyny and prioritized men. They have a few lessons to learn, a lot of bad habits to break, and new mindsets to adopt, but I'll get them there.

The endless possibilities of what we can achieve here keep me up nights, even after I've stayed up too late lost in a good book. One of the very first programming changes I want to make is adding a style segment hosted by Zully. She's been a makeup artist for well over a decade, with a lot of a time working on news sets, so she has firsthand knowledge of the environment. On top of that, she has personality, charm, smarts, and a finger on the pulse of what's hot. The male-dominated executive team at SNC would never see the value in covering style in the news, but yet they whine all day long about losing so many viewers to the likes of YouTube and TikTok. People aren't just going to those platforms for entertainment—they're looking for info, too. Isn't that what the news is supposed to deliver?

That's the sort of stuff SHE is already exploring, and when I'm in charge, we'll go balls to the walls with that type of programming.

Or boobs to the tubes?

I really don't think that's what *balls* means in that idiom, but I'm serious about eliminating the prevalence of maleness in the industry, so I'm going with it.

So serious that I don't need the distraction of stupid boys with big dicks—not that I'll ever admit to Ax that he's packing—and so I leave his message on read and pocket my phone before returning to my original seat.

Then, with my dream clear in my head and the men put in their place, I get to business. "Where are we on putting in our official offer with Bob? Now that Alex is on board, we should have no problem with the loan approval, right?"

"Well...about that." Holt moves to the other side of his desk, sits down, clicks a few buttons on his keyboard, and then turns his computer screen toward me. "If you check the email I just forwarded you, Alex, you'll see what we're looking at."

Nervous, I sit forward and quickly scan the bank document. When my eyes land on the amount we've requested and the word *approved*, I literally gasp. "We did it. We're approved!"

"These look like the terms we wanted," Alex says with more tempered enthusiasm.

"They are. I'm very pleased with the rate we locked." Holt's tone suggests he's holding something back.

I'm sure he's living for the drama, but I can't take it. "What aren't you saying? I feel like I'm being edged."

Holt cringes, probably because he's been forced to think about his sister in sex terms once again, and not because I've already broken the rule I just set.

Alex is the one who addresses the latter. "I thought we were going to maintain professionalism from this point on."

Men *can* learn!

But I'm too interested in Holt's response to give Alex credit, so I cut him off with a "shh" sound.

Holt takes a deep breath. "Seems Bob Peterson has decided he undervalued the company. His new asking price is another hundred on top of this."

"A hundred...*thousand*?" I ask, hopefully.

"A hundred million," Alex says, already a step ahead of me in accepting the new number.

"Million," Holt confirms.

"Oh, shit." I sink back in my chair. *Shit, shit, shit, shit, shit.*

Shock quickly morphs to blame, and I lash out at Holt. "You knew this already, and you started this whole meeting by joking around?"

He shrugs. "A little levity is good for brainstorming."

"What the fuck does levity have to do with brainstorming?" It's not Holt I'm mad at, but he's my brother, so he'll take it.

Yeah, yeah—not the professional environment I was touting, but there won't be any professional environment if we can't get the loan. "Did he say why he changed his mind?"

Holt lowers his gaze. "Just said he reconsidered."

"Uh…" There's trepidation in Alex's tone. "This might be a good time to tell Adly—"

Holt cuts him off. "We don't need to worry her with that. It's moot at this point."

Dread pools in my belly. "Worry me with what?"

I'm answered with silence.

Fuck.

Closing my eyes, I count to five before asking, "If I know, can I do anything about it?"

Here's the thing—I'd also rather not be worried. So if Holt says that I don't need to be, then I'll believe him.

He's the only person I trust in these situations—the only person I trust at all, maybe—so if he says to drop it, I'll drop it.

"There is absolutely nothing you can do, and it might not even an issue," Holt says. "Right, Alex?"

"Yeah. Right." Alex doesn't sound as sure, but it sounds

like a guilty conscience talking, and if he has done something that's going to make me itchy about going into business with him, I would be much happier remaining in the
dark.

Except the price of the company just went up a hundred
million. Out of the blue.

Maybe I'm not so good with being in the dark. "Are you
the reason the price went up, Alex?"

There's a beat of silence. "I'm sorry?"

"Sorry doesn't do much if we can't buy the fucking
company, Alex." I might need to work on the way I
communicate things professionally.

Alex's voice rises to match mine. "We don't *know* that it
was my fault."

"And it doesn't matter." Holt sharply pivots to action.
"What matters is what we're going to do about it. We can
figure out a way around this, I'm sure."

Holt goes on with a list of ideas that he obviously came
up with prior to my arrival and the introduction of levity.
His ideas include bringing on another investor or offering
only a partial buyout or bringing in Grandpa Irving to
bargain with Bob or even causing some sort of destruction
to the network so the value will drop and the new price will
be impossible to justify.

Alex debates each option with Holt while I prop my
elbows on my thighs and hold my head in my hands.
Brown strands of shoulder-length hair curtain my vision,
and I tune the men out while I work through our alternatives by myself in my head.

Doing damage to the network isn't on the table.

Bringing in Grandpa Irving to negotiate for us is as good

as proving to Dad that we aren't capable of handling this on our own.

Only a partial buyout would keep Bob Peterson in the mix, and there's no way in hell that he'll allow a woman CEO. For that matter, anyone we bring on is going to want a piece of the power. I'm already afraid I'll have to battle for it with Holt and Alex. Unless we find a silent investor, but that's easier said than done.

What we need is more money.

And some way to get it without any strings or obligations in return.

A practically impossible option.

Except that I'm a granddaughter of Irving Sebastian, and when I lift my head again, my mind is already settled. Because as much as I hate to admit it, we have no other choice.

"There's only one solution to this problem that will give us all what we want without a significant sacrifice—I'm going to have to get married."

CHAPTER
THREE
ADLY

pride myself on my literal open door policy. Unlike the majority of execs that work in this establishment, I don't shut my office door unless I'm in private meetings. A lot of human resources is about keeping employees happy and giving them a safe place to discuss any issues. It seems like a bitch of a way to create camaraderie with a solid block of oak keeping me shut off from the staff, hence why I keep it open.

It works pretty well for the most part.

Until I'm on the phone with my father, half-heartedly listening to him complain about the cost of the retirement plan I want to implement for SNC's employees before I ditch this place while I say "uh huh" a lot and print emails I want to read later when I'm pretending to pay attention at the executive meeting this afternoon.

Neither task is getting my full attention, but together

they're distracting enough to keep me from noticing Ax wander into my office on this Monday morning.

I'm only aware of his presence when he says, "What the fuck is this?"

I look up to find him standing by my printer, scanning over my freshly printed docs in his hand.

Panic shoots through me, and I forget to cover the receiver. "Hey!"

"'Hey' is not the response I was looking for, Adly. This package is above and beyond what we're required to offer." My father's tone is short. Unsurprising, considering that he hates being interrupted even more than he hates sharing his wealth with the employees who work their asses off to keep viewers from choosing CNN instead.

"Sorry, Dad. A problem just walked into the room that I need to take care of immediately." As much as I'd prefer a different job, I'm stellar at what I do, and so when I say I have an emergency, my father tends to believe me.

I may use the time sensitive excuse more than I should to get out of conversations with him, but we all do what we have to in order to survive our lot in life.

Ax is on my ass as soon as the phone hits the cradle. "There will be an actual problem if you don't explain what the hell this bullshit is."

"Not yours, is what it is." I push my chair away from my desk and rush toward him.

He's quick, though, and holds the papers out of reach so I can't swipe the stack from his hands.

He peers up to read from the pages. "'Grounds for divorce,' 'Engagement period'—this is a template for a prenup."

Ax has the persona of a frat boy, but his mind is sharp. Not much goes over his head, unfortunately. And he's like a dog with a bone when he sinks his teeth into something he finds yummy.

This particular document is the last thing I need him to be interested in. "It's a template for none of your fucking business." I jump to try to reach the papers, but even in my two-inch heels, he's tall enough to easily keep them away. "Give them to me, you prick."

"Why are you printing up a fucking prenup, Ad? And unless you're about to tell me that you're planning on playing lawyer when you come knocking on my door later today, it's the wrong answer."

"Knocking on your door in your dreams." I mean, I do tend to get frisky on Monday afternoons, but eighteen months later, I stand by the notion that our role-played trysts don't count as Adly and Ax hooking up and are instead a string of encounters between strangers. It isn't Adly Sebastian who occasionally knocks on Ax's door, but rather the "cleaning lady" or "FedEx delivery" or a "teenage girl selling cookies."

Over-rationalization perhaps, but necessary to prevent me from drowning in shame.

Ax doesn't budge. "Why do you need a prenup, Adly?"

"Only thing I need right now is for you to leave my office so I can work."

"Prenups are not part of your job description."

"Have you read my job description?"

He just stares at me.

This is the worst. How the hell did I let this happen? The

last thing I need is for this scheme to get out. It could ruin the entire sale. "Why are you even here right now?"

"Doesn't matter. Talk."

I only see the "Quality Inspector" stick-on nametag when he pulls it off his suit jacket. Nice follow up to the doctor scenario we ended up playing out after I left Holt's office the other day, despite my determination to end things. My nipples steeple instantly and my thighs buzz, my body reacting to what that game might have entailed—me undressed while Ax surveyed every inch of my skin. With his tongue.

Or would it have been a performance inspection? With me on my knees and his too-beautiful-for-words cock pointed at my mouth.

Dammit. *This train of thought is not helpful.*

"Ax, just...give them to me. Please." The last word comes out through gritted teeth, and I hold my hand out as if asking nicely has ever led to success where he's concerned.

"Sure thing, little girl." A smidgeon of hope blooms inside me, despite the immature epithet. "As soon as you tell me what you're up to."

I swear there's got to be smoke coming out of my ears.

I can't even be too mad at him. It's my fault for being so careless. I should have printed it out at home. Or better yet, just studied the document on my phone.

Hindsight, and all. Too late now.

"Fine. Keep it. Whatever. It's not even important."

I know as soon as I've said it that I'm trying too hard. Any attempt to minimize the pre-nup's significance is exactly the way to keep him intrigued, but I hold my facial expression and hope he goes with it.

For half a second, I think he might. "All right. I'll just go ask your dad about it." He starts for the still-open door.

It's probably a bluff, but still I cross the room in record time and practically throw myself in front of the threshold. "No!"

His grin is smug. "So there *is* something going on here."

"Just stay out of it for once, will you?"

"If you're thinking of getting married—"

His voice seems five times as loud as usual, and I cut him off with a hiss. "Could you keep it down? For fuck's sake." I peer around outside to be sure no one overhead, then offer a weak smile to my assistant before shutting my office door.

I'm trapped.

Probably because I'm now literally between my door and Ax, and as if he doesn't already know he's got me, he rests his free hand on the door beside my head, caging me in.

My pulse kicks up, not entirely because I'm worried about how to get out of this.

I try a new tactic. "I'm researching, okay? Casually researching. That's all."

"Researching marriage prenups? Addles, research is Googling. This letterhead is official. I recognize that lawyer's name. That's pretty in-depth for just 'casual research.'"

I'm suddenly grateful for the solid door behind my back.

Our roleplay generally prevents us from using first

names—usually I'm Ms. Sebastian or Miss or whatever title helps keep up the pretense. The rest of the time, Ax's names for me are demeaning or banal.

But *Addles* is the one that he occasionally uses in non-roleplaying conversation that gets me, well, addled. My knees feel weak and my stomach is aflutter.

I read too many romance books, is probably why. Pet names are one of my favorite micro tropes.

Not that I'm Ax's pet in any way, shape, or form, of course.

But I'm flustered all the same.

Ignoring the rush of endorphins, I take the opportunity to swipe the papers from him, then duck out under his raised arm. "See this?" I draw a circle in midair. "Some your business," I say, pointing at the empty space. Then I point at the papers. "None your business." I tap the papers to emphasize my point. "This is none your business."

He lets out a low chuckle. "I'm just supposed to forget what I saw?"

"You won't have proof." I tear the papers in half.

Or try to. It's too thick of a stack, though, and I only manage to get a tiny tear before Ax tries to swipe them back. When I turn away from him, his arms come around me, securing my wrists so I can't do any more damage.

"Dammit, Ax, this isn't about you!" Also, dammit, he smells good. Like leather and spice and virile male.

"Like hell it isn't about me. Husbands don't tend to like it when other men have dibs on their wife's kitty. Unless you're adding that to the prenup."

"Dibs? On my...?" I'm so astonished and outraged—okay, maybe there was a heart flip in there, but mostly it's outrage that gives me the strength to push him away. I rush to the shredder and throw the papers in, feeling only mild relief when the implicating document turns into confetti.

Then I turn back to face my demon. "You don't have dibs on any part of me."

No one does. Not my father and especially not Ax Morgan.

"I think your kitty would say otherwise. Should we find out?" Only his eyes touch my pussy region, but I feel it like he's sucked my clit into that devil mouth of his.

And this is when I know I'm in trouble.

Serious trouble. Not just because Ax has stumbled onto my prenup research but because he seems to have some control over my body that I don't ever recall giving him.

My voice stutters when I speak. "Okay, there has definitely been some misunderstanding. We are not..."

He takes a step in my direction. "We are not....what?"

"Anything." I walk backward as he stalks toward me. "We aren't anything other than coworkers. Whatever else you think is happening between us is your own delusion." My calves hit the shredder, and I'm convinced I'm about to be trapped again, but Ax surprises me when he passes me by, heading toward my desk instead.

Without him in my face, I regain my composure. "Do you need me to make arrangements for a mental health consult?"

"Only if you're planning to play psychiatrist."

"Kill me," I mutter under my breath, just as he plops down in my chair.

Leaning back, the asshole has the nerve to prop his feet, three thousand dollar Berluti shoes included, on my desk.

"Some pretty wild things go on in my head, Doc. Should I tell you about them or would you rather I act them out?"

"I would rather you leave my office, actually. If I have any say. Which it seems that I don't."

Just when I think it can't get worse, he seems to spot something of interest on my desk. Before I can trace his eyeline, he puts his feet on the floor, leans forward, and picks up my notebook.

The notebook that I'd been using to make a preliminary husband list.

The names listed are obvious enough that I might as well have written the words *Marriage Material* at the top of the page.

"That's private!" I dive for it, only to be pulled into Ax's lap where he restrains me easily with one arm.

"Tad Murdoch? You can't seriously be considering marrying that prick. And who the fuck is Ishaan?"

"He's not... It's not what you..." I try to come up with excuses while struggling to get out of his grip. Ultimately, I'm too ruffled to do either. "I don't want to talk about this with you!"

"This is about your trust fund."

"How did you...?" *Fuck.* "None of your business!" I point at the empty space in front of me, the place where the papers would be if I were still holding them.

"You want the money, for whatever reason, and you're trying to figure out who would be the best candidate for helping you get access."

"You're spitballing." It's maddening how quickly he unravels my whole plot. Almost as maddening as the feel of his breath skating down my arm.

"What I can't figure out is why I'm not on the list."

"You?"

"I should be the entire list."

I twist my head to look back at him. "*You?* Why on earth would I marry *you*?"

He tosses the notebook back on my desk and wraps that arm around me as well. "Are you really that hardheaded? This is such a no brainer."

"Explain to me how you would ever think you'd be an option. Explain it to me like I'm five." *Explain it to me as though my entire body isn't currently lit up with want.*

"Sometimes, little girl, grownups like to get naked and touch each other's private parts with their own private parts—"

I cut him off before my private parts get the wrong idea. "I'm not getting married just to have sex."

"But you admit you're getting married."

I'm officially the worst at subterfuge.

"I'm not admitting anything. Let me go."

"Okay, then."

He lets go of me so fast that I fall to the floor. *Asshole.*

I barely have time to get to my feet before he picks up my phone. "Hey, Sassy, can you get Samuel on the line for me?"

Yes, my assistant's name is legit Sassy.

And I'm pretty sure she'll do whatever Ax asks without question. Including getting Samuel—aka my father—on the line.

"You wouldn't."

"Wouldn't I?"

I mean, he *is*. There's no *wouldn't* about it at this point.

He dangles the phone out in the air, away from his ear, and I can hear the hold music drifting out from the receiver. This is in no way a bluff. He is literally calling my father, and if Ax mentions prenup to him, the damage will be irreversible.

I silently will Ax to hang up.

He doesn't.

Then Sassy's voice comes on the line. "Putting you through now, Mr. Morgan."

Rushing around the desk, I reach over and click the hang-up button just as my father is still in the middle of his, "This is Samuel," greeting. If this was a game of chicken, I obviously lost.

I hate losing.

I especially hate losing to Ax fucking Morgan.

"He's just going to call back." The superiority in Ax's tone is maddening.

I disconnect the phone all together.

"Cute," he says.

"Clever," I insist.

But Ax's point remains—there's no getting out of this. There's no way I can keep him silenced. If he wants to, Ax will not only tell my father what he saw, but also tell Hunter, his bestie, who would be on top of the world if he found an opportunity to ruin a deal that Holt and Alex are part of.

I don't feel confident that I could make up something believable at this point, but this isn't just my secret to tell.

Which leaves me with few options. "Do you swear on your mother's grave that you won't tell anyone?"

He barely thinks about it. "No."

I groan. "Why are you like this?"

"I'm holding all the cards here. No reason for me to have to prove anything."

"So you'll tell my father whether I explain or not?"

"I didn't say that." He considers for a beat. "But if you don't explain, I'm definitely sniffing around for the truth, no matter where it leads me, so seems like your best shot is to just let it out."

I shake my head, mortified that I'm actually about to do this. Then I brace my hands on the desk between us for support and let it all out in one breath, as if going faster will make it hurt less. "I want to buy something, okay? Something...big. Are you happy now? I need my trust fund to be able to afford the asking price."

"Now you know you don't need money to get access to my cock." He must get the sense that I'm about to throw my stapler at his head, because he switches gears, real fast. "You want to buy...what?"

"I can't say more than that, Ax. There are people involved besides me."

He raises a brow but seems more pensive than smug. Probably trying to put pieces together in his head, guessing what people are involved and what I could possibly want to purchase with one hundred million Sebastian dollars.

My thoughts are confirmed when he next speaks. "And you don't want your dad to know, which means he won't like whatever it is. Are you planning to ditch SNC to go buy the Strand?"

It's hard not to light up at the idea of owning a bookstore, because that does sound like the dream life. "Alas, no."

"A cat café, then." He barely gives me time to shake my head. "A costume shop for lovers."

His smirk says that last guess was about us.

"Don't, please. Don't..." *ever insinuate that we're lovers, and also...* "Don't try to guess. In case it isn't obvious, there's a lot on the line if you keep digging. Not just for me. So please, please don't make me regret telling you."

"You haven't told me anything. The begging is a nice touch, though."

I give him the most serious scowl I can muster. "I mean it, Ax. I've told you too much already."

His face remains stoic, but his eyes soften. "You really don't think you can trust me?"

"I don't...know." There was an actual second where I might have left it just at the first two words. I mean, I don't trust anyone, really.

Then I realized, surprisingly, that Ax might be an exception, which means I really don't know.

Or maybe I just hope I don't know, and that Ax has the capability of not being a dick just once in his life.

He addresses my thoughts as if he can hear them. "I think I've proven I can keep a secret, Addles."

My face goes hot at yet another reference to our year-and-a-half tryst. "You have, but—"

He interrupts me. "Which is reason one why I should be on the candidate list."

I almost laugh.

And then I actually do laugh. "That's a ridiculous reason."

"Is it, though? You seem to want to keep this whole marriage project on the downlow."

It's true that I intend for this whole thing to go off without any fanfare. Whoever agrees to partner with me will have to agree to secrecy. But that's not enough reason to choose Ax as a candidate.

Isn't it, though?

"Do you even have time to vet people?" He crosses one leg over the other at the ankle and leans back, hands laced behind his head. "I'm already vetted."

"Exactly why you aren't on the list."

"And I wouldn't ask for anything in exchange. You know no one else is giving you that deal. How much were you budgeting for payment?"

I hate that my ears perk, but this is an issue I haven't quite worked out yet. We pretty much need every penny of my trust fund for the purchase, so I'd have to come up with a payment plan or hope that I have enough outside the trust to pay whatever I'll have to bribe my groom with in exchange for going through with the scheme. It's not like I haven't been getting paid for my time working at SNC, but I also haven't been the biggest saver since I knew I'd one day have my inheritance.

If Ax would do it for free...

No, that's ludicrous. "I can't marry you."

"Give me one good reason."

"I don't even like you."

He takes a beat before replying. "Who said anything about liking each other?"

For some reason, that stings. Stupid since I said it about him first.

But it's the kind of sting I feel compelled to test. "Right? Because you don't like me either."

"Hate your guts. Let's get married."

I roll my eyes, as irritated at myself for entertaining this conversation as I am with him. "Why would you even want to do it if you aren't getting paid?"

His grin is almost sinister. "I mentioned your kitty, didn't I?"

"This isn't about sex."

"So you're not planning on fucking your husband?"

It's not like I haven't thought about it. Promising sex might be the only way I get a guy to agree to the deal.

But that's not something I'm discussing with Ax. "Remember the some your business, none your business?" I point once more to the imaginary circles in the air.

"Pretty sure you can't get caught fucking me if you want to keep a prenup intact, whether you're fucking him too or not."

I don't tell him that there's no way I'll be caught fucking him at all since I'm officially done with the Ax pastime. Probably. "It doesn't matter who I'm fucking because it's strictly going to be a marriage of convenience. Annulled as soon as the cash hits my bank account."

"And I wouldn't take a single penny of it."

"Then what would you get out of it?"

"Besides total access to your puss?"

I feel a headache coming on, inspired mostly by the way my pussy tingles every time Ax pays attention to it. *Fucking traitor.*

But also inspired by Ax. "You do realize being married doesn't mean you get free rein over your partner's body, don't you?"

"Holding this whole thing over your head is also a pretty decent reward, if you ask me."

"So basically, I should marry my bully so he can continue to bully me under the umbrella of the law."

"I'm going to bully you either way, so why not make it legal? Though I prefer the term torment."

"Terrorize is more accurate."

In one fluid motion, he's on his feet, his hands propped on the desk, leaning over with his face so close to mine that I can feel his breath on my lips. "Doesn't matter what you call it, darling, as long as it gets you wet, and we both know that it does."

I'm simultaneously embarrassed and ashamed. Ashamed that I ever dropped my panties for this dick and embarrassed that he has correctly guessed that my panties are damp.

I'm not going to lie—his power over me has me scared.

"Think about it, Addles. How much fun we'd have."

I slowly shake my head. I can't think about it. I won't. It's too…wrong.

"Then how about this—you want me to keep silent? Then maybe you should be giving me what I'm asking for. What I think I deserve." He doesn't pretend it's not a threat.

And this is exactly why he's the worst.

"Thank you, Ax," I say, straightening to a stand. "Thank you so much for proving why our extracurricular activity has to come to an end, once and for all."

His eyes widen. "Hold up…how did we go from total pussy access to no pussy access at all?"

"Because there never should have been pussy access.

Privileges are hereby revoked. Go and find yourself another kitty because mine is no longer friendly."

It's possible that I subconsciously heard the click of the door behind me while I was ranting, but it's Ax's face that prompts me to glance over my shoulder.

Only to find my father standing in the doorway.

For the first time since Ax walked into my office, my brain acts fast when I turn back to address my tormentor. "...is not something that should ever be said by a coworker. I'll look into it and see that the issue is properly addressed. Thank you, Mr. Morgan, for bringing the matter to my attention. You can see yourself out."

Throwing on an overconfident smile, I spin to face my father. "Hi, Daddy, what's up?"

His eyes dart from mine to Ax's. "Not another sexual harassment case, I hope. Does the girl have anything credible on you?"

I'm both amused and appalled at how quickly my father decided Ax must be at fault in an imaginary sexual harassment situation, but I'm also aware that the person I least want Ax to blab his stupid mouth to is standing right in front of us.

"It's practically already handled," I say, wanting nothing more than to get one of them gone. Both of them gone would be even better.

Ax comes around from behind my desk with a self-assured swagger that makes my heart pound. "I'm trying to help, but your daughter seems to like to take care of the dirty business by herself."

It's obvious he's not talking about what my father thinks he's talking about.

Obvious to me, anyway. Which feels like another threat, one I should probably take seriously.

But I'm a Sebastian, and we don't shrink when caught between a rock and a hard place. "Because it's *my* problem. *My* job. And I don't think your experience is what's needed for this particular situation."

"We'll see about that."

"What's that supposed to mean?"

But Ax walks past me, as if I'm no longer there, straight up to my father. "I tried to call you, Samuel, but there seems to be an issue with Adly's phone." He gestures toward the disconnected device on my desk.

"Mm. I tried to call back, then decided to walk down when I couldn't get through. Was it important?"

"Yes, actually. Adly here..." Ax peers back at me, and my entire body goes tense.

This is it. The moment when he's going to fuck me over.

I can't let it happen.

Crossing the room to them as fast as I can, I put a warning hand on Ax's arm. "How about we talk about this more at a later time?"

"You think it will be a different conversation if we do?" He glances at my hand, which makes it feel like it's on fire, and I drop it to my side.

Hell no, it won't be a different conversation, but I'll say whatever will buy me time. "Sure. Perhaps. We'll have to, you know, see."

Ax isn't buying it. "Doesn't sound the most promising."

If luck was ever on my side, my father would be bored with this discussion and would change the subject or tell us to sort out our mess before bringing it to him.

But luck has been MIA for me today.

"Whatever this is about, now I'm intrigued," Dad says.

"It's nothing," I try to say.

But I still haven't gotten Ax on my side, and he talks over me. "You're right, Samuel. I'm just going to say it. Might be bad timing, but Adly here...told me you were looking to sell your yacht. My father was looking at getting one for his retirement. Might be a nice present from his son."

Relief trickles over me. It's not a pure wash of comfort since I know that Ax won't let this go.

At least for now, my father's satisfied. "Ah, good to know. I'll have my secretary reach out to you with details. Now, I'd like to finish that conversation we were having earlier, Adly. If the two of you are done here?"

"We are," Ax and I say in unison.

"Most definitely done," I say, hoping it means that we are done with everything, and he'll forget all about this.

But the look on Ax's face says that not only will he not forget, but that he just won big time.

And the prize?

I think it might be me.

CHAPTER
FOUR
ADLY

Tad Murdoch's mouth is boring.

It only takes two minutes of conversation after the host leaves us at our table for me to remember that about him.

We're in a private room at Panache, one of the restaurants in the Sebastian Center where SNC is located. Reservations are weeks out for this place, even for lunch, unless you're a member of my family. Convenient when you want a confidential meeting that's offsite without actually being offsite.

It's the first time in years that I've seen Tad in person. He was my senior prom date back in high school, which led to a fairly uneventful hand job in the back of his father's limo, and an even more uneventful kiss goodnight. We didn't speak to each other much after graduation besides the general online niceties, but after scouring his socials and discovering he's newly divorced and stuck in a dead end job with seemingly nothing on the horizon, I thought a marriage of convenience might be exactly what he's looking for to turn his life around.

Also, he was always a bit of a sheep. Just what *I'm* looking for with this marriage deal.

The man rarely posts pics of himself, though, so I hadn't realized he'd taken to styling his hair with a combover, and I'd forgotten about the two thin, flat lines that make up his mouth. The top one disappears every time he speaks.

Such a drastic difference from the lips of He Who Shall Not Be Named.

The same He who has mysteriously been MIA since he left my office two days ago. I wish I thought that meant he'd dropped his interest in my search for a husband, but I know better.

Another thing to Ax's credit—if he were newly divorced, I doubt he'd start a date with a rundown on everything that went wrong in his marriage.

Of course, someone would have to be willing to marry him before he could get divorced, a thought that almost makes me laugh in the middle of Tad's monologue about his "emotional vampire" of an ex-wife.

Vampire. Now that could be fun.

I shake the roleplay scenario from my mind and attempt to engage while laying the groundwork for my proposition. "Honestly, I'm not sure romance even belongs in marriage."

Tad takes it as a joke and laughs. "Right? Not really, but it's funny to consider."

Swallowing a sigh, I open my mouth, intending to redirect the conversation to a less charged topic—at least until our entrees arrive—only to shut it again when the

Manhattan I'd ordered from the host is placed in front of me.

"Thank you, we're—" All speech escapes me when I lift my eyes to our waiter and discover that he is not *Toni,* as his Panache nametag says, but rather a six foot tall, demon mouthed Italian devil who works upstairs in programming.

Goddammit, why does the sight of him make goose-bumps race down my arms?

"We're ready to order," Tad finishes for me. "Is what she was about to say."

Ax stares down at my date with slitted eyes. "I believe the lady can speak for herself."

The hostility in his tone is obvious, even to Tad, who draws his thin lips into an impossibly thinner line.

But why is Ax here?

"Uh, um…" I have to take a sip of my drink before I can talk. It's not just the surprise of seeing Ax right now, but also the dedication to the bit. His hair has been slicked back, his usual suit jacket gone. His sleeves are rolled up to the elbows, exposing the rarely-seen-during-business-hours tattoo that decorates his lower right arm, and he's wearing both a black vest and apron.

It shouldn't be as hot as it is—it's a typical waiter uniform, for fuck's sake—but anytime Ax shows up in "costume" my body is trained to turn on.

Stupid body.

"Yes," I say, not sure my mouth is saying *yes* to the same thing my brain is. "Ready to order, I mean."

Except I suddenly can't remember anything on the menu that I've had memorized since eighth grade. "Um, actually…" I reach for the sheet printed with the day's fare.

"I can go," Tad suggests.

"Ladies first," *Toni* says.

Without meeting his eyes, I glare in his direction. "That's not necessary."

"I insist," he insists. He pulls out a notepad and a Sharpie fine point pen from his apron pocket.

I simultaneously want to melt into my chair from embarrassment—poor Tad doesn't deserve this—and roll up my sleeves to take on Ax with my bare hands. Let's not even talk about what my kitty wants to do, because I'm not inviting her to the conversation.

How did Ax even know where to find me?

Sassy.

Ax saw Tad's name on my notebook, and he probably asked her if I had anything scheduled with him so that he could show up and dig into my secrets or create chaos or both.

I'm going to have to talk to her about the risks of being taken in by a pretty smile. Believe me, I'm experienced.

Speaking of that pretty smile, Ax flashes it now. "Might I interest you in our specials? We have a hot and spicy meatballs dish that will fascinate your palate."

Fascinate your palate is officially chef's kiss in the character composite.

But I refuse to give him the impression that I'm impressed, particularly because I'm fairly certain that the meatballs he's referring to are the ones dangling between his legs. "Hot and spicy is a matter of opinion."

Tad turns his menu over. "I didn't see meatballs listed...."

Ax ignores him. "Perhaps sausage and peppers would whet your appetite."

"I do love a good sausage," Tad says, and kudos to Ax for not cracking up right there.

"Skip it. The sausage here doesn't ever fill me up." I direct the comment to my date, but our waiter knows who it's meant for.

Ax makes a grumbly sound of dispute. "That seems unlikely. Most people describe our sausage as *extremely plump*."

"I can't imagine anyone saying that," I say.

"Your imagination is lacking," he says.

My imagination is far from lacking, and I'm about to remind Ax of how creative I have been on many occasions —kidnapped princess was a particularly good scene—when I remember that the ultimate goal is winning over Tad, not Ax.

"I think I'll stick with the chopped salad." I hand Ax my menu, which he takes with a smirk, tucking it under his arm so he can write down my order on his notepad.

"Of course, Ms. Sebastian. Will there be any meat with that?"

I give him the best *fuck-you* smile I have. "I'm meat-free at the moment, thank you."

As of last Saturday night, but it counts.

There's a gleam in Ax's eye. "Ah, that explains *this*." His eyes dart from me to Tad and back again.

I have to bite my lip so I don't laugh since I'm pretty sure Ax just called my date "dickless."

Poor Tad isn't following. "What was that?"

"I'll put your order in immediately," Ax says with a waiter-like flourish that makes my mouth water.

No one can say the guy isn't committed.

"Excuse me. You haven't taken my order yet." Okay, maybe Tad can say he's not committed, though it's possible the way Ax is treating him is another part of the bit.

Ax returns to our table immediately. "My apologies, sir. I thought you ordered the limp noodles."

"Uh, limp noodles?" Tad looks at me. As if I might be able to explain this weird interaction.

"Did I say limp?" Ax waves his hand in the air. "Slip of the tongue. I meant garlic noodles. Don't know where my mind was."

His gaze lands on me, possessive and intense, and anyone paying attention would know exactly where Ax's mind was.

I swallow hard as heat trickles through my center.

Tad, though, is clueless. "Garlic noodles, huh. That actually does sound interesting."

"Unfortunately, they're not on today's menu," Ax says, as if he hadn't just suggested they were. "Is there something else I can get you? Cold soup? Stale bread?"

Tad's brow raises, and again he looks at me.

"He's joking," I say. "Obviously."

"Right." Tad doesn't sound like he thinks it's right at all, but Ax grins, which seems to confirm my assessment. "Strange sense of humor. Anyway, I'll do the lobster bisque."

"As your meal?" Ax manages to make the simple question sound like he's making fun. Which, of course, he is.

"With the garden salad, yes. Ranch, please."

"Ranch?" Ax shudders as if it's the most disgusting thing he's ever heard. "Whatever you prefer, sir."

Then he turns his attention back to me. "Ah, looks like you dropped your napkin. Let me help you with that."

I haven't dropped my napkin.

But Ax bends, as though he's picking it up, then he drops something in my lap. "Here you are."

My fingers brush over the paper from his notepad as I pretend to smooth my napkin. Immediately, my heart speeds up to rapid-fire, wondering what it says but unwilling to read it in front of him. "Thank you."

"No problem, Ms. Sebastian. It is still Ms., isn't it?"

I nod, my throat suddenly tight.

"Good then. I'll get your orders in right away."

As soon as Ax closes the door to our private room, Tad leans forward. "Was it just me or was that waiter a little...*off*?"

"Must be his first day. I haven't seen him around before." My hands shake as I turn over the paper in my lap and see Ax's scribbled handwriting. ***Tell this tool you need to use the restroom.***

Just so he can corner me and try to grill me about my plans again? No way.

Though I would love to give him a piece of my mind.

I look down again at the paper, realizing that this was what Ax had been writing instead of taking down our orders. In other words, there's a good chance we'll never see our food.

I pop up from my chair so fast it almost topples. "Actually, I'm going to just see that our order makes it to the kitchen. Since he's new and all."

Dropping my napkin on my seat, I keep the note crumpled up in my hand and head after Ax.

Tad calls after me. "I'm sure that's not necess—"

"I'll be just a minute!"

Outside the private dining room, I practically sprint to the restrooms, only to find the hallway empty. The women's room is to the right, the men's to the left. Then there are two gender neutral family rooms a little farther down.

Which one to choose?

The women's room door opens, and a brunette walks out. Before the door shuts again, I glance in and see another woman at the sink. No execs in disguise as waiters in sight.

Cautiously, I push into the men's room. At first glance, it seems empty as well, but the handicap stall at the end of the row is shut.

Stepping as quietly as I can in heels on tiled floor, I approach the closed stall. As soon as I bend to check for shoes, the stall door opens, and I'm abruptly pulled inside. A strong hand clasps over my mouth, cutting off my gasp.

"Hush." Ax's voice is warm and gravelly at my ear. "I've watched you come into this restaurant, time after time, shaking that tight little ass and pursing those red painted lips, and I finally had to shoot my shot and ask you to meet me so I can find out if your cunt is as snug as those pants I've seen you wear. I'm betting it is."

So we're playing, then.

I'm instantly wet.

Without even taking a beat to decide if I should play along or not, I immediately step into character, that of a bored trust fund baby out to lunch with her stuffy fiancé only to be hit on by a too-hot-for-his-own-good waiter.

"He'll miss me if I'm gone too long." As soon as I start to speak, Ax drops his hand from my mouth and grips my hips possessively.

"His bisque will be arriving soon. That should keep him occupied."

I don't even care if Ax is bluffing or if he actually got our order turned in to someone. My pulse is rocketing in my ears and anticipation is bubbling in my belly. "And in the meantime...?"

"In the meantime, you should reconsider the sausage." His hand snakes under the skirt of my dress, quickly finding my clit through the fabric crotch panel of my panties.

My back arches into him, and I bite my lip to stifle a moan as he teases me.

Ax's fingers are as much my enemy as his mouth. They're long and thick, but more importantly, they're skilled. He knows exactly how much pressure to use, and it's only a matter of seconds before I'm panting. The thrill of potentially being caught only adds to the fervor of the moment.

But I'm greedy when it comes to these trysts, and my pussy feels jealous and empty. "I think I'll stick with the chopped salad."

I start to pull away, only for Ax's arm to tighten around my waist. "This is just the appetizer. There's still the main course."

"You think I can just return to my fiancé with another man's cum in my pussy?"

"Fiancé?" With a growl, Ax spins me toward the stall's sink, the crumpled note falling from my hand to the floor unnoticed as he presses my body against the edge of the porcelain. Then he hikes up my skirt and gathers it at my waist. The handicap counter is lower than the typical counter, and the distinct wet spot on my panties is clearly visible in the mirror.

When I lift my eyes, Ax's gaze locks onto mine in our reflection with a predatory intensity that sends a shiver down my spine. "You're in a rush to get back to *that* guy?"

I lift one shoulder in a shrug. "Maybe he's everything I want."

"I promise you, he's not. Spread your legs."

When I don't move fast enough, he uses his knee to nudge my thighs apart. Then he squats down, and my skin tingles as he lets his fingers trace down the back of my legs before swiftly pulling my panties down to my knees.

Even though he's behind me, I can feel his eyes rake over my pussy with a primal hunger. The touch of his stare is as real as the feel of his breath on my skin as he leans in to take in my scent, his nose grazing against the lips of my soaked pussy.

Another shiver runs through my body, and it takes everything in me not to push my hips back in an attempt to urge his mouth to action, resolved not to come off desperate, even if it's a lie.

My reward is a single swipe of his tongue from clit to asshole before swiftly standing again, leaving me more wanting than ever.

"Well, that was unsatisfying." I'm going for nonchalant, but the tremor in my voice gives me away. "One out of five stars on your Yelp review."

"I'm the waiter, not the customer. *I* serve. *You* eat."

He probably intends to get me on my knees.

Fuck that, Toni. "I meant it when I said I'm going meatless."

But as I speak, his hands slide between my thighs. One from the front, one from behind. With the former, he presses a pad on my swollen clit. Then, with his eyes locked on mine in the mirror, the latter slowly slips a finger inside of me.

It's *one* stupid finger. One long, thick finger, inserted all the way to the knuckle, and suddenly, I'm gasping and pushing back against him.

"Are you sure about that?" he rasps at my ear.

I'm no longer sure of anything.

He adds a second finger, and my jaw drops. At the addition of a third finger, the sensation of being stretched by him overwhelms my nervous system and I moan.

Ax finger fucks my body like I'm his instrument. Up and down, in and out, he plays me with such precision that stars form at the borders of my vision. My hands grip the edges of the vanity to steady myself as, with each thrust of his fingers, he drives deeper inside me, sending waves of pleasure throughout my body.

"You're so wet." His hot breath sends more shivers down my spine as his cock pokes against my right ass cheek. "You going to tell me that this is for that limp fuck out there?"

There's enough capability for logical reason left in my mind to suspect that Ax isn't just playing a scene. That this is another version of the conversation we had in my office. Another attempt to convince me to put him on the candidate list.

Despite that, I can't help but answer truthfully. "It's all for you."

"Goddamn right it's all for me."

Outside our stall, the sound of the main door opening makes me tense up. Footsteps follow, along with the sound of someone using the urinal.

"You'll have to be quiet if you don't want this to get back to loverboy," Ax whispers. The stiff shape of his cock seems to grow harder.

I bite my lip to stifle a response as his fingers intensify their movements, driving me closer to the edge.

But it's the exhilaration of possibly being caught that has me most worked up. The scene has become so real that I'm actually afraid this will get back to my fiancé. That I'll lose everything I've built my life around for a fifteen-minute rendezvous with a stranger who's noticed me from a distance.

The thrill is so intense that it clouds my mind with nothing but pure pleasure as Ax takes control of my body.

"Do you want to come?" His voice is thick and husky.

I mean to say *you never make me come.*

"Yes," I breathe out.

He smirks against my neck as he curls his fingers inside me, rubbing me in the sensitive spot that only Ax has ever located—not that I'd ever admit that to him. The sensation is almost too much to handle, but it feels incredible all at once. With each thrust of his fingers, I feel myself getting closer and closer to release.

My knees start to shake, and I clutch tighter onto the basin. Without removing the pressure from my clit, he tightens his forearm around my waist while the other hand continues its relentless assault on my body.

"Look at yourself," he commands.

I watch in the mirror as he perfects his rhythm. My face is flushed with desire and pleasure, and Ax's expression is one of pure satisfaction.

"Does this fill you up? Is this enough for you?" His words are a mix of dominance and desire, sending waves of electricity coursing through my veins. "Does that woman looking back at you belong with *him*?"

I can't let myself answer, afraid what I'll say. Afraid I'll mean it.

"Whatever you think you have planned," he continues, "whatever scheme you're up to, this doesn't end until I say it does, so let me make this clear right the fuck now: You're mine."

His words are new—never spoken in any previous scenario. He's played possessive before, but never actually claimed me as his, and it does something to me.

Something big.

So big it doesn't matter if it's just a game. The real me heard those words. The real me likes them.

Likes them so much that they send me over the edge, and a fierce orgasm rips through me before I can remember to fake it *not* ripping through me. My body trembles as my vision goes black and waves of ecstasy wash over me. Every part of me is hypersensitive, and I try to pull away from his fingers inside me, but he stays there, eking out every last ripple of my climax. Even when his finger leaves my clit, I can still feel him there.

Vaguely I'm aware of the click of his sharpie pen, but I

can only identify it through the bliss when I feel the point draw across my ass. Shapes that I suspect are letters. Six of them? Seven? I'm not sure I could guess more even if I weren't so blitzed from euphoria.

The pen is put away and Ax removes his fingers from my pussy just as the door outside our stall opens again. Ignoring the men engaging in locker room talk as they do their business, I watch Ax in the mirror as he brings his fingers to his mouth and licks them one by one.

"Guess I got to eat too," he says, and I feel a flush crawl up my neck.

I turn to face him, my dress falling in place as I move from the sink. There's more I want to say—more I *should* say, considering how I'm pretty sure Ax thinks this was more than just a finger fuck. He thinks he's made a point, and I'll be damned if I don't get to make one too.

But when I open my mouth to speak, he places one wet finger over my lips to hush me.

"I'd take your panties as a trophy," he says quietly. "But there's no way in hell I'm sending you back to *him* with your cunt on display."

Warmth spreads through my chest.

It's just a scene. He's just playing his part.

But he *always* takes my panties. This isn't how the game usually goes. He's thrown me for a loop.

He knows it, too. "Don't bother cleaning up. I doubt your date recognizes the smell of a satisfied pussy."

"This isn't satisfied," I say, a beat too late, the lie bold when he's had proof to the contrary.

His smile is smug. "Whatever you say, Addles. I have tables to check on."

Then he disappears out of the stall, shutting the door behind him, leaving me very *addled*.

As soon as I can pull myself together, I quickly gather my skirt around my waist again and, backside toward the sink, crane my head over my shoulder so I can figure out what the hell he wrote on my ass.

It's clear to read, thanks to Ax's clever idea of writing the letters backwards. The message in the mirror is only two words, but they make my stomach flip with their powerful statement—*My Wife*.

CHAPTER
FIVE
AX

I t only takes fifteen minutes after I slip out of Panache before Adly shows up knocking on my office door.

Actually, she never knocks. She buzzes past my assistant, who doesn't try to stop her since he assumes Adly's in my face because I'm perpetually in trouble with HR. It's not hard to believe since she's the one who assigned me Krieger in the first place, a gay-as-the-rainbow male assistant—who might be the best assistant I've ever had, as it turns out—after I'd converted the last guy into my wingman and fucked the previous three women that were at the desk before him.

I'm not a pig—I'm an opportunist.

And why shouldn't I be? I'm damn good at my job as programmer, and it's the highest position I'll ever have at SNC—despite my father's wild ideas—so what's the point of following the rules?

Especially when getting in trouble means a visit from Adly Jade Sebastian.

All the better when I'm prepared for it, like I am now. In fact, I'm just pouring the last of eight whiskey shots at my office bar when she bursts in.

"You have a lot of fucking gall."

"That's a compliment, isn't it?" I cap the whiskey bottle and put it back in its place. "Be sure to add it to my next performance review, will you?"

"Do you have any idea what you fucked up for me?"

There's a nerve that sticks out in her neck when she's really pissed. It's bulging now like a bullseye peeping out under her long brown hair. Daring me to take her on, which I will—it's why I've poured the Dalmore, after all—if the impulse to run my tongue the length of that nerve doesn't win out instead.

The urge to taunt her is greater.

"Didn't Tadly enjoy his lobster bisque?" I already know the answer since I paid the real waiter to spill the bowl in his lap. "He gets his name first in the ship name, too. What more does he want?"

She's practically a smokehouse, the way fumes seem to stream from her head. "He was in the process of issuing a complaint with the hostess, Ax."

Shawna won't rat me out after that rendezvous in the coat closet last January.

"They're likely going to look at the security footage to try to find the faux waiter," she continues.

"Good thing there happened to be a weird glitch in the recordings today, then." The security guard owed me after I cleaned his ass out in penny poker last month.

Gives me a new idea for a scene with Addlecat. One where I clean *her* ass out in penny poker but she doesn't have the funds to pay, so then she lets me clean her ass out in a different form.

Weird to plan out sex when I'm a guy who never two-times it with anyone.

But do repeats even count when every time we fuck we're playing somebody else? I haven't pulled the roleplay loophole with anyone else besides the woman standing in front of me.

She's fucking adorable when she's enraged. Scowl all she wants, her brown eyes still sparkle, her light olive-toned skin is radiant.

"This isn't a joke, Ax. You're ruining my life."

"And mysterious other people's lives...so you've said. I was listening. Why do you think I set up?" I pull the bar cart so it's between us and gesture to the already-poured shots.

Her scowl suggests I'm out of my mind if I think she's giving in. I tense when she moseys past my desk first, trailing her fingers along the surface so they skim over the stack of mail I'm ignoring, particularly the high school graduation notice stacked on top of the torn envelope. She pauses as her eyes skim over the image of the girl—woman now—in cap and gown, seemingly curious, but then she steps up to the bar and picks up the first of the shots.

Just like that, we enter Negotiations.

Negotiations began as a drinking game in high school. With all the women Hunter and I shared, he and I learned pretty quickly that we needed to have some ground rules. Establishing them over alcohol turned out to be the best way to keep both of us from entering hothead mode. That's where the no repeat rule came from. One time per pussy unless we're willing to attach girlfriend status to the chick. Won't ever be a problem for me since I'm devoted to the bachelor life, but it does keep competition and jealousy from getting between us.

Obviously, I've never told him about this Adly thing and never will. He and Ad don't get along, but he still might not appreciate me banging his half-sister. I've gone so far as to erase the security tapes in his apartment after she comes over so he doesn't decide to go looking one day for something and find out.

Aside from her, more than twenty years later, our bro code has long been ratified, and the shot tray rarely comes out for anything other than debauchery. Adly's pretty much the only person I need to drunk-negotiate with these days.

Only person I *want* to drunk-negotiate with.

I mean, she's a pain in my fucking ass. She's hard-nosed and way too goddamn serious, which makes it a real win when I can get her to fluster.

For some unknown reason I'm kind of obsessed with it.

And no, it's not about getting my face in luxury pussy. My entire life outside this office building—okay, inside this office building too—is basically pussy buffet. If Adly permanently closed her legs to me, I wouldn't be missing anything in that department.

But the chance to get her panties twisted in a knot (before I steal them for my collection, that is) is real hard to pass up, so here we are, shots lined up and ready to bargain.

With glass in hand, Adly lifts her chin defiantly. "I'm

going to get married to the man of my choice, and you won't interfere."

She knows we're beyond this, but I don't blame her for trying. As soon as she saw those words I wrote on her ass, she had to know there was only one way this was ending.

I lift my own glass, a kind of fake out before giving her a smug grin. "Not a fucking chance."

That's how the game goes—someone lifts a glass and offers their demand. The other counters and so on, back and forth until an agreement is made. Then the shot's taken. Four negotiation points—that's usually what's set up. The strategy being to push the points while you're sober enough to remember what they mean to you while also trying to push off the points important to your opponent so that they'll be too drunk to make a stand.

Literally.

Except that Adly can drink most people under the table, a quality that I consider an entertaining challenge.

Her long lash twitches—her whole eyelid, actually, but I notice it because of the fluttering lash. "God, you're such a fungus."

"Definitely not agreeing to that."

"A foot fungus. That smells." She throws the shot back in one swallow.

"Hey! That's not—I call foul."

She's already at the liquor cabinet with the Dalmore in hand—impressive she identified the brand with one go—removing the cap. "Calm your tits. I needed a warm-up round."

After refilling her glass, she takes another large gulp from the bottle before returning it to the shelf.

I should maybe be offended that it requires this much liquor to discuss marrying me, but I'm taking it for what it is—a two-point advantage for the guy who's sober as a Mormon. There's no way I can't win.

Whatever winning looks like.

She uses the back of her hand to wipe off her mouth, the lipstick not left on the glass lost to the bottle rim.

"Better?"

I don't bother hiding my gloat.

She responds with a display of her middle finger.

"I think the ring goes on the next one," I tell her. Taunt her.

"There will be no rings." When she lifts her glass, I know we're back to negotiating.

"No rings." I lift my own glass in agreement, but don't toss it back yet, in case there are any other amendments she wants to add, which apparently she does.

"No evidence at all other than the marriage certificate from City Hall. No one knows about this, you got it? No one."

"Wait—are we negotiating rings or that no one knows?" I'm a dick because I already see the correlation. Just trying to work out how tipsy the first two shots made her.

"I'm negotiating secrecy. No one can know, which means there can be no evidence. No rings, no pictures, no mentions to anyone. No one can know."

She's repeating herself a little, maybe, but still has her head straight.

I suppose I should make this easy and agree.

But what's the fun in easy?

Without letting go of the glass, I set it back on the cart.

"What exactly do you mean by 'no one'? Because the justice of the peace will obviously know. And who will be our witness? Should we nominate Hunter for the job? Holt? Daddy Sebastian?"

"Oh, fucking hell," she mutters before I'm finished with the torment. "Only those people absolutely necessary can know. You can't tell anyone."

"No one? Not even my dad? Not Hunter?"

"Not our assistants. Not our drivers. Not your dad or your bestie—or Holt—and super definitely not my dad."

She pauses before naming Holt. Like she was only adding him because I had. Does that mean something?

"I don't know if I've ever kept a secret from Hunter before…"

She raises a brow. Daring me to say that I've already told Hunter about us.

I drag it out a beat before continuing. "Except the big giant one about the level of familiarity my cock has with your—"

She cuts me off. "Pretend this is the same secret, and we're good."

She lifts her glass toward me. I lift mine and clink hers before we both say, "*Salute.*" Basically it's cheers in Italy, a tradition I adopted years ago, an ode to my mother's heritage.

Then we both toss them back with one gulp.

Adly picks up the next glass without hesitation. "I'm not giving you any money."

"I already agreed to this."

"I'll need you to sign the prenup saying as such."

I pretend to consider. "But what exactly is the wording about fidelity?"

"Who cares about fidelity?" It feels like a victory when she rolls her eyes. Not just because they're starting to get glossy with liquor but because it means I have her ruffled, and ruffled Adly is my favorite. "It's an on-paper marriage. Like I said before, we'll get annulled as soon as my money is disbursed."

"That's still a matter of weeks we're talking about."

"Don't worry. I'm not going to cock block you. Slut it up all day and night like you do now, as far as I'm concerned. I wouldn't expect a little thing like nuptials to get in your way."

That does seem like something I'd be worried about.

Actually, though, I'd been thinking about her. There's something really bothersome about the idea of us being married, paper-only or not, and my wife fucking someone else.

But admitting that opens up a whole can of worms that I'm not interested in bringing to this negotiation table. So not interested, in fact, that I lift my glass, ready to agree and move on.

"*Salute*," we say in unison. We drink.

"My turn." I slap my glass down and pick up the next before leaning my elbows on the cart between us. "I get to fuck you on our wedding night."

She laughs. That boisterous cackle that she brings out when the liquor starts to hit. I swear she crafted the sound so she'd have a way to grab me by the balls with just her voice. It also has the effect of making my dick go hard, despite spanking the monkey in my bathroom as soon as I got back to my office from our restroom adventure. One smell of her cunt on my fingers was all it took to send me over the edge.

"Why are you laughing?" I keep my voice light so it doesn't seem like I care about the answer. "Married people fuck."

"We are not considering ourselves married."

"Is that a new point of negotiation?"

"It was implied before."

"When? When was it implied?"

"Always! The whole time!" She blinks, her eyes taking a second to focus before she tries to lock them on mine. The alcohol is hitting her.

I manage to hold back a smirk and don a pretend confused expression instead. "This shouldn't even be an issue. We were fucking before the agreement."

"We never—." She cuts herself off and starts again. "You and I were not—" She shakes her head. "No. No. No. We're done, and I'm not transacting sex."

Her last point is fair enough, but the other thing—not the we're done thing, but the thing she tried to pretend that she didn't mean with that little dismissive headshake of hers—that point is even louder. I'm not an idiot. I've known she hates herself for this secret affair of ours. That might be half the reason I think it's so hot. If I had to bet, I'd say that she's convinced herself that it never happened. That it isn't happening. Maybe the roleplay helps her disassociate.

I don't like it.

Probably because I like it better when she's feeling ashamed, and so where's my enjoyment if she's in denial?

Whatever. We don't have to agree on this one. It will be

more satisfying when I end up fucking her anyway. "Settle for the panties you're wearing."

I shouldn't have to negotiate for them since the only reason she still has them on is that I was being courteous earlier. They belong to me already.

"You will? Okay." She slips her panties off before I have a chance to even try to get a peek of the goods. Then she lifts her glass.

Huh. I thought she'd fight me more on that one, on pretense alone.

I resist sniffing her panties before stuffing them in a pocket, but only because I'm already battling with my hard-on.

Then I lift my glass. We clink. "*Salute.*"

This time when she tries to slam the glass back down on the cart, she tips it over. "Whoa, there." She giggles which turns into the cutest little hiccup. "'Oh my God," she says, covering her mouth, blushing. "No idea where that came from."

Her words slur together, and bingo.

My girl's intoxicated. In the middle of a workday, no less.

I mean, not *my girl*, but about to be my wife, so it's an understandable slip of thought.

Thankfully, it doesn't derail me. With Adly's head spinning, I pick up the final glass and level her with my most persuasive tone. "What is it you need the money for, Adly?"

"Oh, no. No, no, no, no." She shakes her head again, so much this time that I suspect she's made herself dizzy when she hooks her elbows on the cart like it's the only reason she's still standing.

"How about yes, yes, yes, yes, yes?"

Another hiccup. "Nope."

"Come on, Addles." It riles her up when I call her that, so of course I pull it out whenever it best serves me. "How can you expect a marriage to work when it begins with dishonesty?"

"Ha!" She moves the empty glasses with a wave of her arm—I barely save the two that are still full before they topple over—then lays her forehead down on the cart and rocks it side to side. "We're not going to really married." She stills, as though realizing her words were wrong. "You mean what I know."

I bend so I'm at her level, which means staring at the top of her head. "I'm dying here, Ad. I have to know."

"You can't know."

"You have to tell me."

"I can't tell you."

Her hair has fallen around her face, and it takes everything in me not to reach out and brush it back so I can see her expression. "You can tell me. I've shown you I can keep a secret. I'll agree to keep it hush. I'll drink on it. You know that's a sacred vow that I'd never break."

However intoxicated I assumed she was, I find out I've misjudged when she lifts her head and looks me in the eye. "I can't, Ax. If that's what you need to agree to this, then no deal. I'm out the door right now."

"Fuck that. You need me."

"I don't need you."

It stings, which is fucking weird, particularly because

it's not true. "No one's marrying you with better terms than this."

"I know." She's solemn and serious, all signs of having too much liquor suddenly gone, and I start to wonder if I'm somehow the one being played here.

Not possible.

After what I did to her at lunch? After so many shots? There's no way I'm not getting this info from her. "I guess we'll have to call the whole deal off, then."

"Okay." She stands all the way up, brushes her hair off her shoulders, and smiles. "Thanks for the drinks."

She starts toward the door.

I call after her. "You walk out, you're back at square one. You can't tell me there isn't a time limit to the deal you're after. Otherwise, you'd wait the three years and inherit your money rather than try to find a guy who will sign up, blind."

She stops, but doesn't turn around. She only swivels her head so it's over her shoulder, in profile view. "You underestimate what men will do just to get close to a Sebastian."

Something about the thought of what men might do to get close to Adly has me seeing red.

"I'll tell your father." I somehow manage not to sound panicked. "Tell him you're planning some sort of inheritance scam."

She turns around to glare at me. "You can't prove it."

"I have my phone on recording this whole thing right now." Reaching into my pants pocket, I pull out my cell and hold it up as proof.

Fake proof since I'm not actually recording.

She shrugs. Like she doesn't care, rather than that she's

defeated. "Go ahead and play it for whoever you want, Ax. The deal will be undermined before it even gets started, and then you'll never know what I was up to."

There might be truth to that, or maybe she's calling my bluff.

"But if that's what you need to do…" Another shrug. "I'll find someone else." Then she turns back toward the exit.

She's almost to the door when I call out after her, "Fine." *Did I just say that?* "It's off the table." *What the fuck am I doing?*

"Really?"

"Yeah, really." I don't fucking know why I mean it or when it turned into meaning it this much. I thought this was just a fun opportunity to mess with the girl's head. Get in her way. Wreck her plans. I don't really want to marry her.

Just if she marries any other man—even "on paper" only—I'm going to have to chop his dick off. Can't explain it. But there's no other option, and that's going to be a fuck of a mess to clean up, and there's nothing more tedious or expensive than dealing with a cleaner.

Adly returns to the bar cart. I wouldn't blame her for smiling like she's won big, but all she does is pick up the final glass. "Why do you want to do this so badly? What's in it for you?"

Million-dollar question, baby.

Correction, billion-dollar, since a million is pennies to a woman with the Sebastian name.

I give her the only guess I have. "It pisses you off,

doesn't it? The idea of being married to me. Even in secret. On paper only. Pisses you off real good."

The nod of her head is so slight, as though it's the last thing she wants to admit.

As though the confession is a concession of some sort, she clinks my glass and says, "*Salute.*"

Her glass is empty before I've even picked mine up.

Just like that, the deal is made, and it isn't until she's left the room before I let the full force of what I've agreed to hit me.

Holy fucknuts.

Mr. Never Even Gonna Have a Girlfriend just got his ass engaged.

Hunter wouldn't believe me if I did tell him.

CHAPTER
SIX
ADLY

wo days later, I hit the elevator call button in the staff lobby of SNC and pray it arrives before Ax catches up to me. Exactly what every little girl dreams of growing up to be—a bride running from her husband.

Just as the elevator starts to open, a voice booms from behind me. "Waiting for me to carry you over the threshold?"

I panic look around to be sure no one heard him before turning to give him a warning scowl. "You agreed to secrecy!"

"What are you talking about? I'm not spreading secrets. I'm simply enjoying conversation with a fellow employee. Who happens to be *my wife*."

We haven't been married more than an hour, and I'm already dreaming about the day I get to file for divorce.

At least Ax whispers the incriminating words.

Still, it's enough to send a shiver down my spine.

A shiver of worry, probably. That has to be what it is since I can't think of any other reason why his sentiments would cause such a visceral reaction.

With a huff, I step into the elevator and try not to dwell on how I ended up in this situation. Married to My Bully. It could be the title of a dark romance that I'd binge in one sitting. Somehow it's not as swoony of a story when it's happening in real life.

Ax follows. As expected. Unfortunately. A paper bag gripped in one hand and a half-eaten street taco in the other.

Pressing my badge to the card reader, I hit the button for our floor and do my best to ignore the brute next to me.

It's harder than it should be. Especially when he's wearing his black Tom Ford double-breasted mohair suit that fits him so well he looks like he was sewn into it. I'd almost wonder if he picked it specifically for today if I didn't already know this is where it falls in the rotation. Yesterday was the Canali linen. Monday it will be the Armani pinstripe. Predictability should be boring, but I find it strangely satisfying to know what he'll be wearing when I see him.

It's almost worth the crumbling devastation that follows when I realize I'm once again surprised at how good he looks wearing...everything.

Ugh, I hate him.

I try to put him out of my field of vision, but our reflections are in every panel of the mirrored elevator, and I swear wherever I glance, Ax is watching me.

When our gazes crash—accidentally—he mistakenly

takes it as an invitation for engagement. "Are you sure you don't want one?" He lifts up the taco he's eating, in case I don't know what he's talking about. "I have plenty to spare."

"Not even a little bit."

My stomach rumbles in protest, but I'm deeply resentful toward those tacos.

They're the reason we're rushing back now. Because Ax couldn't "just get in the car" so we could get back from our lunch break with a minute to take a breath before our staff meeting this afternoon. No, he simply had to try out the street vendor in front of the courthouse, "to memorialize the day," despite our time crunch and the five-deep line we had to wait in to get them.

"Your loss." He finishes his taco and throws the foil wrapping in the bag, his tongue flicking out over his stupid lip to catch a stray drop of salsa that I didn't even for a second consider licking up myself.

God, he's so tiresome.

I'm both grateful and on alert when the elevator stops to pick up one of the interns from the lower levels, hands full of files, most likely a delivery for someone on the exec floor. There's no reason for Ax to say anything that will out our new marriage status, but there's not much reason for most of the irritating shit he does.

Sure enough, as soon as the doors close after her, Ax lifts his phone in the air and points it toward us. I'm absolutely sure it's not a selfie when I peer up and see both of our faces on his screen. "What the hell are you doing?"

"Taking a photo. Special occasion, and all."

"I said no pictures," I whisper-hiss, gaze darting to the intern.

"That's not exactly what you said. Look up at the camera, Ads."

Actually, I said no proof, and since I'm wearing a nothing-special, black pencil skirt and business style blouse—a far cry from what's considered bridalwear—it's probably fine.

Fine except that the intern probably thinks we're freaks or that we got high over the lunch hour, but that's just annoying rather than problematic. Hopefully, she's more engrossed in her phone than us.

"Do you want me to take it?" The intern slips her own phone in her pocket and reaches for Ax's.

So much for wishful thinking.

"No, thank you," I say.

"Please," Ax says at the same time, handing his cell over. "We're celebrating."

I readjust my body so that I can discreetly step hard on his toe.

The intern maneuvers her files so they're under her arm and points the phone at us. "One, two, three, cheese!"

I most certainly do not smile, but when Ax takes the phone back, he grins at the image. "Perfect. Thanks."

"No problem. What are you celebrating?"

"Making it to our destination." The elevator stops and the doors open, and I've never been so happy to arrive at the SNC executive floor. "This is me."

I'm already exiting when I hear Ax behind me.

"This is *us*." It doesn't come out quite like he's correcting me, but I'm irked all the same.

"Did you want to see our picture?" Once again, he's on my heels as I clip down the hall.

"I really don't."

"I should print it out. Put it on my mantle. Or maybe my office. That's what the good husbands do, right? I wonder if Krieger has any unused frames laying around that I could commandeer."

I stop and spin around so fast that Ax nearly bumps into me. "Don't you dare."

"What? It doesn't even look like a wedding photo." He studies the image, still apparently open on his phone. "An engagement photo, maybe."

I swipe the cell from his hand. "Give it to me."

Once I see the image, I'm annoyed at myself for being curious. It doesn't look like we're a couple at all—because we're not. Ax is smiling like the dorkass that he is. My arms are folded, my expression sour, as though I'm deeply uncomfortable. My eyes are even open.

If he puts this photo on his desk, the only question Ax will be asked is, "What's the prank?"

He's not going to tell anyone. But of course he's going to needle me, trying to make me worry because that's what he loves to do. Rile me up.

I can deal with being riled. As long as he keeps his word.

"I swear to God, Ax Morgan, if you ruin this for me…"

"Who, me?" That smirk should be classified by OSHA as hazardous to one's health since I can feel my blood pressure rising every time he flashes it.

I hand the phone back to him. He's lucky I didn't throw it.

Then I turn down the hall branching toward my office, only to spin back at him when he turns down the same hall. "Don't follow me."

He gets so close that his leather and spice scent smacks me in the face, and I teeter a second before finding my balance.

Then when I think he's reaching for me, and my pulse ricochets skyward, he actually reaches *past* me and tosses the paper bag in the trash. "Just throwing away the tacos you didn't want. *Mrs. Morgan*."

I force myself to count to five.

He wants a reaction.

And I've already given him too many.

So with my mouth clamped shut, I swivel away from his shit-eating grin, march to my office, and swiftly shut my door, where I can pretend the goosebumps racing down my arms and the nipples steepling through my bra have everything to do with the blasting AC, and nothing to do with Ax calling me by his last name.

I HAVE JUST enough time to scan and email our newly signed marriage certificate to the officer at the bank where my trust is held and call Holt before our staff meeting.

"It's done," I say when he's answered.

"You're *married*?" There's subtext to the question that suggests the idea is laughable.

"I meant I've turned in everything for the claim for my trust fund, but yes, that too."

"God. Wow. Really? That quick?"

"That quick." I give him a beat of silence while he takes it in. "Normally, you have to wait for the county clerk to record it afterward, but A..." I stop myself just before I say his name. "But the guy, you know, the guy who agreed to... he knew someone who knew someone, and he got it recorded immediately."

Being the son of a lawyer comes in handy, apparently.

Honestly, for as annoying as Ax has been after the fact, he was helpful and responsible through all the important parts, almost like a real grownup. Not only did he arrange the quick recording of the marriage, but he also moved his appointments for the morning and called in a favor with someone in order to get us on today's schedule with the justice. Otherwise it was going to be next week, which felt like a forever wait. I would have had the whole thing done the day that we'd negotiated—I actually did drag him to the courthouse that afternoon—but there was a twenty-four-hour mandatory waiting period after the license was issued, so we had to go back.

At the event itself—I hesitate to call it as such, since it was really so nothing it hardly qualifies as an event—Ax was courteous and quiet, and surprisingly never interrupted the ceremony or cracked jokes. And the way he looked at me throughout, as if the whole thing deserved respect, as if he genuinely enjoyed looking at me...

Let's just say that the court-appointed witness was certainly fooled.

Thank goodness I had enough forethought to tell the justice to skip the kiss at the end, claiming we were both anti-public displays of affection, because if I hadn't—if we'd gotten to that part and Ax had lowered his head and finally pressed that wicked mouth to mine, all while looking at me the way he was—

It's not something I want to think about, is what it is. "Point is, three-to-five business days, and the bank should be able to guarantee funds. Tell Bob Peterson we'll have an offer by next Friday."

That's the part that matters. That's the part to celebrate.

But brothers are dicks.

"*The guy*," Holt repeats, and I prepare myself for the ambush. "And you're still not going to tell me who it is?"

"His name will go to my grave." The thought of anyone finding out that it's Ax makes my insides summersault. I'd prefer Holt and Alex didn't know I was getting married at all, but there wasn't any way around that with the deal.

"Because it's embarrassing...or...?"

My brother knows me too well. "Because it's not important. It's not a real marriage. There's no reason to give it any attention." Then, since I've learned the best way to avoid questions is to ask them instead, I ambush him right back. "Are you sure Grandpa isn't going to find out about this?"

It seems odd that he wouldn't be informed since he set up all the grandkids' trusts, but both Holt and Alex assured me it wasn't the case when they got access to their accounts.

"He's ninety-seven, Adly. All the people he dealt with at the bank when he set up our trusts are dead or retired. He barely looks at his own financial records these days. You think he's worrying about every nickel and dime he tucked away decades ago?"

"You know it only looks bad on you when you treat me like I'm an idiot since I'm going to be your boss soon and all."

"No, it's also fun." His tone grows serious. "Really, though. I wouldn't worry. Even if they send a letter to inform him it's been accessed, his assistant will likely toss it without a second thought. It's not like Elias is going to remember when your birthday is, and Grandpa would fire his ass if he bothered him with shit like that."

"Okay." I take a breath and look at the clock on my desk. Time to head to the conference room. "Anyway, just wanted you to know the status. I have to go now."

"Hold on, wait. Just one more thing."

"Make it quick."

"Is this He Who Won't Be Named?" *For fuck's sake.* He could at least get the name right. "If he's got something going on with his dick, you probably don't want to—"

"Goodbye, assHolt!" I hang up the phone before he can tease me more.

Just wait until I give the toast at his wedding. He's going to find that payback is a bitch.

———

Ax is already at it when I get to the conference room.

Since I'm running late, most everyone's sitting down already, including my father who is running the meeting, but Ax is making his way around the table, handing out cigars.

"What's this for?" Richard from corporate development asks.

"Celebrating, obviously."

I know in my heart that when pressed, Ax will same

something innocuous. That he's only trying to provoke me, and that there's no reason to fuss.

But I'm fucking fussed.

Deciding it's best to ignore the asstwat, I slide into my seat. "Sorry, I'm just getting here. Have we started already?"

Uncle Arthur, my father's younger brother and COO, tucks his cigar into his breast pocket. "Aren't cigars for babies?"

Meade from weather seems confused. "They give babies cigars?"

Meade's an idiot, by the way.

"That's not what he means," Dad says, in a tone that I know means he's eager to get going.

Arthur is one of the few people who doesn't cater to my Dad. "Am I wrong? Isn't that what they do in the movies? Hand out cigars shouting it's a girl! It's a boy! I swear that's what they do."

"Oh. Right," Meade says. "Yes, they do do that."

"They don't do it for weddings?" Ax's question sounds casual enough. He meets my gaze as he takes his seat, which as it turns out, is directly across from me. "I swear that I heard they handed them out at weddings."

I swear that I would jam my heel in his eye, if we were alone.

"I don't think so," I say, since we're not.

"People hand out cigars for whatever important occasion people want to hand out cigars at. But it's not traditional at weddings." My cousin Scott, who's basically the VP of Public Relations, sniffs along the length of his. "Cohibe. Nice brand."

"What is it that they pass out at weddings?" Ax refuses to move his eyes from mine.

If only I could force mine to look somewhere else.

"Rice." This from Trey in advertising.

If only this conversation would blow the fuck over.

"Birdseed. It's more ethical. Or bubbles." My brother Steele is usually the quiet one at these meetings. Why he knows anything about wedding traditions is beyond me.

"Bubbles." Ax's grin feels like it's only meant for me, as if I'd been as interested in the answer as he was.

As if he has plans for said bubbles, and though I can't immediately think of any kinky things that can be done with bubbles, I have to press my thighs together to stop them from tingling.

No, no, no. I do not want to have kinky thoughts about Ax Morgan. I *will not* have kinky thoughts about Ax Morgan.

Mrs. Morgan.

Too late.

"Can we start, please?" Hopefully, I only sound desperate to myself.

Dad looks directly at me before pivoting his head toward Ax. "Is someone getting married?"

"No one's getting married." I pick up the agenda that had been laid out at my spot before I arrived. "'New CEO announcement' is listed first. Is that still happening next month, Dad?"

"That's not true," Ax says. "About no one getting married."

My face heats as all eyes turn to him.

I panic. "Whatever he says, he's—"

Ax cuts me off. "Samuel's oldest and first offspring to wed—Holt. Right? Isn't he engaged? Did he set a date yet? Is he still on the shit list or are we happy for him?"

Everyone waits for Dad to answer. Holt is no longer the CEO for Reasons, and as he was supposed to be Dad's shining star—since he's why Dad had to leave retirement to temporarily fill the spot after Holt fucked up—Dad's the only one who can address the bad blood.

It takes him a beat to answer. "We're happy for him."

Then, because Dad really doesn't like talking about Holt, he starts the meeting, and Ax's antics are thwarted.

Temporarily, anyway.

Because there are at least five other times during the meeting that Ax slips in innuendos meant to make me squirm. The worst being when he tries to convince the team that "secrets are hot right now" and so we should have some sort of secret that we can use to interest our audience.

"Like tease the new lineup for the fall?" asks Irena from the communications department. "We have a secret, stay tuned sort of thing?"

"Sure." Ax doesn't sound like that's the kind of secret he means, but no one seems to notice but me.

Arthur nods. "That could be fun."

"Hot, right?" The timbre in Ax's voice makes my skin burn.

I laugh like it's preposterous. "No."

But sort of also, yes. It *is* kind of hot. Not just our secret marriage—because whatever. That's not real—but our whole secret relationship. I'm convinced that there would only have ever been one time if it weren't for the thrill of sneaking around and knowing a thing that no one else could ever know.

"*Hot* is an interesting term," Steele says, eyeing the man across from me.

Maybe I'm not the only one who's noticed Ax being weird.

"Hot, in, on trend—I know exactly what he means." Dad nods to the marketing officer. "Write up a plan for that, Jason. Great idea, Ax."

Oh, nice. Dickhole got himself a compliment.

"Told you it was hot." Once again, it's as if Ax is talking only to me.

"*I hate you*," I mouth, but I'm not immune to the humor of the situation, especially when he replies with his hands in the shape of a heart, a sight so hilarious on this ass of a grown man that I find a smile start to toy on my lips.

And then, even though it's the last thing I want, my mind starts to create a scenario where the HR nightmare bad boy employee starts fooling around with the boss's daughter. In secret. Sneaking around during the workday, banging in places the CEO walks by every day. Talking about their relationship in front of everyone and no one has any clue.

Wait. That's my literal life.

Except in the scene, the two would never end up marrying at the courthouse on a random Friday in June, so I think I just might be able to convince myself that it is nothing like my life at all, and it could be the hottest role-play yet.

Yeah, I hate myself too. It's fine.

That's where my head is at, mentally calculating the

logistics of a secret bang session after this and before my next appointment—possibly in this very conference room—when the doors suddenly swing open, and Grandpa Irving bursts in.

Bursts in is sort of metaphorical, considering the fact that Elias is pushing Grandpa in his wheelchair, but it's dramatic enough of an entrance that it feels accurate. Point being, his appearance is unexpected, and while everyone else gapes in surprise, my muscles tense.

Can it be just a coincidence that he's here? Today of all days? When he rarely comes to the office of late?

Underneath the table, I cross my fingers. All of them.

Uncle Arthur is the first to address the elephant in the room. "Is everything okay, Dad?"

Grandpa ignores his son. "Where is she?"

I'm the only Sebastian "she" in the room. The only Sebastian "she" in most rooms.

My stomach drops, and I want to crawl under the table.

But right now the main goal is damage control. Grandpa might be on the verge of disowning me, but it doesn't have to be in front of the whole executive team. "Can we go talk about this somewhere else?"

Elias nods in agreement, but when I start to stand, my father puts up a hand to stop me. "We're finishing a meeting right now, Dad. Could you—"

"This involves you, too." Grandpa stands from his chair —he can walk fine, just tires out easily—and points a finger at me. "Were you in on it? Do you know what your daughter did?"

"No…" Dad's interest is clearly piqued.

"No!" I say at the same time, bolting up from my chair,

determined to not let this turn into the most embarrassing moment of my life.

But it's nearly impossible to win a battle of willpower with Irving Sebastian—even at his ripe old age—and though I say no again, I'm no match for the boom of his salty baritone voice. "She went and got herself married without a wedding."

I sink down into my chair and there's Ax's face in front of me, his eyes twinkling with amusement.

He pulls a cigar from his pocket, sticks the end between his teeth, and that fucking stupid mouth of his grins.

CHAPTER
SEVEN
ADLY

Chaos breaks over the conference room.

Half the team has the sense to get up and leave, thank God. The other half are the annoying fucks who like to rubberneck at car wrecks.

And then there's Ax. Chomping away on his unlit cigar like it's made of candy. If I could reach across the table, I'd pull it out of his jerk mouth, throw it at him, and hope it hit him in the eye.

This is the man I married.

I'm going to have to stand and take responsibility for this in a minute, but for the moment, I can't move. Like a deer caught in headlights, I'm frozen in inaction.

Frankly, if I could move, first thing I'd do is send a text to my oldest brother. Sure all the boys got their inheritance with no problem, but the first time a granddaughter qualifies, Grandpa comes charging into the office. The only bright spot is that I'll get to tell Holt he was wrong. Trust me, I'm going to gloat.

Meanwhile, my father is having trouble accepting the news, and understandably so. "Dad, Adly isn't even dating anyone. Believe me, I wish she were. She's officially an old maid."

Yep. My father said that. In front of people.

Elbows propped on the table, I drop my head in my hands and try not to scream.

"Maybe you need to sit back down in your wheelchair," Uncle Arthur says, in that loud voice he always uses with Grandpa, overcompensating for his hearing loss. Then he lowers his volume, but not so much that we can't all clearly hear him. "We should probably make an appointment with his doctor, Elias."

"I'm not loony, you dickweeds! You and your brothers are the incompetent brain sacks, not me." No one can accuse Grandpa of going quietly into the night. He's more outspoken and feisty these days than ever. "I have credible intel. My contact at the courthouse told me our precious Adly had a marriage certificate signed and recorded this very morning."

The courthouse?

Technically that means Holt *wasn't* wrong, since he only reassured me that the bank wouldn't reach out to Grandpa. He never mentioned the courthouse.

Bye-bye, bright spot. Now the whole thing is just a fiasco.

"You have a contact at the courthouse?" Arthur still seems dubious.

"Of course I do. Reaches out whenever he comes across

anything that might be of interest in case I want to bury the news. You do that too, right?"

Both August and Dad talk over each other in their attempts to assure their father that they are capable men who also have government connections.

"Do connections at the FBI count as useful?" Ax asks, low enough that I'm sure I'm the only one who hears him.

I lift my face from my hands to give him an inquisitive tilt of my head. "You have connections at the FBI?"

He doesn't get to answer before Dad gets back to the point. "Adly did not get married without our knowing. That's ridiculous. She's right here. Tell him, Adly."

I feel all eyes on me, but before I can answer, there's a chortle from Steele at the other end of the table, stealing the room's attention. "Someone married Adly. That's funny."

Obviously, I decide the person who needs a cigar thrown at him is my brother, but since I don't have one, I throw my pen instead, hitting him squarely in the side of the head.

Ax seems to realize suddenly that this situation could look as bad for him as for me. He starts gathering his things, a panicked expression on his face.

"You dirty rat," I whisper at him.

"We can play rat catcher later, baby. Right now, I'm out." He stands, ready to bolt.

Simultaneously, Uncle Arthur asks Grandpa, "Did you happen to ask your contact who Adly supposedly married?"

"Of course I did, son, I'm not an imbecile. She married Axel DiAngelo Morgan."

Now everyone's gaze descends upon Ax. Which feels

much better than when everyone had their eyes on me. This horrible situation is once again looking up.

"You?" Dad has known Ax since he was born, but the way Dad's looking at Ax now, it's like he's not only never seen him before, but also like he's an alien creature who crawled out of the sewer and is now standing in front of everyone with shit dripping onto the carpet.

It's kind of nice to be reminded that Dad does love me.

Sure he constantly patronizes and belittles me at the office, he's also a father. Meaning, Samuel Sebastian isn't going to think just anyone is good enough for his only daughter, especially not Ax, whose best friend's name is a curse word around our family. Hunter has tried incessantly to snatch the job of CEO at SNC, even though he's very much not in line for the position.

It's caused a lot of animosity, as can be expected, but even before that, Hunter was a problem since he was the product of a one-night tryst between my mother and my dad's brother.

...and that's how Hunter is both my brother and my cousin, cementing our family tree into real life soap opera territory. It happened before she married my father, but that affair—one that my Dad insists was nonconsensual (can't ask her, since she's been dead since I was four)—has haunted our family for decades.

Point being—there's a good chance Ax might need to beef up his resume after this.

I'd feel bad, but it's his own fault. He pushed to be the guy who married me. If he didn't consider what could happen, that's on him. Not me.

Honestly, it's almost worth whatever punishment I'm sure to face just to see Ax in the quicksand with me.

I stand and open my mouth, ready to give my defense, when something totally unexpected happens: instead of darting out and hiding until I've softened the blow—a move I completely expect from him—Ax solidly faces my father. "It was my idea, Samuel."

"What?" Dad and August and Steele say in unison.

"What?" I say at the same time.

Ax holds a hand up and attempts to clarify. "The secrecy regarding the marriage, anyway. Was my idea."

I'm once again stunned into silence as Ax continues, rounding the table toward me as he does. "Now keeping the *relationship* on the downlow was a bit of both of us. We've been together for...what? A year and a half now? We thought it might cause unnecessary tension among the execs if two of us were dating, and we wanted to see where it went first, so we've been hush about it. Isn't that right, Addles?"

"Uh..." I stare at him, dumbstruck, as he puts his hand around my waist.

Under layers of clothing, my skin feels the heat of his palm.

"But then it got serious." Ax pulls me against him, smoothly, like he's done it a million times before. "We wanted to tell you first, Samuel, but she's been worrying about your heart. Having to come back out of retirement couldn't have been what the doctor ordered, and we thought it would be better to throw this on you—throw *us* on you—after you had the CEO position filled and this stress is gone."

The most incredible thing isn't that Ax knows just what to say, but rather that my father seems to buy it. His features are soft when he looks in my direction. "You were worried about me?"

I blink once before jumping into my role. "Duh. You had a heart attack, Dad."

"And you thought I'd have a relapse if my daughter got married?" He laughs. "I survived my own wedding and honeymoon last fall without any issues, honey. I think I can survive yours."

Great. Now I sound like an anxiety ridden worrywart.

I glance up at Ax, since he's the one who has my father eating out of his palm.

Without hesitation, he steps in. "Adly thought there was too much going on currently to add another wedding to your plate—since she knew you'd want to be responsible for it—and when I pled for her hand in marriage, she suggested we put it off for a year or two. But I couldn't go a day longer without making her my bride. That's why I suggested the justice of the peace in the meantime."

I think I might throw up.

But also my heart does a little flutter in my chest. Obviously, it's confused.

"A year or two?" Grandpa sounds appalled. "I'm ninety-seven. How long do you think I'm going to be around?"

"I could say the same thing," Dad says, though any other time, he'd insist he's the perfect picture of health. "If you're worried about my heart, why would you wait? I can't imagine not being able to walk my daughter down the aisle."

"You'd better be planning a grandfather/bride dance at the reception," Grandpa adds.

"We haven't planned anything," I say.

"You bet we are," Ax says over me. "Remember, honey, when you said that you wanted a wedding dress worth dancing with Irving?"

"Uh. Yeah. That sounds like something I'd say." If it were the key to getting my inheritance and getting the hell out of this place, I'd say anything.

Ax's grip tightens at my hip. "See? We're already on the same page."

"Hm." My father nods his head, staring from me to Ax, taking it all in.

There is no way that anyone believes that me and Ax look good together, but Dad's approving gaze says otherwise.

The knot in my chest loosens. No one's mentioned my trust fund. Are we really pulling this off?

When Dad speaks again, it's as if everything's settled. "You should talk to Giulia. Her planner put everything together for our wedding in a few short months. Reasonably priced, too. I'm sure she can be convinced to drop any current clients with the right bid."

Hold up. I'm not agreeing to an actual wedding. "I'm sure we have plenty of time to plan something for next year. Late next year."

I'll make sure me and Ax "break up" well before then.

"Why wait?" Grandpa asks.

I shrug when no excuse comes to mind. "Why rush?"

Once again, Ax steps in. "We're legal now, Grandpa.

That's what mattered to me. And don't worry, Samuel. We signed a prenup. Her money's safe."

Dad cracks the hint of a smile, which is more than he gives most people. "I'm warming up to you, Axel."

"I have been your employee for seventeen years now, sir. It feels about time."

My father continues to banter with Ax. "Pretty sure I remember you running across my lawn once without a diaper."

"I only streak in my living room these days."

"I approve."

Watching them bond is too much for me, and I gently pull away from Ax's hold before my head explodes. I need my mind. Now more than ever. I'm already running an evaluation of the new situation, trying to figure out whether or not anything important has been affected by people knowing. There shouldn't be any hold-ups with the money now, which is a plus.

Pretending to be lovey dovey with Ax sounds tedious, but not unbearable.

Living the rest of my life with people thinking that I (even momentarily) thought he was marriage material is maybe the worst of it. Holt will never let me live it down.

But then I'll be his boss, so if that's what it takes...

I'm so deep in thought, I don't notice Grandpa has maneuvered his wheelchair over to me until he's speaking. "If you wait for the perfect time, sunshine, it's going to pass you by."

"I know, Grandpa. I just..." Lying to him is worse than lying to Dad. "I have so much on my plate right now."

"Ah, I know about your plans. Alex told me." His eyes

dart to the others, making sure no one's listening before going on. Then he takes my hand. "I fully support the three of you. I hope you know that."

Alex told Grandpa about our plan to buy SHE?

This must be the tidbit Holt didn't want me to know. I definitely wouldn't have approved, though maybe it worked out since Grandpa's given his support.

But it also means that Grandpa knows I'm not above keeping a secret from my father. How long before he draws a line from that purchase to my trust fund? Has he already?

"If you're worried about your father, he'll get over it," Grandpa goes on. "Your dad fell in love with you the second you were born. He might be a bit old-fashioned in his ideas—he's an idiot, we all know I raised a bunch of them—but I do believe, deep down, he wants you to be happy."

I study my father's profile, and a pit forms in my stomach. As much as I'm committed to leaving SNC and starting out on my own, I'm aware my father will take it as a betrayal. "I hope you're right."

Not wanting to dwell on the possibility that I'll never be forgiven, I try to focus on the moment. "It's a lot, though. Too much to add wedding planning to the load as well."

Grandpa Irving pats my hand. "Seems like money should be able to buy you everything, but I suppose it can't buy time."

"No, Grandpa. It doesn't." But it can buy a girl a company. There's literally nothing else I want, except more books and endless hours to read.

"Tell me." Grandpa's tone is abruptly serious. "Does he

make you happy? Does he love you like you deserve to be loved?"

I'm not prepared for such a personal question. I have no idea how to begin to answer. "I...well...you know..."

Grandpa rescues me from my fumbling. "Never mind. That look tells me all I need to know."

When I follow his line of sight, he's watching Ax, who's still talking with my father, buttering him up as only a conman like Ax can, but every few words, he slips a glance in my direction. Heavy glances that linger too long.

The pit in my stomach deepens.

"He's a goner for you, Adly Jade," Grandpa assures me.

But the look on Ax's face doesn't seem to me like one that says he's a goner. Grandpa must see that because that's what he's looking for.

My interpretation of Ax's expression, on the other hand, makes much more sense—it says, *Adly Jade, you're going to owe me, and you're going to owe me big.*

CHAPTER
EIGHT
ADLY

A x manages to escape the interrogation before I do—
because he's still an ass, even if he did save our
asses—but I fully expect him to barrage me with
compensation demands.

So I'm not surprised when I find him waiting in my
office.

I'd meant to talk to Sassy about her unprofessional soft
spot for Ax, but after news that we're married gets around
the office, she'll probably think he's entitled.

Or more likely, Ax will convince her he is.

He's seated on top of my credenza against the window,
his long legs nearly touching the ground. He's made
himself at home, the pillows I keep along the top of the
cabinet now stuffed behind his lower back, and I can't help
but wonder if he knows my secret—that I like to curl up
there and read sometimes after working late.

The Manhattan night skyline and a good book—what more could a woman want?

She could want her cozy reading nook off limits to the most annoying man in the office, but since that wasn't a condition spelled out in the prenup nor our previous negotiations, it's probably irrational to expect.

When I get closer, I realize he's also located my Glenfiddich. I'd had it hidden on the bottom shelf of my bookcase. Totally inconspicuous. Does the man have a superhuman nose for whiskey I should know about?

This time, there are a total of twelve shots lined up, divided into two rows. "*Six* rounds?" Most we've ever done before was four.

"Yeah, I think we have a lot to work out."

Fuck.

I mean, fair. I would prefer to believe that nothing has changed in our deal beyond the annoying reality that people now know, but that's probably unreasonable. There will definitely need to be some amendments to our agreement.

But six rounds?

I don't even keep that many glasses in my office. Ax must have hustled to have time to gather some of his own. There's no way we won't be drunk by the time we're through.

Best strategy is to negotiate quick, before the liquor has time to muddle reason.

I sink into my desk chair and roll closer to him. Then I pick up a shot glass. This should be an easy one. "The truth stays secret."

I'm relieved when Ax instantly lifts a glass of his own.

"The truth being that our coupling is a sham rather than true love?"

I nod. "I know it seems unbelievable that anyone would ever think—"

"Ridiculously unbelievable," he corrects.

"Ridiculously unbelievable that we would—"

"Ludicrous, even."

I slit my eyes and glare at him, waiting to go on before I'm sure I won't be interrupted again. "—that we would be romantically—"

"Preposterous, really."

"Oh my God, are you going to let me finish?"

That grin of his is dazzling. "Just wanted the circumstances to be absolutely clear."

He waits a beat, and when I don't pick up the conversation again—because I don't trust him not to be a dick, obviously—he finishes my statement for me. "It's preposterous that anyone would ever think we're together, but apparently not too preposterous because people believe the lie, and you would like me to keep that lie a secret."

"Yes."

"Are *you* keeping it secret?"

"There are people who will know the truth." Alex and Holt, namely. "But I'm not telling anyone else, and you can't either or the whole thing is blown."

I'm honestly surprised Grandpa didn't call me out already, especially since he was told about SHE. Then he finds out I secretly got married? How is that not suspicious?

Maybe some people believe what they want to believe. As for me, I tend to trust no one.

Whatever miracle that shone on us today, I'm not trusting that it will occur again. Mum has to be the word.

But Ax is apparently in a fuck around and find out mood since, rather than just agree, he tilts his head and considers. "What's my incentive to keep it secret?"

"I don't know, Ax. What *is* your fucking incentive?" It's not like I haven't asked that very question a million times. Maybe we'd get somewhere if, as opposed to pouring the whiskey down our throats, I poured it all over his ten-thousand-dollar suit.

My voice is sharp, and he puts his hands up in surrender, shot still clutched in one. "I'm just making sure we're covering all the bases."

"Look. This isn't that much of a change from the first session. The marriage might have been outed, but the truth was not. We've already agreed—we're keeping it secret. Let's move on."

"Secret it is." His tone is light, in contrast to my elevated volume, and I more than a little want to strangle him.

I settle for clinking glasses and throwing the shot back instead. "Salute," we both say in unison.

I put my glass on the tray and reach for another.

"But Hunter's going to know, no matter what I try to tell him," he says.

"You can't have caveats after we've saluted!" *There are rules.*

But also his caveat should very much be addressed. "Go on," I say.

"You said some of your people will just know. I'm saying the same for me. There is no way that Hunter won't figure this out."

I want to argue with him. Sure, Ax and I have never played nice in public, but he's a good actor. I've seen him roleplay. He can stay in character. Can't he convince Hunter like he convinced my family upstairs?

But Hunter has always been the most likely person to fuck this up for us—besides Ax—and suddenly the stress of the last few hours seeps through my veins like caffeine injected through an IV. I'm anxious and jittery and every minor crack in our plan seems like a wide-gaping hole.

"You're right." I push out of my chair so I can pace. "You're absolutely right. Hunter's going to think of my trust fund right away. He'll figure it out and tell Grandpa. What if Grandpa already knows? What if the whole thing upstairs was a ruse? It would make sense, wouldn't it? Grandpa Irving knows and was trying to catch us in the lie, and then we didn't break, so now he's going to keep pushing us to prove our relationship like an absurd game of chicken and everything he said to me about understanding and the way you look at me was just an attempt to get me to confess, and oh my God, I'm not going to survive this. There's no way. There's no way!"

"Hey!" As I pace by, Ax grabs my arm and pulls me to face him, placing a hand on each of my shoulders. "Cool the fuck down, will you? You're spinning. Deep breaths."

This isn't spinning. This is freaking.

But I force myself to take a deep breath.

"Good girl." In a strange turn of absurdity, the praise settles me more than the breathing. "Now what was that about the way I look at you?"

My heart starts to pound again from the look he's giving

me now, and my skin tingles under his grip, and every-where feels hot.

The first shot taking effect, probably.

I wriggle out of his hold. "Nothing. You just really had them going. Laid it on a little thick, actually."

He shrugs. "Got the job done."

"But what if it didn't?"

"Well." This time he reaches for my hand to pull me to him.

Then he takes both of my hands in his and rubs along my wrists with his thumbs. "Game of chicken? Okay. That sounds typical Sebastian. Then we just have to play better, right? We can't break. We're already married. What else can we be pushed into?"

A hilarious vision pops into my head of me in a hospital, Ax at my side, as I red-faced push a baby with a big-ass head out of my who-ha.

The big-ass head clearly being inherited from his father.

I shake the image off, refusing to let the melodrama win. "Nothing." No one's going to force me to birth Ax Morgan babies, anyway.

"Exactly."

Following the worst-that-could-happen logic, I arrive at the same place we always were. "My trust fund could be rescinded."

"If they can prove we aren't real."

The only thing I hate more than when Holt makes sense is when Ax makes sense. "So we just have to play the game better."

"And we're fucking great at games."

"We are." My nervous system finally registers the caress of his thumbs, and goosebumps pop up along my arms.

I tug my hands away and cross my arms over my chest. "...And if Grandpa's really clueless? What do we do about Hunter? He's going to make sure Grandpa knows."

"You let me handle Hunter." Ax is too confident for my liking.

"You think you can convince him otherwise?"

"I do."

"How?"

He dismisses me with an expression that says he knows my half-brother better than I do—he's not wrong—then picks up the next shot glass. "Guess you're going to have to trust me."

That's not happening.

The problem is that it's out of my hands. Hunter won't keep his mouth shut for my sake. If anyone can convince him not to bother tattling, it will be Ax, and if Ax can't do it, then I'm already screwed.

I pick up the shot, not because I trust Ax, but because this is my only plan. "*Salute.*"

"*Salute.*"

The heat of the whiskey down my throat kindles a determined fire. We're going to pull this off. We have to.

After I set down my glass, I cross to the opposite end of the credenza and hop up. I let my dangling shoes fall to the floor. Then I steal one of my pillows from Ax for my back, getting as comfy as I can while still wearing business attire.

I pick up the next shot. "What else?"

He shifts so he's facing me, and loosens his tie. "If your

family thinks we're together, we're going to have to *be* together."

"Not all the time."

"But some of the time."

I wrinkle my nose at the idea of Ax invading my personal life. More than he currently does, that is. "You're already always at family events."

"Not the smaller ones."

"I'm going to need you at the smaller ones," I say with reluctant acceptance. Sunday dinners at my father's house, birthday parties for the cousins, weekends in the country. It's potentially a lot of Ax.

Strangely, it doesn't make my stomach turn the way I would imagine it would.

Fortunately, Ax can't tell. "We'll have to actually stand next to each other," he says, as if hoping it will get a rise out of me.

"I know," I say, without a rise.

"We're going to have to act like we like each other, too."

"I can act like I like you." This one feels personal, considering how many times I've very much acted like I've liked him.

"In front of people." He leans forward. "We'll have to be touchy-feely."

A strange sensation flutters in my chest.

And between my legs. I press my thighs together to dull it. "I can be touchy and feely in front of people."

"We might have to kiss."

"We won't have to kiss." But that stupid mouth of his is taunting me, and I find myself wondering, not for the first time, if that mouth would feel as good against my tongue as it has against other parts of my body.

Wait…do I actually want to kiss Ax?

I shudder. "No."

"No?"

Whoops. Forgot he wasn't part of that conversation in my mind. "We won't have to kiss," I repeat.

"Are you sure?"

No.

But I'm sure enough to try to reason it out. "We're not going to be together long enough to have to worry about a wedding." In case that isn't obvious. "And It's not like my family is into celebrating PDA. I just can't imagine why we'd have to kiss."

"*Get to*, baby. This mouth is a master at kissing." He puckers his lips, which is somehow both comical and alluring at once.

I lower my head so I'm not looking at him. "Kissing ass? Yes, you've told me."

"And if your grandpa is trying to break us…" The shrug is in his voice. "Game of chicken and all."

If I *did* want to kiss Ax, I wouldn't want the first time to be in front of other people. Should we practice? Is that what he's suggesting?

Do I want to practice?

As if he can hear my internal struggle, he starts to bawk. Like a chicken. "Bawk. Bawwwk."

"So immature. Oh my God." I'm definitely not kissing a child. "If we have to kiss, we'll kiss. It will be fine. Otherwise, no kissing. And I'll hide my impulse to throw up if you have to touch me."

Our glasses clink. "*Salute*," we say.

And I'm officially feeling the alcohol.

I pull one of my feet under me, not caring how much thigh is exposed in this new position, and waggle a finger at Ax. "While we're discussing your manwhoreness—manwhoriness?—you can't be seen with other women." I lift a glass, figuring that this is an easy one to settle.

But alas.

Ax doesn't reach for his. "You can't just ask a man to keep his cock in his pants and not think it's going to require some debate."

"That's not what I—" Mumbling to myself isn't helpful.

Louder, and more direct, I start again. "Did I say anything about your cock? When did your cock come into play?"

"My cock is always in play."

I pause to evaluate whether or not I appreciate the innuendo and decide it's too complicated to determine. "I don't care what you do with your cock, as long as no one finds out."

Ax has the gall to look offended. "You honestly have no feelings about who I'm fucking?"

"None at all." For some reason, I can't look at him when I say it.

"People will assume I'm fucking *you*."

"As they should." If my body wasn't reacting to him before, it is now. Maybe it's begun to associate alcohol with roleplay since our trysts always begin with liquor.

Except the trysts that happen stone cold sober.

I've trained myself to never think about what trysts Ax

participates in without me. Not because it bothers me. Just...gross.

And a little bit ouch.

"It's only a few weeks, right?" He picks up a shot, and though I'm still not looking at him, I can feel him studying me. "I can manage to keep my extracurricular activity on the DL until then."

"How noble." *Translation: I don't care.*

"I'd remind you that you can't date either, but we both already know the last time you had a *real* date was senior prom."

I flip him off. Then pick up the next glass.

Clink. "*Salute.*"

This shot leaves me feeling prickly. Images of Ax with other women flash through my mind. Times I've seen him flirting. When he's left the club with someone that looks barely legal. "Maybe you fucking around can be why I end up breaking up with you."

Yeah. That's definitely how it will go down.

"Hold on—what?"

"We'll have to have a reason. You cheating seems kind of inevitable." It's funny how mad I feel about it. Considering it's a fictional scenario and not at all real.

"There's absolutely no precedent for that statement, since I've never cheated on anyone."

"Only because you've never been committed to anyone in your life." The closest he's come to a long-term relationship is...well, whatever we've been doing for the last year and a half.

Is that right?

I fight the urge to throw back another shot.

When I look back at Ax, he's shaking his head. "It can't be my fault."

"It has to be your fault. No one will believe it's my fault."

"Fuck you, and think about my position. Your father will support you no matter whose fault it is. Want to imagine what he'll do to me?"

While I don't believe that my father would have enough support from the board to fire Ax without a work reason, he could certainly make the job more difficult. Not to mention, I won't even be here if all goes as planned. Ax will have to weather the "breakup" in front of my father. Alone.

It's probably the only fair thing for me to agree. "Fine."

Actually, the idea of Ax having to play brokenhearted over me is worth the concession. I'll just tell people the truth—I'm not the marrying kind. End of story.

I raise my shot.

Ax puts a finger up, as if to say wait. "I know you said you'll have the money in a few weeks, but isn't that going to be awfully coincidental, to break up right after you cash the check?"

I've been so preoccupied with how we'll convince people we're together, I forgot to think about the optics of a breakup. "Fuck."

"We should wait longer before breaking up. Three months?"

Warmth spreads through my chest, as if I've just thrown back a shot, but the burn from my last one has already dissipated. "You'd be willing to do that?"

"Why do something if you aren't going to do it right?"

That's a notion I understand, even if I don't trust it coming from him.

He brings his glass to mine to clink. "*Salute,*" he says.

"*Salute,*" I repeat.

The whiskey only heightens my skepticism. He's not just willing to do this for me—for free, no less—but he's also offering to stretch the charade out for my benefit?

It doesn't make sense. "Why are you doing this?"

"Oh, God. This again?" He pulls a leg up and rests his foot on the credenza, so he can face me better. "You really don't trust me?"

"It doesn't make any sense." Unless he's playing me. Is he playing me? Is that something people do or is that just in books? Is Ax Morgan about to make me the biggest fool on the planet? "Why would you fight so hard to do me a favor that absolutely puts you out? It's weird."

He turns his head toward the window and gazes out over the city. "Admittedly, it's not the same thrill as when your dad didn't know. But then?" He lets out a sound of amusement. "Fucking around with the boss's daughter? Literally and figuratively—how is that not a grand time?"

He turns his gaze back at me, and I can read all over his face just how grand a time that would be for a bad boy like Ax. How he must have felt like he was getting away with something. Something really naughty. Something his boss could never know.

I get it.

I won't admit it, but I get it.

But that was when our trip to the courthouse was a secret. "And now?"

His answer surprises me. "Now it's a different thrill. Your father's never looked at me like I could be a contender before today."

I feel gut punched.

How many times have I hoped for an approving look from my father? I'm not sure what I'd be willing to do to get it. Buy a new company, maybe. Go to crazy lengths to acquire it. Marry my enemy.

I never imagined someone like Ax could feel the same.

I feel vulnerable even entertaining the idea. "Shut up. You're a top exec in his company."

"Because of the board. I don't even think Samuel voted." His pain is palpable.

Or I'm projecting.

"He hasn't fired you," I say, as though that's a comfort.

"Also not that easy when you have a board. That my father is on." He gives a half smile and immediately takes it back. "This job was an appreciation token to my father for all his years playing creative lawyer for the Sebastian family. Nothing more."

I'm still holding the last shot glass. I roll it absentmindedly between my palms, trying to clear my head of the buzz so I can really think. Ax is a good actor, but what he's shared is so specific. So relatable.

I peek up at him, and it feels like I'm baring my soul. "You really have no ulterior motive?"

"What ulterior motive could I possibly have?"

"That's not an answer."

He reaches across the wasteland of shot glasses and lifts my chin up with two fingers until my eyes are locked with his. "No, Addles. I don't."

My throat is tight, so I simply nod.

"One more round left," Ax says after a beat of silence. "Anything else?"

There's nothing I could negotiate that would protect me if I'm playing the fool, and if I'm not being fucked over, then he's the one who should be making demands because, in that case, I owe Ax big. "You?"

He doesn't hesitate. "What are you buying?"

I make a sound like a buzzer announcing an incorrect response on a game show. "Nice try. Next."

He considers. "Since I can't fuck you on our wedding night—because there's no wedding, I know, I know—I'll settle for a blow job."

"A blow job."

"Do you need me to explain what it is? I can't decide if it will be more or less entertaining if I have to teach you."

"I know how to give a fucking blow job." It's been a while, but I'm not inexperienced. Oddly, blow jobs have never made it into the Adly-Ax repertoire. It's not like we haven't played scenes where they'd be appropriate. Or like I'd refuse. It's like the kissing—we never discussed we wouldn't, we just never did. Same with the BJs.

Would I mind that?

The thrum between my legs returns, so apparently not.

"When? Now?" My mouth waters in anticipation.

But Ax shakes his head. "Sloppy blow jobs are a boner killer. I'll let you know when I'm ready to collect." He jumps down from the credenza.

"I'm not sloppy at jo blobs." When I hear the words out loud, I realize just how drunk I am. "Oh. Right. That's fair."

He chuckles as he moves in front of me. Then he picks up one of the last shots and offers it to me.

I blatantly choose the one still on the counter instead. We clink.

"*Salute.*"

Ax takes the glass from me and stacks it with his on the counter. Then he holds his hand out to help me down.

I think about pushing it away—I don't fucking need his help, and all—but I *do* need his help. More than I ever wanted to need anyone's help.

So I place my hand in his. Sparks shoot up my arm, sending heat throughout my body. I try to cover my shiver with my jump down, only to stumble forward, despite having his support, when my feet hit the floor.

I fall directly into Ax. His free arm wraps around my waist to steady me. My palms come to rest on his shoulders, for no other reason than that I don't know where else to put them.

Then I realize how close our mouths are.

His breath hits my lips, and without thinking about it, I tilt my face up.

In response, his head lowers. Half an inch. Three-quarters. "You sure we won't need to kiss?"

My heart pounds in my chest. "You sound nervous about it."

"I'm not."

"Why'd you bring it back up then?"

Another quarter of an inch. "Trying to be helpful."

"Or are you the one who needs practice?" Expectantly, I lick my lips.

"More like I'm afraid you won't be able to take it."

"Ha."

His mouth dances around mine. "You'd come on the spot."

"You never make me come," I lie.

"On the spot. And everyone would know." His lips graze mine. Once.

Twice.

The phone on my desk rings suddenly, jarring me from my haze. I jump out of Ax's arms, ashamed I'd found myself in them at all, and realize it's still early. "Fuck. It's still work hours."

And I'm drunk.

Middle of the workday drinking is not typical Adly Sebastian behavior. This whole Ax/trust fund situation has really thrown me off my game. I'm definitely not fit to answer a call so I ignore it. Two more rings, and it stops.

"Anyway." Ax's eyes glance at my lips, but the moment has passed.

Thankfully.

Miraculously.

That fucking mouth.

I can't look at him anymore.

"I have work to do." Pretending that I'm in control enough of my faculties to be productive, I bring my chair back to my desk, sit down, and jiggle the mouse to waken my screen. "Don't worry about the mess. I'll deal with it later."

"Yeah? Cool." He sounds aloof.

Which is fine. It's perfect. That's how he should be.

Still, I watch him as he leaves, shot glasses bulging from his pockets, despite my instruction to leave the mess, and a random inspired-by-too-many-romance-books thought floats into my mind—we should have agreed that neither of us would fall in love.

But talk about a preposterous idea.

CHAPTER
NINE
AX

s anyone close to their father?

I'm not.

The man is not really close to anyone, really, except maybe Henry, Irving's oldest son who runs the Sebastian Industrial Corporation, which is how Kevin Morgan became the lead lawyer for the Sebastians and was later given a spot on the SNC board as a reward for loyalty.

With no details or proof, I'm sure that "loyalty" is interpreted as "did sketchy things and got away with them."

SIC is also headquartered at the Sebastian Center, so for many years, Dad worked just floors above me, unless he was in court. Despite the close working proximity, I rarely saw the guy. Now that he's (mostly) retired, I see him even less.

Even so, juicy secrets spread like wildfire, and I'm not surprised when I get back to my office and Krieger announces that my father is waiting for me inside.

Fanfuckingtastic.

Dad's standing over my desk when I walk in, perusing the papers that I have laid out with his eyes only, since his hands are clasped behind his back, as though touching my things might give him a communicable disease.

I'm too used to this sort of treatment to find it that annoying, though I might feel differently if the graduation notice I'm avoiding was still on my desk instead of buried in my drawer. "Didn't know you'd be in the city today, Dad."

He finishes his inspection before lifting his head. "I was consulting on a trial downtown. Stopped over here when I heard the news."

I don't pretend I don't know what news he's talking about. "We would have told you eventually," I lie. "We didn't think we'd have to deal with people knowing until next year."

He wrinkles his nose, as if he smells something unpleasant, or as if the idea that he'd care about my marital status is appalling. "I'm sure you had your reasons for keeping it quiet. What I'm concerned with is how you plan to capitalize on this new position."

"You mean the position of husband? If this is a birds and the bees talk, I'd say you're twenty years too late." Since it doesn't look like my father has any intention of relinquishing my desk area, I slump down on the sofa instead. "Twenty-five years, actually. But who's counting?"

"You married a Sebastian."

"That I did." The judge's pronouncement of man and wife replays in my head and my heart starts to thump like it's trying to get out of my chest. It's been doing that all day, every time I think back on the moment. Trying *not* to think about it has been rather unsuccessful.

I pick up a throw pillow and play a game of toss and catch to distract myself instead.

As usual, my father misreads my actions as attitude. "This is the problem with you." He comes around the desk and leans against it as he lectures. "You have no momentum. You have no goals. You don't even see the opportunities when they're in front of you. You've spent your years as a lackey. Where is your ambition?"

I catch the pillow and hold it in my lap. "What the fuck are you talking about? I'm the VP of Programming. I'm a literal exec. I've hit the ceiling. There's no more up from here."

He draws his lips into a thin line, tilts his head and stares at me, like I'm purposely being obtuse.

I could say the same about him, because this is not the first time we've had this conversation. CEO is the job Hunter's after. He has the right last name, too, so as far as I'm concerned, the seat has his name on it.

I mean, sure, he hasn't ever worked at SNC, and everything he knows about the company and what it needs to run, he's learned from me.

But isn't that a form of job security? I've assured myself a spot as Hunter's right hand. He could create a new position just for me with a significant raise attached, when the time is right. Maybe what Dad likes to call lack of ambition is really just patience.

Suggesting that to my father feels like a waste of breath. I keep to the simple facts instead. "The CEO position always goes to a Sebastian. You know that."

"And now *you're* a Sebastian."

I swear I almost throw the pillow at him directly. "That's funny, because it was Morgan that I signed on the marriage certificate."

"But the other name on that certificate was a Sebastian and that's practically the same thing. Better than, since you're a man."

He's oversimplifying.

On the other hand, Samuel does have influence on the board's decision. Since Holt fucked up the opportunity to follow in his father's footsteps, the two names that have been floated around the board have been Samuel's other son, Steele, and Hunter. Steele doesn't want it, and Samuel knows that. But he'll never rally for Hunter, even if he's a favorite of the board's.

Would he rally for a Morgan who is married to his Sebastian daughter instead?

Maybe. My resumé is solid enough.

But Hunter is my best friend. He's the asshole who wants the power. Why would I betray him like that?

"Look." Dad, seeming to sense he doesn't have me convinced, folds his arms over his chest, looking very much like the stern parent who rode my ass to always get "better" grades in high school and college, even when I was top of the class. "I understand your reluctance, but Hunter will come out of this just fine. You, on the other hand, have always had to rely on skill and strategy, and a part of you must understand that or you wouldn't have married the boss's daughter in the first place."

"Her name is Adly." The sharpness of my tone startles me. Something about the way my father has reduced her to her usefulness to my career has me annoyed. "And I married her for the reasons people usually get married."

"Nothing wrong with that. You can put a picture of her on your desk when you take over Samuel's office."

This is standard Kevin Morgan. His marriage to my mother was over by the time I was ten, and he never remarried. Too devoted to his job to have time for romance. That's what ambition looks like to my father—career before anything else.

Didn't I appropriately emulate him? There's very little I have in my life besides my work. Haven't I done everything he wanted? Isn't VP of a world renowned business enough?

Honestly, I don't think there is an 'enough' as far as he's concerned.

But I have work to finish before the weekend and a headache starting behind my eyes, and I just want my father gone.

"Okay, Dad." It's the best way to put an end to this. Just say okay, even if it's a lie. I'm not actually going to go after the CEO position—even in the unlikely event that I'd ever be a candidate—and more importantly, my marriage to the boss's daughter has an expiration date, meaning so does my advantage. "I'll look into it."

"That's all I'm suggesting. And before I forget, this came for you." He reaches inside his jacket pocket and pulls out an envelope that I immediately recognize.

Jesus, how many places did she send them? One was forwarded from my old place, one sent here to the office, an email invite came through as well, and now this one sent to my father. As if I've lived at his home any time in the last twenty years.

I stand to take it from his hand and throw it on the desk behind him. "Thanks."

"You should probably update your address."

"Yeah, good idea." *Mr. Obvious.* The problem is more likely that I haven't responded to any of her attempts to reach me. Sooner or later, she has to take the hint.

I ignore the tight band that forms across my ribcage at the thought. "Don't mean to rush you, Dad, but—"

He pushes off the desk and cuts me off. "You have work. I'm sure."

"I do." Eager to shut the door on his ass, I walk him to the door.

"Ax," he says when we get there, turning to me, "Congratulations are in order. I should have led with that."

I wave my hand dismissively. When has he ever led with anything nice?

Then he reaches out and lays a hand on my shoulder. And the way he looks at me? It's an awful lot like the way Samuel looked at me earlier—like I did something good. Something worthy. Like he's not ashamed of me, for once. "I'm proud of you, Son. This is good. This is real good."

It feels like an explosion of warmth in my chest and a sock in the nuts at the same time. It's an expression I never thought I'd see on my father's face. It's a statement that I never dared imagine would cross his lips.

But proud of me for *this*? For marrying a woman who needs a favor? Proud of me because she has the *right* name?

It's fucked up, and I don't want any part of it. Especially if it means taking advantage of Adly.

So why am I suddenly fantasizing about what it would take to make him say it again?

HUNTER'S IN THE DEN, shooting pool, when I walk in. The sound of the balls clacking gives him away.

I set down my briefcase and throw my keys in the dish by the door, and call out, "Hi, honey, I'm home."

It's an overplayed joke that still makes me chuckle every time. The living situation with us in general is laughable. We're both pushing forty years old, and our bank accounts are stupid fat—not the typical roommates scenario.

Yet here we are.

This wasn't always the arrangement. I had a condo of my own for a bunch of years, but then I started spending more and more late nights at Hunter's, supporting him through what he calls his mandatory shitty years at the Industrial Company, then when he was old enough to inherit his trust fund, coaching him on SNC. Sharing my ideas. Getting him pumped for his time to shine.

Partying, too. A lot. More than a lot.

Too many too-drunk-to-go-home incidents led me to claim a room of my own at his place. My clothes migrated over. Then my computer. Then my bong. Eventually, Hunter suggested I might as well rent my place out and treat it as an investment and stay with him, sort of like a live-in mentor, at least until he gets the CEO position.

He'd never say it, but I think he doesn't like being alone, and I'm just not that particular about where I sleep, so it works.

Until he finds out I'm married to his sister, anyway.

The intensity with which he shoots the ball when I make it to the den says he might already know.

"What's she paying you?" He doesn't look up from his game, but the bare restraint in his tone says he's decided what the story is, and he's not pleased.

"She isn't." I know this came out of nowhere, but his attitude makes it hard to want to be forthcoming.

Hunter's head swings toward me. "Then what are you getting out of it? You're not fucking her, are you?"

I lean against the doorframe and give him a look that says, are you fucking kidding? It's either that or lie outright, and frankly, it's neither relevant nor any of his goddamn business.

Anyway, I told Adly I'd handle him.

A beat passes before he lets out a laugh. "It was just as ludicrous in my head. I only said it because I can't think of a goddamn good reason you would marry my fucking cousin and not think to tell me."

"Sister," I correct, because I'm an asshat, and it annoys me that he's always trying to distance himself from that side of his family. Yes, I'm a hypocrite, considering my own family relationships.

"*Half*-sister."

"Exactly why I married her. So we could be half-brother in-laws. Half brothers-in-law? We're going to have to Google the terminology." I pull my phone from my pocket and pretend to do just that. "Seriously, it's a dream come true. Should we break out a bottle to celebrate?"

Hunter's not in the mood. "You know she's only after her inheritance."

He's so irritatingly serious sometimes, and now I'm not in the mood either. "Yeah, I know she's after her inheritance. I'm not a fucking moron. I was doing her a favor." I pocket my phone and cross to the bar to pour some Macallan. Not to celebrate, but to soothe the sudden urge to kick Hunter in the head.

"Since when do you do favors for the Sam clan?" The hint of betrayal in his voice does not go unnoticed.

I get it, but it's unwarranted. "Are you jealous, baby? Don't worry. I still love you best."

"Quit with the jokes, Ax."

With my back still to him, I take a swallow of my scotch and remind myself I'd be pissed too if he got hitched without telling me. Don't get me started about what I'd do to him if he hooked up with my sister.

When I turn to face him, I'm sober. "She needed a favor. I needed the amusement. I figured, what's the big deal? She wants to buy something. Let her buy it."

"She wants to buy SHE."

I scoff. "SHE? The news network for women? Her inheritance isn't enough for that."

"It is when she combines it with Holt's and Alex's."

He has to be dicking with me. "How do you know this?"

"Alex told me. Told Grandpa Irving too, apparently, so that I won't try to mess with the deal."

My heart drops to the bottom of my stomach. "Adly's leaving SNC?" It's stupid that I hadn't put that together before. More stupid that it bothers me so much.

"Apparently, yeah, since you've now made it possible for them to afford the price tag after I got Bob Peterson to jack it up."

So much for Hunter not messing with the deal.

I take another sip of my drink, taking in the new information while I wait for the alcohol to float my heart back up to where it belongs. In that beat, I realize that Hunter's also been keeping secrets.

It's a realization that stings as much as his bomb about Adly's departure plan. "Might have been nice to be included in your scheming."

He shrugs and shoots another ball. "It didn't occur to me that my best friend would personally aid my enemies."

"Enemies? Come on." I'm not dissing the rivalry between his dad and his uncle—they have legitimate beef, from what I've gleaned. I'm not even surprised that Holt and Hunter hate each other like they do, both of them blaming the other for the loss of their mother.

But Adly and Alex? Hunter's *enemies*? It's a little extreme.

On the other hand, I can't lie and say I don't feel animosity toward Adly at the moment. She couldn't tell me about her plans, but Hunter knew? It feels personal to have been left out. It feels bad.

Whatever. She wants to leave, she should leave. "So what if they buy SHE? They're out of our hair. Isn't that a good thing?"

"They'll be our competitors."

"Against the giant that is Sebastian News Corp? In a niche market?" The more I think about it, though, the more bothered I am. And pissed. At no one in particular.

Or maybe at everyone in particular. At Samuel for always treating me like an afterthought. At my father for never being satisfied. At Hunter for his secrets. At Adly for hers. It's strange how anger makes me petty, but that's exactly what it does. "What you should do is create a rival division of SNC. Steal SHE's market. Kill the competition."

Another swallow from my tumbler washes away the guilt. Another swallow after that, and I can't remember why I felt guilty in the first place.

Hunter freezes over his shot, staring for so long that I can't tell if he's considering my suggestion or trying to hit the ball with his mind.

Then a better idea occurs to me. "Or you could buy SHE first."

Hunter sinks a solid before he straightens. "Unfortunately, I don't have the cash. And that whole thing where I'm not supposed to interfere."

"But you already interfered and got the price changed."

His smirk is spiteful. "Prove it."

In other words, Grandpa isn't what's holding Hunter back. The money is a real obstacle, though. I should leave it there as a bitter fantasy and move on.

Adly's leaving.

For some fucked up reason, what I really think is, Adly's leaving *me*. No more barging into her office pretending to be from the US Department of Labor. No more playing naughty secretary over lunch hour. No more sending dirty texts to her while she sits across from me in the middle of an exec meeting.

It feels more than bad.

"You might not have the cash, but SNC does." I hate myself a little, but the idea rolls like a snowball. "Adly doesn't have the cash yet. The deal can't go through until she does, which is at least another week or so. If you tell Bob to hold off on accepting the offer, you could buy some more time. The board is supposed to announce the new CEO soon. You could pull it off."

Hunter nods, slowly, the wheels turning in his head.

"And if you're CEO, you work for the benefit of the board, not Grandpa. They'll want you to do what's best for the business. Since Samuel and his brothers don't share their father's feelings about family before profit, I bet they'll be on your side."

He leans his cue stick against the table and runs his hand through his hair. "Fuck, do you think you can find out her bid? Since you're married and all. Then we can make sure our bid is higher."

Doubt it, but I shrug. "Maybe."

"You should try." Hunter's cackle is abrupt. "Samuel's approval. Can you imagine?"

I *can* imagine. Vividly.

The memory of my father-in-law's earlier admiration turns my stomach into a hard pit.

The marriage is temporary. I don't owe Adly anything.

And she's leaving. I'm not. My loyalty is to SNC.

Hunter lightly punches my shoulder. "You're a goddamn legend, Ax Morgan. 'Doing her a favor.'" He laughs. "Doing us a favor, more like."

"Right?" Exactly, right. No reason for guilt.

Because we're all looking out for ourselves here, and Hunter's the only Sebastian who has ever said "us" and meant it.

CHAPTER
TEN
ADLY

When I arrive at the Ida Sebastian Academy annual fundraising auction on Saturday afternoon, I realize I have vastly underestimated the extent of interest in my marriage. It's not even the media on my heels this time—far as I can tell, they still don't know—but a much worse group of people who are hounding me: my family.

The second I walk into the cultural hall, I'm swarmed.

My stepsister, Lina, is the first to grab me in an uninvited embrace. "I can't believe you didn't tell us!"

Her boyfriend (and my cousin) Reid, is less effusive. "Ax Morgan? I'm dumbfounded. You're not pregnant, are you?"

Then there's my stepmother Giulia. "I have tons of catalogs saved and websites bookmarked from my own wedding."

"I mean, Ax isn't really the kind of guy anyone thought you'd bring home," Lina says. "Not that I've really thought about who you'd bring home, really, because that's really weird, and also there's just no guy who would be good enough for you, but if this is the guy you love, then I completely support you!"

Holt's an asshole of a brother, so of course he joins in. "We could *tell* people she's pregnant."

Thankfully, his fiancée, Brystin, is a reasonable person. "We're not telling anybody any such thing."

"Who's throwing the engagement party?" my cousin Brett asks.

"I think they skipped the engagement part," his fiancée, Eden says.

"Then a reception," Brett says.

"Except they're still planning a wedding in the future, right?" Reid asks.

"They goddamn well better be." From my father, obviously.

"I can introduce you to my coordinator," Giulia says. "I'm here for anything you need."

"Did I forget to say congratulations?" Lina's question sparks a cascade of congrats from so many people that I can no longer pick out single voices as the best wishes turn into an interrogation.

"Where's your ring?"

"Are you both living at your place?"

"Are you not doing rings?"

"Are you moving someplace new?"

"Where *is* Ax?"

"You didn't come together?"

Right when I'm thinking I should have texted Ax a reminder, when I'm convinced there's no way I can do this and I'm going to be caught in the lie of it all, his gruff voice pierces the cacophony. "I'm right here."

Ax Morgan is never going to be anyone's knight, yet here he is, riding in again to save me like he's in armor instead of bespoke Bogliolo.

My stomach spins like I'm on a merry-go-round, and a smile breaks out on my face before I think to put it there. "Here he is," I repeat, my voice sounding breathy.

I clear my throat, then proceed to choke on my own spit, when a warm hand lands unexpectedly on my hip. My *bare* hip, since my dress happens to have cut-outs on each side of my waist.

In seconds, his hand heats from warm to burning.

"I slipped a few bids in while you were all playing tea party over here." Ax digs his fire fingers into me, a quiet reminder that I'm supposed to act like I like him. "We have our eye on the Matisse, don't we Addlebug?"

Addlebug?

I will my face to not cringe, which is admittedly not as hard as I would have imagined. Almost not as hard as it is to lean into his embrace and place my hand on his chest. "We could finally fill the spot in the foyer."

The heat radiating from his body to my palm is both foreign and familiar. I've touched him many times by this point, but with our clothes on, in front of my family, this feels strangely more intimate.

Ax tilts his head like he's considering, despite never

having been in my foyer. "I was actually thinking it's a good look for your new office."

There's a bite underneath his words, but the words alone are enough to put me on edge. "*New* office?" I feign laughter. "Am I going somewhere?"

Holt meets my panicked gaze with a raised eyebrow, and my mistrust in Ax suddenly feels very valid.

But then he says, "Ah, slip of the tongue, baby," and the endearment slides so naturally from his mouth that I shiver. "I meant it would make your office look new. Freshen the place up a bit."

"Oh." Most of my office walls are windows or covered with shelving, but I play happy couple and nod. "Hm. Yeah. That's, um, something to think about."

Fuck, he knows.

Or he's just fishing. He already knows I'm buying something big. Maybe he's just guessed now that any big purchase would need my full attention, and that I'll be leaving.

Or somehow, he fucking knows.

The thought of not being the one to tell him makes me feel like some kind of traitor. Stupid since I haven't broken any promises, and this is not actually a partnership in any way, shape, or form.

But still.

It's Holt who breaks the awkward silence, drawing attention away from the topic of my office. "My vote is the foyer."

Brystin, who I'm sure is in on the ruse, considering Holt tells her everything, is quick to agree. "That bare spot is really an eyesore, Adly."

"Unless they're planning to move," Giulia says. "That apartment isn't set up for a growing family."

"Growing family?" Then Lina gasps. "Oh my God, *are* you pregnant?"

With that, the onslaught of questions resumes. How did we get together? When will we have a ceremony? Why didn't we tell anyone? Questions that will be answered speculatively if we don't put our own voice to them, but I'm once again reminded that I'm not the best with on-the-spot improv and constantly relying on Ax to be my rescuer does weird things to my ego.

How did we not think to come up with a story?

We're obviously going to need a moment alone.

"I'm sorry, everyone," I say, pulling away from Ax. "My stomach is on the fritz today. If you'll excuse me..."

I push through the throng, ignoring the mumbles of, "Maybe she *is* pregnant," and all its variations. When I'm on the other side and realize Ax isn't following, I find his eyes and jerk my head pointedly toward a side door.

It seems to do the trick.

"I'm just going to check on my wife," he says, and my whole body shivers.

I turn back quickly toward the exit, hoping he didn't see the effect his words had on me.

My wife.

Is it going to do a number on me every time he says it? I'm sure it's because I'm conditioned. It's just a phrase, but it's a popular trope in some of my favorite books, usually when the characters are in a marriage of convenience, and though I'm very much only married to Ax for the convenience of getting my trust fund early, I'm not going to compare us to the romances I like to read.

This is real life.

No one is accidentally falling for their pretend spouse.

Neither of us will decide we want to stay together.

It's a practical arrangement, nothing more, with an end date that I am very much looking forward to.

Wanting to avoid more crowds, I choose an exit at the back of the auditorium. It's probably off limits to the public, considering the hallway is dark and empty, but the private school has Sebastian in its name, and I feel like that gives me privilege.

Not that there's anywhere to go now that I'm here. Metal gates block off one corridor. The gym at the end of the other hallway is obviously chained. I'm usually too much of a princess to sit on the floor, but if that's my only option, it will have to do.

I don't turn around when the door opens behind me until Ax speaks. "Your family's fucking brutal," he says.

"You think?" I'm trying not to stress, but between the plans to buy out SHE and my current full-time job, I'm busy as it is. There was no budget in my schedule for building and nurturing a fake relationship.

But I'm a woman of action. Between the two of us, we should be able to tackle this. "We need to come up with some answers to feed them."

Ax is barely paying attention. "Sure. Do that." He starts down the hall and tries to open the first door he sees, only to discover it's locked. "Let me know what you come up with."

I stand, my jaw dropped, as he tries another door. "You're not going to help?"

"Why would I?"

"Because we're in this together."

He's farther down the hall now. He jiggles another locked doorknob. "You're in this, and I'm in this. It doesn't mean we're in this together."

Irritation quickens my pulse and makes my jaw feel tight. If he's dropping his part of his bargain, so help me God...

I scramble to catch up so I'm not yelling after him. "What happened to *we have to play the game better*?" Fairly sure I didn't imagine the *we*.

He passes a janitor's closet without attempting to open it. "I believe we were talking about your grandfather when I said that, and I didn't see him here today."

"But we have to be on all the time, Ax. Shit gets back to him."

He shrugs, his hand on another knob. "Better hope he doesn't believe everything he hears."

"Thanks. Helpful."

"Anytime."

The next door he tries opens. He reaches in, flips the light switch, and the classroom is suddenly lit with fluorescent bulbs that give everything a greenish hue. Rows of desks with attached chairs face a whiteboard and smart screen. The walls are bare, though, and the desks cleared for the summer holiday.

"Ah," Ax says, apparently having found what he's looking for. Then he disappears inside, letting the door close in my face.

My irritation level notches up to pissed. He wanted to be part of this. He blackmailed me and sabotaged my other candidate, and now he's acting like the results of all that cajoling are my problem.

That fucker.

My feelings are only validated when I open the door and find him sitting behind the teacher's desk, his feet propped on top of it, and his jacket hanging on the chair. His arms are folded over his chest, and he's leaned back with his eyes closed.

That mother*fucker.*

After making sure the hall is cleared and no one's watching, I stomp into the room, and close the door behind me. "I knew you were a bad choice. Second day into this, and you're already bored and flaking out. This is why I didn't trust you. I knew this would happen."

"I'm here, aren't I?" He doesn't open his eyes. "That's what I committed to. I don't remember saying I'd help you create a story about us. I do remember you promised a blow job."

A blow job that I was willing to give yesterday, when he was my ally instead of my obstacle. "Don't hold your breath waiting."

I reconsider my words. "Actually, pretty sure I don't need my husband to be alive to collect the cash so *do* hold your breath."

"Real spirit of partnership you have, Addleby, for someone who is doing you a favor. For basically no compensation and very little info. I don't know what you're buying or what you intend to do with it." He almost sounds hurt.

Guilt hits me, but it's outweighed by the feeling that he's just trying to needle me for information that I've told him I'm not giving him. "Not this again."

Especially not this *now*. He can be butt hurt all he wants —we have things we need to sort out. Movement always seems to help get my brain working, so I set to pacing.

Ax continues to pester. "For all I know, this purchase of yours is going to come back and bite me in the ass."

"Shh. I'm trying to think." Though I'm somewhat relieved that he's still poking about my purchase. He must not know after all. "We could say you and I are a recent thing. Maybe say we got close when we were arranging your latest assistant. But I wouldn't want people to think we rushed into our relationship. What's a good time length between first kiss to 'I can't wait to get hitched?' Three months?"

He scoffs.

Admittedly, I've had little experience with relationships that weren't just sexual. The Sebastian way is career first, and I've followed the rules. With little reward, I might add, hence why I'm trying to leave.

I make another attempt. "Six months? Is that long enough?"

When he doesn't answer, I'm convinced he's fallen asleep. "Goddammit, Ax. This would be a hell of a lot easier if you would provide some input."

I'm in the process of pacing away from him when I hear the distinct sound of fists hitting laminated particleboard. "Mrs. Morgan," Ax growls. "You need to take a seat. Now."

It's a tone I've never heard from Ax. Bossy and irrefutable and a little bit mean. Plus using that tone with those words—Mrs. Morgan—it has my thighs vibrating and my skin suddenly feeling warm.

It also has me obeying. Without a second thought, I scurry to a desk and sit down before I realize the power he has over me with a mere sentence.

I need to tell him I'm keeping my last name so he doesn't use his like a weapon. Not now, since I'm still tongue-tied and subdued, but later.

With my attention fully on him, Ax stands. He unbuttons one cuff, tucks the cuff link in a pocket, and rolls his sleeve up. "You know why you're in detention today, don't you?"

Oh, it's a game.

It takes a second to figure it out because I'm too busy watching him roll the other sleeve up, his flower-entwined cross tattoo boldly appearing, but once I do, I'm back to being annoyed.

Well, I *should* be back to being annoyed. This is so not the time for this, no matter how intriguing Ax the Teacher is. No matter how fast my heart is pattering in my chest. No matter how distracting his bare forearms are.

Next thing I know, he picks up the yardstick laying in the whiteboard marker tray, and smacks it against the desk with a thwack. "I said, do you know why you had to stay late today, Mrs. Morgan?"

"No," I say, before I can stop myself. Before I can decide if I'm actually playing.

"No, *sir*," he corrects.

…and instantly I'm wet.

Just as quickly, I make the decision. It's not a responsible one—my decisions rarely are where Ax is concerned. But

I'm overwhelmed and stressed, and what's wrong with a little escape into fantasy? Roleplay with Ax gives me the same sort of getaway that reading does. I can leave the pressures of the world for a while and hide in the reality of a character whose problems can all be solved by being railed by a hot man with a big cock.

Where do I sign up?

CHAPTER
ELEVEN
ADLY

J ust because I'm down to play doesn't mean I'm not still annoyed with my scene partner. "You want me to call you *sir*?"

Ax doesn't miss a beat. "You can stop with the fucking attitude right now. You're already in a shitload of trouble, young lady."

"Didn't realize teachers were allowed to swear."

Ax takes the ruler and thwacks it across his palm. "Did I say you could talk?" His voice is gravelly. Menacing and mesmerizing and mega hot.

It stuns me into silence, as if I'm really a student who's in trouble with her teacher. As if I'm really about to be punished.

Except silence seems not to be what he wants.

Using the yardstick like a cane, he stalks toward my desk until he's looming over me. "Answer when I ask a question directly, Mrs. Morgan."

"No, you didn't." I swallow before I add, "*Sir*."

"So you *can* learn. Good girl."

When I peer up at him, his eyes are dark and his expression is pleased. It's the first time I've really looked at him today. He fit himself to my side as soon as he arrived, and then I was too busy panicking to pay attention, and now I think if I had really looked at him before, my panties might have been ruined a whole lot earlier.

His dark hair is unruly, as if he's had his hands in it a bunch of times since he woke up, but the high and tight cut keeps him looking military sharp. His silver tie brings out the glints of silver in his hair that are really only noticeable when looking for them, and he's trimmed his beard so that wicked mouth of his is center stage.

His appearance is both dazzling and disarming, and I'm sufficiently dazzled and disarmed, even when he switches from praise to scolding. "So now your offenses include disrespecting authority, talking out of turn, not finishing your assignment, and then trying to rope your teacher into giving you the answers."

The eye roll comes naturally. The assignment is *our* story. He *should* help. Not that I'm going to say that right now when his alpha side has been triggered. I always suspected he had it in him, but I didn't know I'd find it so...intriguing.

I'm so very intrigued.

Seemingly not finished listing my wrongs, Ax takes several steps backward where he can properly observe me. "And then there's this outfit."

"What's wrong with–?" I catch myself too late, remembering I'm not supposed to speak out of turn.

Mr. Teacher ignores the slip to focus on my real *offense*. "Too short to comply with school policy."

My face gives away my *oh, come on* thoughts. My dress is a cut-out halter mini dress, with ruffles that give it a bit of volume. Yes, it's short, but it's modest, and I'm pretty sure my high school uniform wasn't much longer.

"You disagree?" he asks. "Let's test it and find out. Come here."

Like before, my body responds to the command without thought, and I approach him at the front of the room.

"Kneel down," he says.

The tile is harder and colder and more uncomfortable than I imagined, yet I comply, and absentmindedly pull at my dress, as if it might stretch it to be long enough to give comfort to my knees.

Ax seems to consider that cheating. "Hands behind your back," he snaps. The action straightens my spine, and he props the ruler next to me to measure. "Your skirt is supposed to hit the floor. It's a good two inches from that. Add that to your other offenses, you're looking at suspension."

"I can't be suspended. It will ruin my college applications." I pitch my voice higher so I sound like I'm near tears.

He doesn't show me any pity. "Are you asking me to bend the rules for you? The rules are in place for your benefit. For your education. It doesn't serve you to let you walk out of this institution without..." He pauses for half a beat. "Learning anything from me."

For a second, I think that he meant to say "without *me*,"

but that doesn't make sense from a teacher. Or from Ax. Even if he really knew I was leaving.

Just a stumble in his improv, I suppose. The words he chose fit the scene and inspire my response. "Sir, if you please. That's not true. I *have* learned from you."

The bulge in his pants is eye level, and I feel a smug satisfaction when it grows.

He traces my jawline with a single finger and tilts my chin up to meet his dark gaze. "Not the lessons I've wanted to teach."

My stomach flips. "Which lessons are those, sir?"

"Obedience. Responsibility. Perseverance—I'm not sure you can complete a task to its end." He draws his finger up to rub roughly along my bottom lip.

It takes effort not to stick my tongue out and lick, knowing I need permission first. "I can. Just…test me or teach me. I can learn, sir. I swear."

"Let's see if that's true." He sticks the finger in my mouth, thrusting it deep like it's a tongue depressor.

I close my lips around him, saliva gathering on his skin.

"Have you done this before? Sucked a man?"

With his finger still in my mouth, I shake my head ever so slightly.

"I'm not talking about sucking fingers, either. I'm talking about sucking cock. Have these lips ever been wrapped around a man's cock?"

This time the shake of my head is more pronounced.

He brings his second and third finger to my lips and pushes them in as well. "The boys your age don't count. They think it feels good just to have a mouth on them.

They're as uneducated as you are." He pulls his fingers out, slowly, drawing saliva with them that he drags down my chin. "The online sites you read will give tips and tricks, but they'll never teach you what a real man wants you to learn."

"What does a real man want me to learn, sir?"

"How to take what he gives."

He rests the yardstick against the desk, then without any warning, he grabs the back of my head with both hands, pressing it against his crotch. He bucks his hips, rubbing his cock against my face through his pants. "You think you can take what I give? You think you can learn?"

It's more aggressive than he's ever been with me. Still, when he lets me up for breath, I don't have to think before I gasp my answer. "Please, teach me."

It's the consent he was looking for. "Undo my pants."

I do as he's ordered, quickly working the buckle on his belt, then the button and the zipper. This close, the musk scent that only belongs to Ax fills my nostrils, and my pussy clenches with familiar anticipation, as if she's about to be rewarded.

Sorry, kitty. Not this time.

"Now take my cock out."

I fumble for a few seconds, too eager to find the opening in his boxer briefs. Then his cock pops out, hard and fat and dripping at the crown. It's a nice looking cock, really. Long and thick, with a prominent vein running down the middle. The skin is a smooth golden brown and his head is pronounced.

While Ax has been more than generous with going

down on me, he's never shown an interest in bjs. Or maybe I was the one who never showed the interest. Whichever, I haven't had a real opportunity to be this close and personal.

Seems I was missing out.

"Do you want to lick it?" he asks, and I do. I really do.

"I'm not sure how."

He wraps a hand in my hair as he speaks. "You stick out your tongue—I'm sure you're capable of that—and swipe it along my tip."

With a deep breath, I lean forward. My tongue flattens against Ax's tip, and I taste the slightly salty tang of pre-cum. It's both unfamiliar and enticing, and my mouth waters for more.

But when I bend to do it again, he yanks on my hair. Hard. "Uh, uh, uh. I said I was teaching you how to take, not give."

My scalp stings from his pulling, which only seems to heighten my arousal. "Teach me how to take, sir."

He nudges at my lips with his crown. "Open your mouth. When I shove inside you, close around me, but only then. Whenever I pull out, you keep it open and waiting. When I'm inside you, relax your throat and take it. Even if you're choking, even if you're gagging on my cock, you keep taking it. You understand?"

I answer by opening my mouth as wide as I can.

Abruptly, he shoves his cock inside.

His force catches me off guard as much as his size, stretching my lips wide around his girth. I fight for air, swallowing saliva and trying not to gag, but the command in his voice echoes in my mind.

He thrusts deeper, going past the point of discomfort,

into a burning pleasure that fills my throat, my chest, my entire being. I swallow hard, the muscle in my throat pulsating as it adjusts to his invading cock.

When he pulls back slowly, my saliva glistens over his flesh like a slick, wet membrane. As his tip approaches my lips, I remember to keep my mouth open, and he rewards me by sliding right back in.

This is an even harder thrust, and I gasp for breath, the saliva pooling near the back of my throat as I gulp it down. The sensation is overwhelming, and I feel a wave of nausea. At the same time, my pussy throbs like a jealous mistress.

Ax draws back again, and this time when he shoves inside he stays there, pushing so far in that I can't breathe. My eyes water, and I gag. Instinct has me trying to lean away, but he holds my head in place and jiggles his cock inside my throat.

"Deep, like that." His voice is gruff. "You feel so good choking on my cock like this." He lets me up for the briefest gulp of air before driving back in, deeper, harder. "Fuck. You take cock so good."

I love the praise. It's one of my kinks.

But I'm even more turned on by this dominant side of Ax. It's new and exciting, and while I'm struggling not to gag all over him, I'm also squirming and pressing my thighs together, trying to stop the ache between them.

My wiggling seems to catch his attention.

"This turns you on, doesn't it? Let's see." He pulls back. Not all the way, just enough that my throat gets a tiny break while he picks up the yardstick. He uses the end to lift up my skirt. "Spread your knees, sweetie. Let me look at you."

I suddenly wish I'd worn white cotton panties instead of

nude, but apparently Ax has the view he wants because he groans.

"You have a wet spot. Fuck. You're killing me." He bucks his hips forward, pushing his cock in deeper, then retreats. "You got that wet just from sucking me. Answer me, baby."

"Yes, sir." It's hard to speak with my mouth full so I nod at the same time.

"Put your hand in your panties and get some of your wet for me. I want to see it on your fingers."

He continues to fuck my face, slowly now, while I do as he asks and slide my hand in past the waistband of my panties, and down to my pussy. It might be cheating, but I rub against my clit on the way, which only makes me wetter.

Gathering the slick, I bring my fingers out for him to see the moisture glistening on my fingers.

"So fucking wet." He pulls out of my mouth until only his tip is still between my lips. "Put it on my cock."

As soon as I rub the moisture on his cock, he pushes back into my mouth. The new flavor is instantly noticeable. His salty taste mixed with my arousal, and this time when he deep throats me, I moan.

Without permission, I stick my hand back in my panties, desperate for friction.

Suddenly, I feel a sharp smack against the side of my thigh as Ax brings the yardstick down against my skin. "Get your hand out of there. I'm teaching you to *take*. You take what I give you. You come if I let you."

If my panties hadn't been ruined before, they are now.

Why the hell does that turn me on?

Whatever the reason, touching myself feels too good, and I keep right on doing it.

"I said *no*." His voice is sharp as he yanks my arm away.

He yanks so hard that he pulls me off his cock and to my feet, and before I know it, he has my arm twisted behind my back and me bent over the desk. With one hand keeping me pinned, he maneuvers my panties down my thighs with the other.

Then in rapid succession, he smacks each ass cheek, one then the other, back and forth, too many times to keep count. Until my cheeks are stinging, and my eyes water.

"I was going to give you a yummy treat down your throat, but now I'm going to have to put it in your cunt. It wasn't the lesson I had planned, but you give me no choice when you refuse to learn."

My arm is still wrenched behind my back, my ass still on fire, when I hear the sound of the condom wrapper being opened. Thank God for man sluts who always carry protection in their pockets, because even though I'd been prepared to finish him off with my mouth, my pussy is begging for the attention.

And attention she gets when Ax abruptly shoves in.

The sensation is fierce, but also exquisite. My body throbs with desire, my muscles clenching around his invading cock, trying to adjust to the sudden assault. My free hand reaches up to grip the edge of the desk, bracing myself against the forceful entry. My back arches, pushing my ass back against him, lodging him even deeper.

He feels good just like that, buried inside me to the hilt,

but he doesn't stay still, drawing out only to shove back in. Every thrust is hard and deep, his hips slapping against my sensitive ass with each powerful stroke. The sharpness of the desk against my thighs heightens the pleasure, creating a harsh yet erotic mix of sensations.

"Take it," he growls into my ear, his voice low and demanding. "You want it."

My mind is consumed with the raw intensity of his words, the sting of the spanking, and the exquisite stretching of my pussy around his thick cock. It's as though I'm living on the edge, every nerve ending electrified by the intense sensations.

"Please, sir," I moan, the need rising within me, not sure what I'm begging for exactly. Not trusting him to deliver what I can't articulate, I let go of the desk and slide my hand underneath me, searching for my clit.

Ax pulls my hand away and twists it so that he's gripping both wrists behind my back now. "No cheating. No coming until you deliver your assignment."

When I don't remember what that is immediately, he reminds me. "The story. What is it? Tell me."

Our story, he means.

He has to be kidding. The task was hard when I had full control of my faculties so I expect it to be near impossible now that I'm so completely preoccupied.

Except it's not.

"It started during a holiday party." My focus is surprisingly dialed in, and though my voice is breathy, the words come easily. Possibly because they're the truth. "Not last Christmas, but the Christmas before."

Ax doesn't let up on his thrusts. "Keep going."

"We were looking for stronger liquor. Even though we were both already tipsy."

As I speak, he shifts his grip on my wrists so he's holding them both with one hand. Then the other slips around my waist.

When his finger finds my clit, I jerk. Not just from the startling intensity of his touch, but from the presence of his touch at all.

For the most part, my orgasms have been my secret. My responsibility. I've faked so many not Os with Ax, that I'm pretty sure he has no idea how easily he makes me come.

More importantly, I don't want him to find out. It feels too vulnerable. Too revealing. Because then he'll *know*. He'll know that I get pleasure out of this. He'll know that he gets me off.

As though it's his intention to unravel me just this way, he only increases the pressure on my clit.

"No," I gasp.

He ignores me. "Finish the story, Mrs. Morgan."

I can't. The pleasure is too distracting. Too demanding. It feels like a whirlpool about to suck me into its vortex.

My hesitation makes him snap. "Finish the story."

I close my eyes and concentrate. "One thing led to another and then we…we…"

It's impossible to go on. My voice cuts off as my orgasm accelerates its build, but the rest of the tale plays out in my head. *We fucked, and it was unexpected and unexpectedly satisfying. Horrifying too, because of our history. Because he's my brother's best friend.*

Without discussing it, we both decided to pretend it hadn't happened. Even when it happened again. And again. And again.

We just doubled down on the pretending. Becoming new characters every time so we never had to admit that we didn't really hate each other.

So I never had to admit that we were growing closer.

That being with him was the favorite part of my day. That I woke up every day thinking of new scenarios we could play, and that every time he texted, I was silently elated, and when he bullied me into picking him to be my husband, I didn't really feel bullied.

I felt secretly… glad.

The revelation sends me over the edge, and I cry out in pleasure, my body trembling beneath him. Ax doesn't slow his thrusts, but he does remove his hand from my clit, just as touch becomes painful, and tightens the grip on my wrists.

I writhe underneath him, my body wracked with the force of my O. It overtakes me with such fierceness that there's no way to deny this one. No way to pretend it away. It feels like it goes on forever, all the tension that had built, cascading in sensation after sensation after sensation.

The drama of my orgasm seems to lead Ax to his own release just as mine finally crests. He collapses on top of me, his ragged breaths blowing hot across my neck, echoing my own gasps for air.

Neither of us move for several seconds. My heart starts to settle. My head, on the other hand, starts to panic. Is that really how it went between us? Do I actually want Ax more than I let on?

Eventually, he asks the inevitable. "What happened next?"

I'm grateful that I'm facing away from him, afraid he

could read my thoughts in my expression if he could see it. The story—the *real* story—spins in my head like the sweet buzz from a glass of champagne, and for the briefest of moments, I consider asking him if that's how it went for him too.

Then immediately decide the idea is ridiculous.

It might be the real story for me, but I'm positive Ax's version is much different. Like he said yesterday, he gets off on knowing he's fucking the boss's daughter. Nothing more.

So with my cheek still pressed to the desk, I quickly make up the rest of our story. "You called and asked me out the next day, for a real date. We kept it secret because of all the politics, but one date turned into two and then three, and then you proposed one night out of the blue over an employee review, and here we are."

A beat passes.

"Here we are." His voice sounds off. It's most likely post-sex exhaustion, but it's the same bite that it had before the sex.

I didn't understand it before, and I can't stand not understanding it now. "Are you mad at me or something?"

It would explain his dickish demeanor. Although, if today is the outcome of his rage, I'm not necessarily complaining.

He goes still before he answers. "Have you done something that I should be mad at?"

It feels like a trap of a question. A different kind of game. One I'm not interested in playing.

When I don't answer, he lifts himself off of me and the

loss of his weight feels like having the covers pulled off suddenly on a cold morning.

"Seems like you were able to finish the assignment on your own, after all." He bends to collect my panties, which have fallen to my ankles, maneuvering them over my shoes then stuffing them in his pocket. "Good work, Mrs. Morgan. A plus."

He offers his hand to help me up, and once I'm on my feet, we're done pretending we're teacher and student and back to pretending we're man and wife.

When we get back to the cultural hall, there are more members of the family gathered with the others, including Hunter.

My mood had been boosted from the orgasm endorphins, but it instantly deflates. Especially when, before we're spotted, I overhear the conversation he's having with Reid and Cole, another one of my cousins.

"I give them two months," Cole says. "I'm sure she's just after her trust fund."

They're obviously talking about me and Ax.

Even though I knew some of my family would have their suspicions, I hadn't expected it from Cole, and I scowl.

Reid considers. "How much you want to bet? A thousand dollars? I think they'll go all the way."

Hunter butts in before Cole can respond. "They'll make it a year. No more, no less."

"That's awfully specific," Cole says. "Do you have some insight we don't?"

It reminds me to ask Ax later how he handled Hunter, a question that seems far less relevant when Hunter answers. "Rules of the trust. She'll get the money released now, but if they're not married in a year from now, she has to pay it back. Didn't you know?"

No. I most definitely did not.

CHAPTER
TWELVE
AX

Hunter is a ballbreaker, but he's not a bullshitter. He's the kind of guy who brings people to their knees with the truth.

In other words, there is every reason to take his pronouncement at face value, which is probably why Adly's expression is one of pure horror.

Not very complimentary to the guy she's currently married to, but I'm trying not to take it personally.

Thankfully, we've yet to be noticed.

"Adly," I whisper, reaching for her hand, in hopes to calm her ass before her family decides her reaction is odd for a woman who's supposed to be in love.

Holt catches her eye at the same time, apparently also having overheard. "That's not exactly true."

Her fingers skim past mine as she moves forward to confront him. "What do you mean it's not *exactly* true?"

Holt scratches at the back of his neck like he's been caught with information he's been withholding.

His fiancée Brystin's eyes widen. "You didn't tell her?"

"Tell me," Adly demands.

"There's a process to appeal." Holt's eyes dart to Hunter and the others then back to her.

"What process, Holt?" She's too preoccupied with grilling him to pick up on the cue. The cue being that the others have discovered her and are watching.

I contemplate letting her hang herself. She's not going to get SHE in the end either way, but if there's a challenge to her inheritance now, it will save her the torment of a bidding war with her family's company.

Maybe part of me wants her to hurt, because it turns out I can't just stand by.

Coming up behind her, I wrap my arms around her waist and rest my head next to hers. "It doesn't matter, though, because we didn't marry for the money, did we, Addlibear?"

Nicknames have always just rolled off my tongue, but never have they been so sickeningly adorable. I can't decide if I deserve a medal or a prison sentence for that last one.

Important thing is that it does the trick.

Awakened to the attention, she leans back against my chest and brings a hand up to cup my jaw. "No we didn't, Ax. Baby."

The endearment is an obvious afterthought, but she gets the rest right. The cuddling, the caressing. The smell of her perfume mixed with the faint scent of sex wafting from her body. My cock just got fed, and it's already stirring again.

We present as pretty fucking legit, if you ask me.

Apparently, Holt thinks she needs some help. "Of course that's not why you got married," he says.

"No one said that's why you did," Brystin adds.

"I was just curious." Adly is tense in my arms, and understandably so since Holt and his girl are being Obvious as Fuck.

"That's my Addles. Always learning." Shit, I'm just as bad.

A few minutes later, Samuel takes the stage to thank donors and ask them for money—typical Sebastian duty shit—taking the spotlight off of us.

Best to stay as we are and keep up the show, in my opinion, but as soon as Daddy starts speaking, she shoves out of my arms and tows her brother away for what I suspect is going to be quite a tense conversation.

It's a good opportunity to have one of my own with Hunter.

"You didn't say anything to me about the year deal," I say, after pulling him aside. Didn't last night's conversation confirm we were a team?

"I figured you already knew." He punches my shoulder lightly with his fist. "Don't worry. Thanks to you, the SHE buyout will be my first order of business as CEO. As soon as Adly realizes she doesn't need the money, she'll ask for an annulment."

The words *thanks to you* sit like a bad meal in my gut. It's the best idea for both businesses, really, but I'm not sure I like the idea of being credited for it.

As for the rest of what Hunter said…"You're awfully certain about shit that's out of your control."

"Not out of my control—I talked to Bob Peterson this

morning. He agreed to hold off on accepting any offers until I have a chance to bid. He let it slip that he doesn't care what happens to the company after it's bought. He wants it off his hands at the biggest payout possible. If there's a bidding war, SNC will win. Alex, Holt, and Adly don't have anywhere else to draw from."

I wouldn't underestimate the AHA trio. They're Sebastians. Sebastians make things happen.

And anyway, when the deal does fall through for Adly, what are the chances she'll still want to stay at SNC with Hunter? Knowing her, she'll look for another escape plan, and I doubt she'll find one that's worth it for her that doesn't involve an investment.

"I don't think Adly's going to want to give up the trust fund, even without SHE on the table." In other words, she's going to want to meet the year requirement. "Then what?"

Hunter shrugs. "You're the one who married her."

Honestly? The new terms of the deal don't have me in a frenzy. She might be leaving SNC, but if we're still married…

Unable to bring myself to continue that train of thought, I sweep my gaze back toward Adly and Holt. She catches my eye and gives me a look that's both panicked and apologetic.

Then she starts toward me, and I cross to meet her. "Holt says I can appeal…" Her voice is quiet, careful not to distract from her father's speech. "But only if *you're* at fault for our divorce."

I'm instantly defensive. "But you agreed to take the blame."

"I know." She wipes imaginary sweat from her brow. "Holt didn't realize that was what we agreed."

"So what's his suggestion?"

"He told me to get you to change your mind." She smiles up at me with a hesitant plea in her features.

The truth is, I *could* change my mind. If Hunter's going to be CEO, my job is protected. I don't need to worry about Samuel's approval. Who cares if I'm the bad guy?

But there are so few things I asked for in this agreement, and Adly's already willing to renege on one of my conditions. The fact that she chose that specific one—that she'd rather cast me as the asshole than even ask if I'd be willing to stay in the marriage longer—shows she's hoping to be rid of me as soon as she can.

For reasons I can't explain, it pisses me off.

And so I lie. "It's nonnegotiable, Adly. Your father would fire me so fast. I'm not blowing up my life for you."

"I know, just…" She sounds like she feels bad, at least. "It's our only option. That or actually be married for a year."

I stare at her, not sure if there's a question at the end of her statement.

She sighs. "Look, you already offered three months, and that was generous. I don't expect you to blow up your life, and I know I don't have the right to ask for anything more from you, but I need the money, so you choose, Ax. You decide which option."

I take a breath in and scan the room, pretending that I need a second to think about it.

But I've already made my decision.

"Looks like you're stuck with me for a year." I beckon to

a waiter as he passes by. "We're going to need shots. Whiskey, whatever you have top shelf. Two at a time. Keep them coming until I say otherwise."

Right at that moment, Samuel finishes his spiel and the room breaks into applause. It feels like an appropriate way to start off a round of Negotiations.

Adly claps for her father, but when she glances at me, her lips seem to be fighting a smile.

Did I choose the option she preferred all along?

There's no time to examine that thought. With the presentation over, the family once again breaks into conversation circles.

Brett, one of Adly's distant cousins, and his fiancée, annoyingly decide they want more deets on our relationship. It's the whole reason we needed a "story" so immediately, but inconvenient since my wife and I have some things to work out.

"So where are you living?" Brett asks, addressing Adly. "Your place?"

"Mmhm." She quickly deflects. "And you're both living…where?"

"We moved into Brett's place," Eden says. "We've been thinking about finding some place a little bigger though. It's hard since we want to stay downtown."

Fortunately, more relatives trickle over, and others jump into the conversation, taking the focus off of us.

Adly moves closer, her hand up to her mouth to cover when she whispers in my direction. "People think we should be living together."

"Shocking."

"I thought we could pull off separate places for a few months." She lifts her shoulders in a shrug.

For as much thought as she's given to this whole scheme of hers, it seems some of the details regarding the logistics of our marriage have been looked over.

I start to respond, only to shut my mouth when Eden once again turns the attention back to us. "What about you guys? Will you stay where you are or are you looking for something else?"

"Uh..." Adly stammers.

"Staying put for now," I interject.

"I could never part with my place in Brooklyn," Lina says, "Reid's stuck. The house is part of the package."

While the girl runs her mouth, I lean in toward Adly. "Do you have a guest room?"

"Not furnished as such, but I can convert the yoga room."

She has a yoga room.

It's not an interesting fact, per se, but it's something I hadn't known, and like all things Adly, my brain lights up like it's worth noting.

"I mean, if it really came down to the house or Reid, of course, I'd choose him," Lina rambles on, "but that would be a weird ultimatum for him to make, and if he did, he wouldn't be the guy that I thought he was, and I don't know if that would be the kind of guy that I'd want to stay with, so I guess it's a really good thing he's never tried to push that."

"I go where you tell me." Reid's face glows like he's a fucking pregnant woman.

"He's so pussy-whipped," I say under my breath.

"We need to be like them," Adly whispers.

"Guess we're roommates, then."

"For a year?"

She says it a little too loud, and I have to wait until people aren't looking at us again before I answer. "I'm a workaholic, Adly. I spend very little time outside the office. I just need a bed and a closet, and I'm good."

The others laugh at some joke, and I join in, as though I've been paying attention. "Good one," I say, before whispering again to Adly. "You're taking care of the mortgage, right?"

"I own it outright."

"Then all good."

"The closet will be an issue, but whatever. I'll make it work."

As if on cue, the first round of shots arrive. In unison, Adly and I each take one from the tray and clink. "*Salute.*"

The waiter's gone again before I have time to remind him to send another round. I look back toward the bar and wave. He nods in return, but so does a fairly attractive woman who seems to think I was trying to get her attention.

I quickly put my hand down, but she's already waving back when Adly turns her head, tracing my line of sight.

When she spins back toward me, there's a scowl on her face. "You can't bring women to my apartment."

Not gonna lie—I'm annoyed. "I'm not going to bring women to your fucking apartment."

"And if you don't want to be at fault, you can't get caught with them anywhere else either."

Does she really think I'm going to be renting out hotel

rooms or going on secret dates? I know I come off as a bit of a slut, but to be fair, it's mostly only Adly that I've been with over the last few weeks.

Or last few months.

Maybe since the beginning of the year. Exact details don't matter. The point is, I'm not really whoring it up as much as she seems to think. And while I would never call myself anything close to religious, I do have morals. One moral specifically, ingrained in me by my devout Catholic mother before she died—marriage is sanctified.

Fake marriage or not, I'm not fucking around on my wife.

It feels weird to admit that, though. When it was just a three-month marriage term, it was easy enough to pretend I was making a sacrifice without it being a big deal. If I volunteer for twelve months devoted to her, she might get the wrong idea.

If she suggested it, on the other hand...

Unlikely if she thinks I'm boning every woman in sight.

All I can do is assure her it won't be a problem. "There isn't going—"

I stop short when I hear some guy next to us talking about SNC. "Are you anywhere closer to choosing a permanent CEO?"

I turn toward the voices and see the question has been addressed to Samuel, who narrows his eyes, darting his gaze toward Hunter before answering. "Unfortunately... yes. It should be announced beginning of next month."

He's been dead set against Hunter taking the helm, but the rumors that have been floating around are that the board has the votes without Samuel.

Seems the rumors are true. Hunter nods in my direction, a silent confirmation that his plan is already in motion. He'll be CEO in a matter of weeks, and SNC will go after SHE.

My stomach feels like I've been drinking lead.

On my other side, Adly hisses at me. "I mean it, Ax. You can't fondle the waitress or do body shots with the ladies at Spice or take the bunnies with you to try out the trampoline room."

I'm about to dismiss her wild assertions when I realize that all of her examples are oddly specific. "Ah, Addles. You've been watching me. How long have you been obsessed?"

She raises her hand to wipe the corner of her mouth with her middle finger.

Fuck it.

I shift my body so I'm facing her directly. "If you're really so concerned, maybe you should take it upon your-self to make sure my needs are met so I don't stray."

She laughs, her eyes scanning the room. "I truly doubt any one woman could handle the task."

"She could try."

She looks back at me, her forehead pinched as if she's trying to decide if I'm serious.

I'm going for "guarded" with my expression, so it's probably hard to tell.

The next shots arrive, and she's made her decision. "I'll be close to you in public. To keep up the pretense. Your needs beyond that are your responsibility. If you fuck it up, then you can't blame me for blowing up anything."

Yeah, I'll be fucking Adly when my needs arise, but she doesn't have to understand that yet.

"*Salute.*"

A few more shots and we've agreed to spending holidays together, sharing a car to and from the office, and family weekends at Adeline, Holt's country estate. I've gotten some things out of it too. She's promised to remove all my offenses from my employee file, arrange for me to have more paid personal days and a second assistant, and to give me a nudie pic of herself, cropped with no distinguishing features, that I've sworn not to use as my cell's screensaver.

Didn't say I wouldn't use it as my wallpaper, though.

Of course, we're also confronted with more questions about our relationship. We volley back and forth as we tell the story she concocted earlier. A story that starts very much like our own.

If we had a story, that is. We're probably better described as a series of happy endings, despite her unwillingness to say so. Hard for her to keep denying it after that orgasm she had today. It rocked through her body so fiercely that I can still feel a phantom pussy clench around my cock.

Then, naturally, there's talk of the wedding. "Have you pinned a date down for the ceremony?" Fairly harmless question, but it feels like an interrogation coming from Samuel.

He somehow manages to appear as though he's looking down his nose at me, even though we're about the same height, and I swear his subtext is saying it's my duty to make sure the wedding happens sooner rather than later.

No one else can make me panic answer the way he can. "Sometime next year."

Samuel starts to smile.

"Or the year after," Adly says, and her father frowns.

"Summer, maybe," I say, desperately wanting to reverse the frown.

"Or late fall," Adly corrects again.

The frown remains.

"I'll still be the first kid getting married, Dad," Holt says. He can't possibly think it's helpful since he's been on Samuel's shitlist since he followed Brystin over to SHE.

Sure enough, Samuel's frown deepens.

"We should go bridal shopping together," Giulia exclaims, in stark contrast to her husband's demeanor. "Brystin and I are going next month. Adly, you should come too!"

"It's too early," Adly says, quickly.

"So far away," Brystin agrees—she probably knows about the ruse.

"Eons," Holt says, because he can't seem to not be a part of things.

"Nonsense. It's never too early." Giulia pulls her phone from her clutch purse and starts texting as she talks. "I'll let the coordinator know to add you to the reservations. This will be so fun!"

"A joy," Adly says in monotone before whispering at me, "At least, I'm inebriated."

So inebriated that she sways into me.

I put my hands at her waist to steady her, and she peers up at me. "That should be everything, right? We don't need to order more shots?"

She's beautiful like this, all dazed and radiant. Her light brown hair falls in waves on her shoulders, framing her apple cheeks and milk chocolate eyes. Her expression is soft and inviting, and though I don't *need* anything else from this negotiation, I suddenly feel a desperate want for something I can't name.

Her respect? Her trust?

"What do you need the money for?" I already know the answer, but I want it from her. Want her to respect me enough to tell me herself. Want her to trust me to keep her secret.

For once, she doesn't evade my gaze when posed with the question. Her mouth parts.

"Adly!" a female voice squeals.

Adly's head turns to the person. "Tess! It's been weeks since I've seen you."

Just like that, the moment has passed.

I drop my hands from Adly's waist so she can greet her cousin Scott and his wife. "How's the baby?"

"Not a baby anymore," Tess says. "He's a professional racewalker. We can't keep up. But who cares about him— you're married!"

Adly gives her insincere smile. The one that doesn't quite reach her eyes. "I am."

"To Ax Morgan," Scott says, eyeing me.

"That's me." I feel a strong urge to pull Adly back into my arms. As if I need to make some sort of statement, but she's drifted too far from me for the move to look natural.

Tess squints from me to Adly. "It's just so…"

"Unexpected," Scott finishes.

"I kind of always thought you hated each other," Tess admits.

"Fine line between the two and all." Adly moves to me on her own, like she feels the same tug I do, and when she wraps an arm around my waist, I draw her closer into my side, and my pulse quickens, but steadies.

Tess lights up. "I can see it. They look good together, honey."

"You're much more..." Scott considers his wording. "*Reserved* with each other than I was as a newlywed."

"Some people have a handle on their libido," Tess tells him.

My grip grows tighter on Adly's hip. "Was that an attack on my manhood?"

Scott answers for her. "I think she forgot the man she was talking about is a man*whore*."

"Former," I say, which sounds like a bigger lie than it is. "Surprising what happens when you find The One."

"Aw. You should make out," Holt says, and now I understand why he's earned the assHolt nickname.

Adly and I shoot him a death glare. Brystin does too, though hers is much more subtle.

He quickly reverses. "Kidding. PDA is tacky."

But then Hunter chimes in. "Actually, maybe they should."

"What?" Adly says, the color draining from her face.

"Kiss," Hunter says.

"What?" Adly says again. She's so dismayed, I swear I can hear her heart thundering.

I pierce him with a sharp dagger stare.

He only smirks. "That's what everyone loves most about

weddings—the kiss. You robbed us all of one of the greatest
joys in life by having a private ceremony."

"Oh, Hunter," Giulia says. "You're a secret romantic."

I'd laugh if I weren't on the verge of murder.

Hunter feigns modesty. "I just think the family feels left
out. We share so many special moments. We deserve to see
the kiss."

My pulse trips, and I get that feeling in my stomach that
I get when I'm going down fast in an elevator.

It's not like I mind the idea of kissing Adly. I may have
even imagined it a time or two. Or twenty. She's just so
fucking sassy with that mouth of hers. It's only natural to
want to whip it into submission with my lips and tongue
and teeth. I wonder what she tastes like. I wonder what it's
like to swallow her moans. The only reason I haven't kissed
her before this is...

Huh.

I don't know why exactly.

Except that it felt like it would be crossing a line. It
would be *real*. It's easy to forget who I'm fucking when
we're both playing characters.

Scratch that.

It's easy to *pretend* I've forgotten who I'm fucking—I've
never actually forgotten. But face-to-face, looking into her
eyes—there's no way I would be able to convince myself
she was anyone but Adly.

And that feels like the kind of thing that shouldn't
happen at all, let alone in front of other people.

But it's too late.

Several pairs of eyes are on us now. Many belonging to

people that still probably need a bit of convincing that we're an honest-to-God love match.

I know what needs to happen.

Adly is slower to come to Jesus. She tries to stammer out an excuse, which is really just a string of single syllables. "Uh...um...hmm...I...we..."

Her mouth is still parted when I spin into her, place a steady hand at her neck, and ignoring her yelp of surprise, I bring my mouth to hers.

She tastes like the whiskey we've been drinking all night and strawberry lip gloss. It's the most delicious taste I've ever encountered. I take small sips from her, her body rigid in my arms.

But then her lips yield under mine, soft and pliant. I feel her gasp against me, her hands fluttering uncertainly before settling on my chest.

The world around us fades into a distant hum as I deepen the kiss, losing myself in the sensation of her warmth pressed against me.

Then everything silences, and it's just us. Adly and me.

Hunter's plans, Holt's antics—all of it falls away as our connection deepens with each passing heartbeat. We're suspended in this moment. Completely aware of each other and no one else. The tension in her body melts away, replaced by a different kind of tension altogether. Our kissing becomes more frantic. She wraps her fingers in my dress shirt. My hand finds her ass. My cock is rock hard as it nudges against her lower belly.

I want her suddenly. Like I've never wanted her before. Want her in a bed, all night long, just us. No roles played.

Masks down. Me and my wife and her fucking amazing lips and no one else.

It's an epiphany that wakes me up.

Or else it's the cat calls that finally break through the haze as someone shouts out, "Get a room."

Whatever the trigger, I remember we are most definitely not alone.

Worse, we're only a handful of seconds away from dry humping at a highbrow social event with her father in the audience.

Abruptly, I break away from her.

Everyone around us erupts into applause and cheers. Adly's hand flies to her mouth, her cheeks flushed. Her breath comes in ragged gulps, mimicking my own.

Hunter gives me a slight nod from across the room, his earlier mischief replaced by smug satisfaction. Brystin and Holt exchange a glance, while Giulia claps enthusiastically. Samuel looks genuinely impressed for once, and also slightly uncomfortable, which is fair since I did just practically molest his daughter in front of a crowd.

Adly refuses to meet my gaze. "There. Happy now?" she asks the onlookers.

Another tray of shots arrive. Incredible timing since, despite already being pretty intoxicated, I could really use another drink.

Adly too, if how fast she reaches for the glass is any indicator. She clinks her shot against mine and finally looks at me, her eyes dark and muddy.

"Told you we might have to kiss," I say.

She rolls her eyes, but her blush deepens. "Hunter's

going to give you hell," she says, bringing her glass to her lips.

I follow suit. In unison we say, "*Salute.*"

The alcohol's warm but nothing compared to how hot my temperature is running. Silently, I pray that no one notices the bulge in my pants or how off-kilter I am—from the booze, most likely. And there's a strange knot lodged in my chest, one that gets tighter with every glance in Adly's direction.

But at least the family is mollified.

"Hunter is completely right," Giulia says, a phrase rarely spoken by another Sebastian. "We're all dying for the wedding, and I just decided that we have to start planning because it's going to be fun. Cancel your car. Samuel and I will drive you home."

"Oh no, that's okay," Adly tries to argue.

"You're on our way," Giulia says. "It's perfect."

"But—"

Adly's cut off by her father. "We insist."

Knowing no one argues with her father, she closes her mouth, only to open it again.

"*Both* of us?"

Fortunately, I'm not too drunk to remember our supposed living situation. "Of course both of us, Addlyboo. We're headed to the same place, and all."

As panicked as she was about a kiss, it's nothing compared to the alarm registered on her face now. "You're coming to my...?" She catches herself. "You're coming...home."

"Yes, Addles, I'm coming home."

Strangely, it's the easiest lie I've told all night.

CHAPTER
THIRTEEN
ADLY

bobble as I step out of the car, saved only by Ax's firm
hand at my back. I probably should have passed on
that last drink from the limo bar, but Giulia kept
adding more and more things to the planning list for a
wedding that's never actually taking place. She grilled me
on everything from venue preferences to guest list to menu
items to party size to colors.

Then, every time she took a breath and my brain had
more than a second of downtime, my thoughts would
scurry back to that kiss.

That goddamn kiss.

I felt it from the roots of my hair to the tips of my toes,
which is saying something since my super cute shoes are
uncomfortable, and I lost feeling in my feet about two
hours ago. A man like Ax Morgan has no business having
such a blessedly wicked mouth, let alone the talent to use it.

That kiss was trouble. It might have legitimately wrecked me.

Hard to tell when I'm this drunk, but what I do know is that a whole bottle of Glenfiddich couldn't wash away the trauma of it.

Hopefully, by tomorrow, I'll be too hungover to remember.

At the moment, I'm struggling just to walk from the curb to my apartment building. I'm not sure if it's better or worse that Ax is at my side, considering that he's also fairly drunk, and more importantly, is the owner of that godforsaken mouth.

But like it or not, we have to keep up pretenses. "Don't look back," I tell him as we step into the lobby. "Keep walking."

"Why would I look back?"

"I don't know. Just don't."

We make it to the elevator, and I wonder out loud if it's far enough. "You can see the elevator from the street, so I think you have to ride up with me."

As I push the up button, Ax turns his head, as if verifying the sightlines.

"Don't look at them!" God. How is this confusing?

Immediately, he turns back to face the opening elevator's doors. "I think they might already be gone."

"Well, don't check." I step into the elevator, push the button for my floor, then hug the side of the elevator.

Ax follows suit, but he plants himself in the center of the car, spreading his arms across the railing that runs along the back.

The doors stay open for what feels like eons. Pushing the button to close them several times doesn't do anything.

"Are they still there?" I don't know why I'm whispering. We're the only people in sight beyond the doorman. It's not like my dad can hear me all the way from here, even if the car is still idling at the curb.

Ax shakes his head, then seems to immediately regret it when he brings his hand up to steady his skull. "I don't know. You told me not to look at them."

I'm pretty sure the guy's an idiot. "You can look *now*. Since you're facing them."

"Am I?" With one hand remaining on the guardrail, he pivots to face me instead.

I fight not to smile. "You're such an Axhole."

He's suddenly way too close. Of course the doors choose this moment to shut, and the small space feels drastically smaller. That stupid mouth of his beckons like… like…something that beckons.

Unable to look at him, I watch the floors as they flip by on the indicator.

Axhole.

Abruptly, I realize what I've done. "Oh my God! Did you hear what I said? *Axhole.* It was a mistake, but it's so perfect!"

"Yeah, ha ha." He doesn't seem sufficiently amused.

"You can't deny how good it is." At the very least, it's a good distraction from the heat emanating from his body. "I can't believe I didn't come up with it before."

"You can't think you're the first to ever say it."

"Why doesn't everyone say it then?" An idea that feels

pretty solid emerges. "You should have it trademarked!" Or *I* should have it trademarked since I came up with it, but maybe it should wait until after we break up because it might seem odd for a new bride to have such a crass name associated with the husband she's supposed to be in love with.

In any case, it can't go to waste. I pull my phone from my purse. "I'm changing your name in my phone."

I pull up *He Who Shall Not Be Named* and push the edit button. Then I hesitate. Somewhere in the back of my head, a warning alarm sounds, and I have a feeling this is a big step. Adding Ax's real name to my contacts, I mean.

Or "almost" real name. It's an obvious leap from Axhole to Ax, is the point. He's no longer tucked away like a dirty little secret, but I probably should have thought about that before I married him.

I type the letters in. A-X-H-O-L-E.

Then press SAVE. "Done."

"Cool. I'm changing yours in my phone too." He pulls his phone out as I pocket mine.

"To what?" I peer over his shoulder trying to see what he's typing, but he pivots away from me. "What are you changing my name to?"

Another question—what was it before? Have I been stored in his contacts under an equally anonymous moniker? *FukBud?*

1-800-Get-Laid?

She Who Comes When Called?

I try again to see what he's typing.

"See this?" He draws an imaginary circle in the air and points to it. "This is some your business." Then he draws another imaginary circle and points. "This is none your business." He moves the phone into the second circle. "This is none your business."

He's stolen my bit. It's much more annoying having it said back to me. "You are such an Axhole."

Thankfully, the doors open. I brush past him. "This way."

I don't look to see if he's following, but I sense him behind me. We walk down the hall to the corner unit. It takes a few seconds to find my key and wrangle with the lock.

When the door's open, I step inside then have a moment of doubt. "Hold on."

I close the door in his face. Not all the way so it latches, just enough so that there's a solid barrier between the two of us while I try to figure out why there are more alarms ringing.

Then I realize that it's my actual alarm.

I quickly put my four digit code into the wall panel, which is the release date of one of my favorite series—0624. Then I open the door again. "You can come in."

Ax steps into my foyer, and my stomach does some weird flip-flop thing that I'm blaming on the alcohol, though it does seem to slightly improve the farther I am from him.

I drop my purse on the floor and put several more feet between us before leaning my hand against the wall to steady myself while I take off my shoes.

Behind me, I feel Ax's eyes taking in my apartment. Noticing my things. Taking inventory. "That painting *would* look good in your foyer," he says.

"Minimalism is a thing." Toes relieved from pinching, I head barefoot to the balcony door.

"You have too many books to be a minimalist," Ax calls after me, and I try not to let it feel like an invasion. He's moving in soon. He's going to see my stuff. He's going to learn things about me.

I'm probably going to learn things about him too.

I banish the thought before it spirals out of control and walk out onto the concrete patio.

"What are you doing?" Ax asks.

It seems pretty obvious, since he finds me peering over the balcony wall. "We have to make sure they're gone before you can go back down. In case they're waiting."

"Who's *they*?" He steps to the wall and looks down to the street. "Your parents?"

"My dad and stepmom. Yeah."

"Is that something they'd do? Wait at the curb for a long time? Have they done stuff like that before?"

"I don't think so?" When he says it like that, it makes it sound like I'm overreacting.

But I'm a Sebastian. There's no telling what my family will do.

I lean out so I can see all the way to the corner. "I don't see their car."

"Don't do that."

The sharpness in his voice catches my attention. "Don't do what?" Then I realize what he's freaking out about, and I can't resist leaning out even farther. "Don't do this?"

"Addles." It's a warning.

"Or do you mean don't do this?" I lean out so far that my feet come off the ground.

"Adly Jade!" He crosses to me in a flash and grabs onto my hips, pulling me to safety.

I giggle as I turn into him. "What...are you rescuing me?"

"Yeah. I'm rescuing you."

The sincerity in his expression robs my breath. My giggle turns into a gulp, and my pulse flutters more than it did when I was leaning over a balcony, twenty flights from the ground.

My gaze flickers to his lips.

When I catch myself, I close my eyes. His mouth really needs to stop being so...tempting.

"Anyway." Opening my eyes, I back toward the door. "You should be safe to go now. I'm sure they're gone."

I step inside the apartment only to spontaneously poke my head right back out. "Want another one for the road?"

"You're crazy," Ax laughs.

"So that's a yes?"

Without waiting for an answer, I cross the living room to the bar, pull out a bottle of Pendleton, and pour two shots.

I'm not sure the last time we drank together voluntarily in a non-negotiation setting. It feels odd not to make some sort of toast. "To...uh..."

Hmm.

There's a beat where I think I should be thinking, but all that I'm aware of is the slight tint of my lipstick smeared on the corner of Ax's bottom lip and the bom, bom, bom of my heart thudding.

He's the one to break the silence. "To Axly."

Heat creeps into my face. As though he's said something much more intimate. As though he's something scandalous.

He mistakes my expression for misunderstanding. "It's our ship name. You know, like when you take the couple's names and—"

"I know what a ship name is, you Axhole™." The use of my new sweary version of his name brings levity, and my breath slowly returns to my lungs. "I just hadn't..."

Hadn't ever thought about us as a couple. Hadn't really gone there. Hadn't reframed the idea of us from concept to reality.

Admittedly, Axly has a nice ring. "It's actually kind of good, isn't it?"

"It really is." He's biased, obviously, since he came up with it, but my opinion is valid.

I raise my glass. "To Axly."

We clink. In unison, we, "*Salute.*"

The alcohol's smooth as it slides down my throat, but it's only a matter of seconds before it hits my stomach.

Instantly, I have regrets. "Oh fuck. Maybe I didn't need that."

"You definitely didn't need that."

I feel judged, but I'm too fuzzy to call him on it. "I need to pass out. You can call your car now."

Thankfully, the nausea doesn't last.

But very much in need of my bed, I'm pleased when Ax brings his cell phone out again.

Until he says, "Shit. My phone's dead."

"Dead?" I grab it from his hand.

"Go ahead, see for yourself."

Ignoring his sarcasm, I try to turn it on only to be met with the red battery emblem. "You were just using it in the elevator."

"It was on two percent."

Then he should have been saving his battery instead of fucking with my name in his contacts. Has he never used a phone before?

I don't have the wits to argue. "Mine's...um." In my purse, which I dropped off in the foyer, which feels a million miles away right now, even though I can literally see it from here.

With a groan, I take a step toward the door, then stop. "How does it work to call an Uber for someone else?" There's a possibility that it's not complicated. For a sober person. Which I'm not. "You know what? I'll find a charger."

I reverse direction and step toward my office, then stop. Then look toward the living room. Then down the hall toward my room.

This process also seems complicated. First, I have to remember where a charger is. I have, like, five, but that somehow doesn't make any of them easier to find. And if I do find one that fits his phone, we'll have to wait until it's charged enough for him to make it home before I can even think about sleeping.

Or *he'll* have to wait because I'm already blacked out on my feet, and I need to thoroughly sweep my apartment for anything embarrassing before I leave him awake alone.

"You could just stay here. I guess." It's against my better instincts, though to be fair, I'm not in any state to be evaluating one instinct from another.

Ax cocks his head. "You said you don't have a guest room ready?"

I don't realize I've mirrored the cock of his head until

the dizziness hits. When I straighten my head again, another wave of nausea washes over me. This time it's accompanied by a storm of panic. "No, I, uh...oh no." Elbows braced on the bar, I cover my face with my hands. "Oh, no, oh no."

"What's wrong?" His tone is full of concern. "Adly?"

I can barely bring myself to say it. "There's only one bed."

"What?"

Uncovering my face, in case that's why he doesn't understand, I try again. "There's only one bed, Ax! Only. One. Bed. I only one-bedded myself."

It's maybe unfair to assume that he would understand the only one bed trope, since I'm pretty sure he's never picked up a book in his life that had any semblance of story to it, let alone a romance book.

But as a girlie who is very aware of the common plot point where two people, who are already experiencing sexual tension, are somehow put in a situation where there is only one bed, and they have to share...I love the trope.

Despite that, I am the first to admit that I'm not always on board with the believability of only one bed. Do hotels really make that many booking errors? Are cabins in the woods specifically furnished for single people? Does no one own fold out couches anymore?

I've been pretty high and mighty about it at times, and now here I am. My how the mighty have fallen.

Ax still doesn't understand the significance of my lament. "What do you do with guests?"

"Book them a room at the Four Seasons?"

"Such a fucking princess."

I lift my head to scowl at him directly. "Who's going to stay with me?"

"Me, it turns out."

It's fine. It's fine. I can be practical about this.

I glance past Ax at the living room couch. It's an Italian traditional design with a tufted back and rolled arms.

He follows my gaze. "Hell, no. I'm not sleeping on that sofa."

"Why not?"

"Besides the fact that it's at least half a foot too small for my frame, it's pink."

The actual description was champagne, but yeah. I can see where he gets pink. Not that I consider the color a valid argument. The length however…

I'm all of a sudden indignant. "Are you suggesting *I* sleep on the sofa?"

"We'll share your bed."

"No. No. That's not happening." I've read enough of those books to know the shared bed situation always leads to the main characters waking up tangled in each other, having had the best night's sleep of their life.

I can't think of anything more traumatizing.

Ax places his forearms on the bar next to me. "I thought you weren't chicken."

"Fuck you, I'm not."

"What are you afraid of?"

"Having to share my bed." My bed is an oasis. I like space to stretch out. I want the room set at my preferred temperature. I do not want to compromise my sleep.

Ax leans toward me. "Bawwwwwk." It's quiet at first. Then, louder. "Bawwwwwwk."

Romance books aren't accurate representations. I shouldn't make a big deal about a fictional tendency to turn ordinary trials and tribulations into opportunities for love to bloom. This is real life.

And the reality of the situation is that I need sleep.

"Fine. Whatever." With a sigh that comes off more as a harumph, I push off from the bar and head down the hall toward my bedroom. "You better not steal covers."

"You better not snore," Ax says, right behind me.

"I can snore all I want to. It's my bed. My bedroom. My apartment."

Except now I'm married. And though our whole relationship is fake and temporary, for the meantime, it seems I'm going to have to learn a word that I've never been very good with—*ours*.

CHAPTER **FOURTEEN**
ADLY

At my bedroom, I flick on the light and brace myself for disaster since I don't actually remember the state that I left it in.

Ax peers over my shoulder, taking it all in. I try to see it from his eyes, the sparkling champagne walls and accents of lavish gold. The bed with its shimmering fabric and showstopper headboard with its intricate metal inserts and contrasting chardonnay trim. The materials are luxurious silk. The hardwood floor is bleached oak planks set in a herringbone pattern, adorned with a plush white fur rug. A crystal chandelier hangs elegantly above, casting a dreamy glow throughout the room.

All in all it's ultra feminine.

Fortunately, the housekeeper was here, which means the bed is made.

Unfortunately, she was here this morning, which means there are several outfits that I tried on and decided not to wear flung over my bench, a pink bra on the floor, a black bra hanging from the lampshade, an open bag of trail mix and an empty Ben and Jerry's ice cream carton on the nightstand, and a book open on the bed where I spent the early afternoon reading.

Ax takes several seconds to articulate his assessment. "This...tracks."

"Fuck you." Though it's possible he was talking about the design and not my mess.

I shift into clean-up mode, gathering the clothes over my shoulder, tossing the ice cream carton into the trash, digging out the phone cord from my nightstand drawer. "Here's a charger."

He easily catches the cord when I fling it to him.

"Don't touch my stuff." I start toward the closet only to spot a familiar pink-tipped object sticking out from under the book on the bed.

Goddammit.

I snatch the vibrator from where I left it and throw it in my nightstand drawer, hoping Ax wasn't paying attention.

A quick glance in his direction says I'm not so lucky. Judging from the smirk on his face, my dildo is not safe in his presence.

Obviously, I retrieve it from the drawer and take it with me to the closet, turning once to scold him, pointing the toy at him as I do. "Don't! Not a fucking word."

He puts his hands up in surrender. "I'm innocent. Don't even know what's in your hand. Want to demonstrate it for me?"

"Axhole!" As soon as I'm in my closet, I drop all the items on the floor, including the toy, lean against the closed door, and take a deep breath to steady my pulse. I definitely feel annoyed, but I'm also…giddy?

The alcohol's fault, probably.

Though that doesn't explain why my stomach does acrobatics every time I think about sliding under the covers of my bed next to Ax. It makes me want to giggle. My cheeks already hurt from fighting not to smile.

Luckily, it's Ax who reminds me why giddiness is inappropriate. "Holy hell, this book is basically porn!"

For fuck's sake. I told him not to touch anything!

Though tempted to hide out in my closet for the rest of the night, I force myself to find something to change into then slip into the bathroom to wash my face and brush my teeth.

Leaving the light over the vanity on, I return to my bedroom. The chandelier has been turned off and the nightstand lamp turned on. Ax is stretched out on top of my covers, fully dressed, including his shoes, reading from my book with a dirty grin on his face.

He looks so natural in my space that I have to take a breath.

"Can you please remove your scummy shoes from my luxury bedding?" I reach over and snatch the book from his hands.

Great. He lost my place.

Deciding that's a problem for tomorrow, I throw the book into my nightstand drawer, and grab two water bottles from the mini fridge hidden in my dresser. Ignoring Ax's very hot gaze, I toss him one.

"That's what you're wearing?" he asks, catching the bottle with one hand.

Maybe it was a judgy gaze, not a hot gaze.

"What's wrong with what I'm wearing?" I glance down at my oversized t-shirt and short shorts. It's an outfit that I usually wear working out, but I figured it was comfortable enough to sleep in.

He lifts a shoulder in a shrug. "Not how I pictured you dressing for bed."

He pictures me dressing for bed?

That shouldn't make my chest feel fizzy like it does. Is this another wave of nausea?

Maybe I'm just dehydrated.

I open my water bottle and take a careful sip before downing several gulps.

Ax continues to study me. "Thought you'd sleep in something...I don't know. More feminine. Silky. Sexy."

"I usually sleep in my panties."

His brows raise with interest. "By all means, don't let me intrude on your routine."

"Nice try." I tug at the covers, hinting for him to move, or at the very least, get his fucking shoes off the bed like I asked.

He picks up on the cue. He stands up, removes his jacket, tie and belt, then toes his shoes off.

Meanwhile, I slide under the sheets and get myself situated on my side, turning off the lamp and moving his phone—which is now charging on my nightstand—away from the edge so I can put my water bottle there instead.

When I turn back to Ax, his shirt is gone, and he's in the process of pulling down his pants.

"What are you doing?" A better question is *what am I doing* because I can't seem to stop myself from staring at his bare chest. It's a display of defined muscles and smooth skin, the light from the lamp illuminating the ridges and curves of his torso.

We're usually mostly dressed when we fuck. Is that why I haven't noticed how insanely cut the man is? Talk about washboard abs. His body is what book boyfriends dream they look like.

"I'm not sleeping in my suit." Ax kicks off his pants, leaving him standing in nothing but his boxer briefs.

"Yeah, but..." I feel a flush of heat rise to my cheeks as I try to tear my gaze away from his sculpted physique. Even his thighs are toned. He is not a man who skips leg day.

"Okay," I say. "It's fine." If I keep saying it, I might start to believe it.

Ax's eyes twinkle with amusement at my flustered state, and he saunters over to the bed, his bare feet padding softly against the floor.

Forcing myself to stop ogling, I turn away and turn off the lamp switch, throwing the room into darkness except for a single shaft of light streaming from the bathroom.

I can feel the bed shift as Ax slides in next to me. He lets out a sigh. "This is what I'm talking about."

I glance over my shoulder to find him stretched out on his back, his hands laced behind his head. Glad he appreciates my bed. There's even more to appreciate about it when I get it all to myself.

Satisfied that we're settled in for the night, I close my eyes.

"But now one of us has to get up and turn off the bathroom light."

I grit my teeth. "No, we don't."

"I'll do it." He starts to climb out of the bed.

I roll toward him. "No! Don't."

He narrows his eyes. "Adly, do you sleep with the light on?"

There's mockery in his voice, and I already know how this conversation is going to go. "Shut up." I turn away from him again, considering the subject closed.

But of course it isn't. "Are you afraid of the dark?"

"I'm not afraid of anything," I lie.

"Ah. Thirty-three-year-old big girl, Addles, and she still needs a night light."

Furiously, I roll back toward him. "For your information, I like to see when I wake up in the middle of the night." Like when I want to pick up my book and read a few lines or when I need to peek under the bed to make sure no one's hiding underneath ready to stab me in my sleep.

Ax pretends to be reassuring. "I'll protect you."

"I'm *not* afraid, you dick."

He looks on the verge to argue further until I fix him with a glare. "Well, I can't sleep with a light on," he says instead.

With an impatient huff, I reach into my nightstand drawer and pull out my pink silk sleep mask. "Here. Use this."

He cringes, probably at the color. "Why do you have a sleep mask if you're afraid of the dark?"

"I said, I'm not afraid." Dangling the mask on my finger, I hold it out for him. "Do you want it or not?"

He thinks for a moment. "I want it."

I watch him put it on and have to smother my laugh

with my hand. It's not just pink, but also frilly, and while I'm a top supporter of men being able to wear whatever color they want, Ax Morgan in pink frill has got to be emasculating.

On that happy note, I sink my head into my pillow and close my eyes. No longer quite as drunk as I was, I'm unable to get comfortable. I'm both too hot and too cold, and Ax's even breathing is loud and intrusive. I shift, trying to find a better position. My foot cramps, and I stretch it out, only to draw it back in a hurry when I accidentally kick my bedmate in the shin.

Propping himself up on his elbows, he pushes the mask onto his forehead. "What the fuck was that?"

"My foot?" Duh.

"It's like a block of ice."

"I have cold feet."

"Keep them on your side."

"It's all my side. You're the one who doesn't have a side." I didn't want him here in the first place. If he's going to complain, he can sleep on the floor.

Perhaps sensing that I'm at my limit, he clamps his mouth shut. Then he pulls the mask back down over his eyes and lays his head down.

The next time my foot brushes him isn't exactly on purpose.

He's just really warm, and my feet really are ice blocks. They can't really help being drawn to his heat.

"Fuck, Adly," he hisses, without removing the mask.

"I could turn on the bed heater." I suppose.

"You could put on socks."

"I'm not putting on more clothes for you."

When he doesn't reply, I grab the remote for the mattress heater from the nightstand and turn it up all the way. This is my usual routine—I get the bed hot and toasty so I can fall asleep. Then I wake up in a couple of hours dripping with sweat.

Someday I should really figure out how to set the timer.

For the next five minutes, we're quiet. My appendages are heating up, and Ax's breaths are steady, and I'm half convinced he's asleep until...

"Adly, why does the bed suddenly feel like a sauna?"

"I told you I was turning on the heater. I'm freezing."

He sits up and pushes the mask again to his forehead. "Jesus. Give me that." Without waiting for me to hand him the remote, he reaches over me and turns the heater off.

Then he rolls to his side, facing me, holds the covers up, and gestures for me to snuggle up to him. "Come here."

No, I want to say.

I gape instead.

Swearing under his breath, he nudges closer.

"What are you do—?" The obvious is answered when he spoons himself around me. "Oh."

Ohhh.

His body is hot at my backside. Hot and inviting. When he puts his arms around me, it feels like a trap. And also like a hug.

I don't really do hugs.

"It's a compromise," he says, his breath at my neck.

"Right." I'm completely tense and can no longer get air to move through my lungs, but sure. It's a compromise.

"You have goosebumps." He rubs his palm up and down my left arm. "Warmer?"

"Yeah." Though I think the goosebumps didn't show up until after he tucked me into his embrace. And my heart is thundering so loud, I'm sure he hears it.

But crazy thing—the more he draws his hand up and down over my skin, the calmer I feel. My heart settles. My breathing evens. My body temperature feels just right.

Little by little, his caress slows. Then his stroke lengthens, passing my wrist to dance his touch over the back of my hand.

Mesmerized, I watch as he threads his long fingers through mine.

"You need a ring," he says, out of the blue.

"I told people we weren't getting them until the ceremony that we'll never have."

"You need an *engagement* ring." His voice is a low rumble. The frequency must have a direct line to my pussy because she starts purring as though she's the one being petted.

It's a disconcerting feeling. Weird since Ax has certainly got her going on more than one occasion.

Just never in a bed. Never with such a nonsexual gesture. Never because a man suggested that I needed to promote a tradition that is antiquated and unfeminist.

"We didn't have an engagement." But I can't bring myself to pull my hand away.

"It doesn't matter."

"I think it's kind of the whole point."

"The whole point is a man telling the world how much he values his woman."

His machismo ruffles my feathers. "That's incredibly patriarchal."

I don't know why it makes my chest warm at the same time.

He traces a single finger down each of mine. "It makes me look bad."

"There's already a long list. No one will pick you apart specifically for this one."

"They won't because I'm getting you a ring." He says it like the matter's closed.

Something strange happens inside me. I very much don't want to wear a ring.

Also, I very much want him to put a ring on my finger. "That's…weird," I say, more to myself than him.

Since he can't read my mind, he doesn't understand the complexity of my statement. "It's the details that make the lie, Addles."

"It does seem like telling a good lie would be your area of expertise."

"Go fuck yourself." There's no bitterness in his voice, though. Just teasing. "Actually, based on the evidence, I guess you already did. Am I currently laying in Adly spooge?"

I kick his shin, pushing my body back against him so I feel the distinct shape of his erection at my backside.

"Careful," he warns.

I close my eyes and pretend that it's not a big deal to feel his cock twitching against my ass. Yes, I've had sex with Ax. In the near dark of my bedroom, I can admit it.

But I must have sobered up some because I'm also very aware that fucking him in my own bed would be a vital mistake.

Letting him touch me like this is a mistake too.

So what do I do? I distract myself from his touch by bringing my hand to his forearm where I trace the intricate cross he has etched there in his skin. "What does your tattoo mean?"

It seems like violating some secret oath to ask. Like we've both silently agreed to only know enough about each other as necessary.

But all agreements go out the window in the dark. "I mean, I know what it is. But why did you pick it?"

He keeps on playing with my hand while I rub up and down over his design. Several long seconds pass before he answers, and I almost think he's not going to.

Then he does. "It's for my mother. She was a devout Catholic, and she wore this cross necklace her entire life. Her mother gave it to her when she had her first Communion, and um...I didn't inherit the necklace when she died, but it's such a vital part of my memories of her, so I had a replica of it designed."

"And this is it?"

I can feel him nod behind me. "She carried her mother with her always. I wanted to honor her the same way."

It's the most sentimental thing I've ever heard him say. The most real thing too, I think.

"That's lovely, Ax. Really." I swallow past the tightness in my throat as I move my finger to the lavender wisps of flowers entwined around the cross "Is this...heather wrapped around it?"

"Mm. Yeah."

My skin feels like it's tingling, almost as if there are tiny electric shocks running through it. My fingers twitch slightly against the smooth surface of Ax's tattoo, the adrenaline causing a slight tremble.

I shouldn't tell him.

I will my mouth to stay shut.

It doesn't. "Some versions of the name Adly mean 'heather field'," I say quietly.

His response comes after a beat, just as quiet. "I know."

I'm warm now, but new goosebumps pepper down my arms. Ax fucking Morgan has my name inked on his skin.

I drift to sleep pretending it means nothing, but I'm glad he isn't facing me, and that he can't see the ghost of a smile haunting my lips.

CHAPTER
FIFTEEN
ADLY

don't wake up with my legs tangled in Ax's.

I wake up alone.

Once again enforcing that romance books are lying liars and not real life.

Surprisingly, my head isn't pounding as much as I would imagine. Probably thanks to the water I drank at bedtime, as well as the full glass I guzzled at five am when Ax was snoozing away with the sheets wrapped around his midline like a toga.

I'm not going to pretend I didn't take the opportunity to get up close and personal with those abs. If anyone asks me if I brought my tongue out to trace along the fuck me lines that vee down at his hips, I plead the fifth.

Despite feeling refreshed, it's Sunday. I gather the blankets around me and roll over, planning to go back to sleep, when two things happen almost at once.

First, I wonder if Ax's absence means he left or if he's nosing around my apartment without supervision. .

Second, I smell coffee brewing.

Throwing the covers off, I jump out of bed and, after a quick trip to the bathroom to pee and brush my teeth, I scamper to find my home invader.

Is it still considered an invasion if I invited him in?

Also, notably, home invader would be hot to roleplay.

But not right now or in my actual home since that would be odd, somehow.

About as odd as it is seeing Ax, still clothed only in black boxer briefs, standing at my kitchen island, slicing strawberries and drinking coffee from a mug that says *Spread those pages like a good girl.*

It's a sight that kicks me in the ovary. First, his ass is truly divine—I could look at it for hours—but more importantly, domesticated Ax is the most delicious thing that's ever greeted me on a Sunday morning.

"There's coffee," he says, not looking up from his task.

Without replying, I tear myself away from the mancandy, leave the kitchen, and glance around. Surprisingly, nothing in the apartment looks rifled through. Guess that means we're not playing home invader.

Also means Ax is more respectful than I predicted.

When I return to the kitchen, he's pouring coffee into a mug that says, *They better have smut in hell.*

He reads it before handing it to me. Then holds up his own. "I'm sensing a theme."

"I'm sensing cooking preparations." There's a large mixing bowl on the counter and a griddle sitting on the unlit stove, and the sliced strawberries have joined a dish with blueberries and bananas. "What are you doing?"

This might be the most action my kitchen has ever seen.

"Making breakfast." He says it like it's the most natural thing in the world. Like we often get drunk, kiss in front of everyone, and have sleepovers that end with Chef Morgan in my kitchen in his underwear.

I have so many questions.

"Where did you get the food?" I'm pretty sure I had the fruit, but I'm also pretty sure I didn't have the bag of flour or the pint of milk. Or the sugar. Or the eggs.

"I had stuff delivered." He picks up a sieve kind of thing that I think is literally called a sifter and adds baking powder and flour to it before shaking it over the bowl.

The bowl is not familiar. And I'm pretty fucking sure I'd remember if I had a sifter.

Maybe.

It's hard to know since I really only use my kitchen for coffee and heating up takeout. "Where did you get the equipment?"

This time he looks directly at me when he answers, enunciating every word. "I. Had. Stuff. Delivered."

The delivery bags from JB Prince on the counter are a helpful clue, I suppose. "It's an awful lot of stuff you're bringing into *my* apartment."

"And I haven't even officially started moving in yet."

The comment jitters my nerves. I haven't let myself think about what living with each other entails. Honestly, I haven't had time. But if it's going to be a lot of Ax putting his things in my places, I'm going to need time to adjust.

Worded differently, anyway.

Needing to sit down whilst I adjust, I climb onto one of the barstools and cradle the hot mug in my hands as I watch Ax make a sort of crater in the sifted together dry mix. Then he adds milk and butter and cracks an egg into the center.

Truly fascinating. Like...how does he know how to do that?

"You have plans for today?" he asks, interrupting my ogling.

I'm instantly suspicious. "Why are you asking?"

"Just making conversation, Addles. No need to get your hackles all hackled."

Perhaps I overreacted. It's just complicated having him here, for some reason. It feels like there should be boundaries established.

Probably not such explicit boundaries that we're unable to carry out small talk. Which is what this is. *You definitely overreacted.* "I was really hoping to get to the bookstore. I'm out of things to read."

Was that so bad?

Sort of, considering that he now looks like I'm off my cracker. "That's not possible. You have bookshelves covering every spare inch of wall in this place and maybe another hundred books that seem like they don't have a place."

So he did look around. "I feel judged."

"Have you read everything you own?"

That is beyond the point. "I'm not going to explain myself to someone who obviously doesn't understand mood reading."

Ax finishes cutting off the tag from one of the new utensils that I'm pretty sure is called a rubber spatula. "Is it like mood fucking? Because I understand that."

I consider that as I sip my coffee. Is there such a thing as mood fucking? Is that the itch that roleplaying scratches? Allows the activity to fit whatever the fancy of the day is?

It's an interesting idea to pursue, but discussing sex with my roommate might be one of those things that should be boundrafied. "Anyway. I'm going to have to wait until another weekend. I slept in too long."

He lifts his wrist to check his watch. "It's barely ten."

I set my coffee down and bring my feet up to the stool, hugging my knees to my chest. "The place I like to go is this romance only bookshop over in Brooklyn. It's called Under the Cover, and it's an adorable place with every subgenre of romance you can imagine, lots of them indie published special editions, which are sometimes hard to acquire. They're always closed by the time I leave work, and they host events on the weekends. If I don't get there super early, it's too crowded to really browse."

"This is New York. There are a million bookshops."

"Not a million like this one. It's my dream place. They have a reading nook under the stairs and a mural of Stevie Nicks." I sigh. "There's no place like it."

"And that's why you're using your trust fund to buy your own bookstore."

"Tempting." Guilt tugs at my conscience. Should I just tell him? I almost did last night, before we got harassed into that kiss.

Fuck, that kiss.

My thighs are jello just thinking about it. Which is why I shouldn't think about it, and somehow related, though I don't know exactly how, it's also why I should keep my secrets to myself. "Sadly, no. I am not on the verge of entering the bookselling business."

Ax turns back to the mixing bowl, spatula in hand. "You should think about it."

"Think about starting my whole career over from scratch? No, thank you."

"I don't know. Why not spend all day doing the thing you love while getting paid for it?" He seems strangely invested in convincing me.

It's kind of sweet. "I'm not sure I'd want to ruin my hobby by requiring it to be revenue producing." I could do a whole PowerPoint on all the reasons I'm not drawn to making books my business, but at the moment, I'm so much more intrigued by Ax and the specific way he folds the dry and liquid ingredients together. "Speaking of hobbies...is this one of yours?"

"What do you mean?"

"Cooking. Do you do it often?"

"When I'm hungry and near a kitchen, so yeah. Fairly often."

If I had something to throw at him, I would. It's not an unreasonable question. I've known the man my entire life, and not once have I ever seen him step aside to whip up a meal.

I guess food has never been a subject that's come up.

Now that it has, I'm trying to fit this new fact into the image I've previously created of Ax. "But how do you know how to do it?"

He pins his gaze on me. "I'm making pancakes, Adly.

It's the simplest recipe on the planet. I didn't even have to Google. Do you really not cook at all?"

Do Pop Tarts count? Though, I usually eat those without toasting them, so probably not. "I burned water once. I wasn't really allowed in the kitchen after that."

"Even after you grew up and moved out? You never got the urge to try again?"

"This was after I moved out," I admit. "In this apartment. I'm the one who kicked me out."

Ax drops the spatula in the bowl then props his elbows on the counter and rub his forehead. "For fuck's sake, this is..." He abruptly bolts upright. "Get over here."

"Why?" I drop my knees, but I don't get off the barstool, half afraid he means to spank me with the spatula that he's once again wielding.

"I'm going to teach you pancakes. My mom taught me when I was seven. You should be able to handle this at thirty-three."

Once more, I feel judged. "Is this what it's going to be like living with you?"

"Get over here."

It's that sharp tone I've only heard him use one other time—when we were playing teacher/student yesterday at the fundraiser.

And while I don't feel the same compulsion to obey as when we were in the scene, it does motivate me to get my ass off the stool. "Aye, aye captain."

"It's chef," he corrects as I circle the island to join him.

I laugh. "*Chef.*"

But then he looks at me with a brow arched and the

spatula raised, and I realize he's serious. Like in-scene serious. "Oh."

A battle happens inside my head. Part of me feels like fooling around right now with Ax is a bad, bad idea, but no part of me can explain why. We've fooled around plenty. Sure I keep saying it's the last time, but that's almost part of the game now. What's the harm in playing one more time? "Okay. Chef."

I almost miss his smile since he hides it so fast. "In my kitchen, everyone helps cook." He hands me the spatula and pushes me toward the bowl. "Mix this together until it's smooth."

Only ten seconds in, I'm convinced I need to do more upper arm training. "I think I have an electric mixer somewhere."

"No electric mixer. Hand only. If you overmix it, your pancakes will be rubber."

How does he fucking know this?

He comes behind me to demonstrate, setting one hand on my hip and using the other to help me stir the batter with long lazy circles. My stomach flutters with excitement, mirroring the movements of our hands.

"How will I know when it's done, chef?" My voice is breathy.

"When everything's wet."

Is he still talking about the batter? If not, bingo. Goal achieved.

He steps closer, bringing his hips tight against me. "You want to make sure there aren't any lumps."

"I don't think I feel any right now." Except for the large one pressing against my backside.

My mouth starts watering, and it's not for pancakes.

"You're right. It's good."

So good that I'm pushing my ass back against his firm ridge, trying to get a little friction.

But Chef Morgan is more interested in cooking, it seems, when he lets go of me and moves to the stove. Maybe we aren't playing a game after all.

I bite back my disappointment.

"Now we heat the griddle." After lighting the burner and turning it to medium heat, he cuts off some butter from a stick and throws it onto the pan. "Put in enough to cover the surface when it melts."

"And then we add the batter?" When he nods, I realize there's an important step missing. "How do we make them round, chef?"

"Oh my God, you're such a princess," he says, more to himself than to me.

It still merits a response. "Yeah, well..." I tap my chin with my middle finger, the rest of them folded down.

His hand comes down hard on my ass. It's not too painful since I'm wearing shorts, but it does surprise me. "Hey!"

"The chef deserves respect."

The restaurant owner deserves some respect as well, if you ask me.

Admittedly, that's not as fun. "I'm sorry, chef. Please tell me what to do next."

I'm pretty sure Ax has a weak spot for the word *please*. At least when I say it, anyway. His eyes flash dark and hungry, and I wonder if it's safe to presume he's not thinking about pancakes anymore either.

"I have an idea," he says. "We're going to practice. Hop up." He pats a clear spot on the counter, on the island, away from the stove, then helps me up.

Once I'm up, feet dangling, he moves in front of me and wraps his hands in the band of my shorts. Then he starts to pull down, silently urging me to lift my hips.

"What are you doing?" I ask, not because I'm opposed to undressing, but since I'm still unclear what is actually happening here, I need the clarification.

"We need a clear space."

"A clear space requires me to be half naked?"

He smirks. "It does when we're making pussycakes."

Then we are playing.

My pussy contracts at the mention of her name.

I lift my hips without another word. Ax pulls my shorts down, his eyes widening when he realizes I was too lazy—read *drunk*—to put any panties on last night. "Slept all night next to you not wearing panties, and I wasn't the wiser."

After dropping my shorts to the floor, he bites his bottom lip and draws a single finger down my slit from clit to pussy hole. "Yeah, this will work."

Without being told, I spread my legs and lean back on my elbows.

That's exactly when Ax leaves me to return to the griddle. *GODDAMMIT.*

"Eyes on me," he says, picking up an ice cream scoop. He narrates as he dips it into the batter and dumps it onto the griddle. "Scoop, and drop." Then he does it again, until there are two blooming circles of batter sizzling on the sheet.

I recognize the ice cream scoop. It's one kitchen utensil I

definitely know I already owned. "The scoop is what makes the circle shape?"

He takes a patient breath. "Whatever you use, it's going to spread in the shape of a circle."

"Why?"

He brings the bowl and the scoop over to the counter next to me. "Science, baby."

When I frown at his simplistic answer, he explains. "Gravity, surface tension. It's always going to make a cake, hence the name." He hands me the scooper. "You try."

I lift myself up onto one elbow so I can scoop the batter with my other arm.

Once I have it collected, Ax rubs the tip of his finger over my clit. "Put it right here."

With a shiver, I drop the scoop where he's asked, anxiously anticipating what he'll do next. "I don't think it's going to get hot there."

"Hm. I think it might." Then he bends down to lathe his tongue through the batter, making sure to linger as he passes over my clit.

"Oh, actually. That is...very...hot."

He chuckles against me, and I feel his warm breath on my pussy. He swipes his tongue across the pussycake again, hitting my clit from another direction this time. Then again, and again, each time raveling tension in my belly.

When most of the batter is cleaned up, his tongue flicks back and forth, dancing around my most sensitive spot, and I feel myself getting wetter from his touch. Especially when his lips surround my clit, and he sucks.

Throwing my head back, I let out a moan. "Fuck. Chef."

Ax continues to suck and lick my clit, his hands roaming

over my body, grasping at my breasts and hips. I feel myself getting closer and closer to the edge, my body trembling with anticipation.

Suddenly, he stops sucking, and as I whimper in frustration, he picks up the ice cream scoop. I watch him with wide eyes as he taps it so most of the batter falls into the bowl before bringing the opposite end toward me.

The metal is cold against my skin, the coolness spreading as he inserts the handle into my pussy, and I moan again, louder than before, feeling the sensation of the object entering me.

Peering down my body, I watch as he starts to really fuck me with the ice cream scooper, shoving in and out of me like he would with his cock. Batter drips from the other end onto his hand. Onto the floor. "You're making a mess."

"A mess of your pussy, or a mess on the counter?"

I try to laugh. "Both, I think."

Particularly when his mouth returns to latch onto my clit, his tongue licking at the same time as the scoop moves in and out. My hands fly to his head for support, my thighs shaking as the sensation overwhelms me as the pressure builds, and my body trembles, teetering on the edge of orgasm.

But even more, he's making a mess of me. My brain is fuzzy with lust, the pleasure radiating from my core dominating all my thoughts.

Still somewhere beneath all that I can hear the warning alarms go off again. Telling me that this is too intimate, too real, too out of control.

"Ax," his name floats from my mouth—his legit name— and while I'm sure that I'm no longer playing, I'm not sure if I'm asking him to stop or begging him for something else. Something I can't name. Something I so desperately hope he can give me. "Ax, I..."

"Oh, shit!" he says, and that's when I realize that, once again, the alarms aren't just in my head. This time, it's the smoke alarm.

Ax jumps away from me. The ice cream scoop clatters to the floor. The alarm's shrill sounds bounce off the walls, piercing my ears and making my heart race even more than Ax's mouth had. As he bats at the flames with a dish towel, smoke fills the room, and the smell of burning batter mingles with the musky scent of my pussy.

My body still tingling from pleasure and frantically trying to catch my breath, I jump down from the counter and run over to the fire extinguisher box on the wall. The burnt water taught me not only to keep one in the kitchen but to also know how to use it. Quickly, I aim the spout at the fire. The red hot flames hiss as the cold mist makes contact, and within seconds, the blaze is put out, leaving the kitchen covered in white powder left from the spray.

"Now who's made a mess?" Ax asks, a playful smirk on his face as he uses a broom handle to stab at the the smoke alarm until it stops shrieking. "Next lesson—never take your eyes off the stove."

It's an opportunity to laugh, and I'm tempted.

But it also feels like karma. Like this is what I deserve for letting things get out of hand. There's a reason I'm not allowed in my kitchen—things get burned.

Luckily, this time, it was only pancake batter and not me.

"Actually, this is, um, good." I pull at the hem of my T-shirt, even though it fully covers my body, as if I can hide what he's already seen.

"I didn't know burnt pancakes covered with sodium carbonate was your thing." His tone is guarded, though, and I have a feeling he senses what's coming next.

"Ha." My laugh comes out forced. "It's just...if we're going to be living together for the time being, this place needs to be a safe space for both of us. It's too..." Intimate, maybe. Too dangerous, for sure. "I don't think that we can do that if we're...you know. Making pussycakes and what not. Not in the apartment, anyway."

"Okay." He drags out each syllable, like he's not quite on board. "Are you saying you felt unsafe?"

He follows my gaze to the burned pancakes and speaks before I can answer. "Stupid question."

He laughs, but his expression is guarded.

"I'm sorry I gave mixed signals. I hadn't quite worked it out myself. I haven't lived with anyone since I lived at home. I'm new to this whole..."

He finishes for me. "Marriage thing? Yeah. Me too."

His tone is hard. Cold. I want to fix it, but I don't know how, and every instinct I have to step forward and touch him feels...terrifying.

So I step back instead. "Then you understand?"

"Mm hm. I understand, Adly."

"Okay, well. I'm going to go clean up." And probably finish myself off in the shower with the nozzle because I now I really need that rush of endorphins.

"I'll work on this," he says, pointing to the mess. "We still have enough batter to make another batch."

"You don't have to do—"

He cuts me off. "Hey now, I slaved over this meal. I'm not letting it go to waste."

It feels like an attempt to regain the lighter mood, but I can't go there with him. It's dangerous. This isn't the time to lose my head, and Ax makes it real hard to remember that.

"Okay," I say. "Thank you." Maybe I'll even eat them.

I leave the kitchen with the scent of smoke clinging to me like a black cloud.

It lightens somewhat when he calls after me, "This just means we're going to be spending an awful lot of time outside the apartment together this year."

The thought makes my stomach flip despite the simultaneous sinking feeling of dread.

CHAPTER
SIXTEEN
AX

By Wednesday, everything feels strangely back to normal.

The congrats have died down from coworkers, Samuel is treating me like a steadfast, overlookable employee, and my father has emailed to let me know he's disappointed in my "apparent willingness to let my wife be the man in the family."

In other words—normal.

Since I'm not set to actually move in to Adly's until this weekend, I've still been staying at Hunter's. There's not a lot for me to pack, but I've used that excuse to get out of spending any real time with him. I'm not exactly avoiding him...just keeping things as uncomplicated as possible. Our friendship is a conflict of interest to my marriage, and while I've chosen my side, I don't like to think about it too much.

As for my wife, I've barely seen her since I left her apartment Sunday morning. I didn't even stay to eat the second batch of pancakes. She stated her boundaries, and they were a punch in the gut, but she's right. Fucking around and playing house is a bad combo. Best to remember what this is and what it isn't and avoid the latter all together.

Which is why today's text message from her remains unanswered.

> Can you do Saturday for furniture shopping?

In addition to my bed, there are a few other pieces we need. Her living room set is far too feminine for me, and anyone who knows me at all would never believe I'd move in without making some changes. But I have half a mind to let her deal with it on her own.

Better yet, we could handle it online. She can send me a link, and I can give her the thumbs-up or -down. No need to physically be together where her fingers could accidentally brush against mine, or she could laugh too hard at one of my bad jokes, or her lips could part and I mistake it for an invitation.

Or it's not a mistake, and I ignore my better instinct and accept the invitation, which could be equally consequential if not more so.

On the other hand, is it really considered playing house if we aren't actually in the "house"?

I'm mulling it over as I mosey to the conference room for a meeting with my programming team, too lost in thought to realize that the man headed toward me down the hall is not an employee until he's right in front of me.

"Shit, Hunter."

"My man!"

We do our bro handshake—thumb clasp, hug with a back pat, hand slide, fist bump. A quick recalibration of my brain at the same time, and I remember that he had a meeting with the board today. "So? How did it go?"

Hunter's smile is victorious. He glances over his shoulder, making sure no one's around before leaning in to boast. "Perfection. They formally vote and announce in two weeks, and Samuel is still grumbling, but it's a lock. You're looking at CEO, Ax. We did it."

I'm genuinely excited for him. Years of planning, a decade of me sharing ideas and gripes about the company with him, night after night of strategizing and imagining a remodel to the outdated corporate policies—it's all finally playing out.

At the expense of Adly, sure, but that's business. If there's anything she understands as a Sebastian, certainly it's that.

And my father says I have no ambition…

Still, I have to swallow past the ball of shame in my throat to share in the congratulations. "We fucking did it."

"Grand slam, I'm telling you."

There's a relief exuding from him that I haven't felt since maybe ever. His own father's expectations weigh even heavier than mine. The things he's endured to get here are tenfold the hardships I've had to endure, even with the privilege of his name. Maybe more accurately *because of* the so-called privilege of his name. I've been through it all with him, so I know what he's done to get here. I know he deserves it.

Relief flirts with my emotions as well, only I can't seem

to embrace it the way he has. Too much yet unsettled, perhaps. Too much still unknown.

It's not the place for details, but my curiosity is a deep seated need to know. "You presented the buy-out?" I don't have to say the word SHE for him to know what I'm asking.

"I didn't, actually," and now the relief starts to settle over me. Until he adds, "Saving that for when I take over, as the first item on my agenda."

Admittedly, it's the best course of action. I can't be surprised he hasn't abandoned it.

Down the hall behind him, the conference room door opens and board members start trickling out, their meeting evidently adjourned just in time for me to set up for mine.

Hunter glances back at his uncle Henry, who gives him a reassuring thumbs-up before pausing to chat with another one of the board members.

When Hunter turns again to me, he looks even more smug. "I, uh, sold them on some other reorganization ideas." His voice is just above a whisper. "We can talk about it later, obviously. Don't want to jinx anything right now."

"Sure. Later." I give him a fist bump. "Good job, man. I knew you could do it."

He claps me on the shoulder. "*We*, Axelrod," he says, lengthening my name incorrectly, to be a shit. "It was always *we*."

It should make me feel celebratory along with him.

It doesn't.

Maybe I'll feel it when it's official. Meantime, I'm getting good at this thing called pretend. "I know you got my back." The words are honest, even if the enthusiasm behind them is less so.

Hunter doesn't acknowledge the statement, and when he looks back again and sees his father step out from the conference room, along with my father, I don't expect him to. "I really should take off."

"Can I come with you?" I joke.

"Heh. Right? Fuck all those old men. Soon it will be our place." He punches me lightly on the shoulder, then he's gone.

I pause before heading again toward the conference room, waiting for the rest of the board to clear out. Relief finally does kick in when our fathers take the other hallway to the elevator, thereby alleviating me from having to talk to them. The last thing I'm in the mood for is Dad berating me in front of his friends. It wouldn't be the first time. There's nothing he loves more than using someone else's success to put me in my place.

When everyone seems to have left, I finish my trek to the room, only to find a board member lingering. "Sorry, Samuel. I didn't realize you were still here. I have the room scheduled in fifteen—do you need it?"

"No, no. We're wrapped up." He slides a Montblanc pen into his suit pocket, picks up a spiral bound packet from the table, and stands up from his seat. "And it's Dad."

"Uh, right. Thank you. Dad."

He's corrected me no less than five times now. I'd hoped he would stop pushing it when I blatantly never took him up on the offer, but it doesn't seem to be the case. It makes for awkward engagement at the office. Despite having had my position for a few years—a job that I have worked hard to earn—having to refer to the current man in charge as Dad feels like it negates all of my skills and ability.

At least when Hunter takes over, I won't have to worry about that anymore.

Probably won't have to worry about my father-in-law at all at that point, since there's still a chance Adly will suck it up and stay when she can't buy SHE, and then she'll have no need to stay married to me.

Maybe Hunter will even let Adly run the division that the buy-out creates. Her father might want to keep her sequestered in HR, but he won't be in charge anymore.

The idea is so satisfying that for the first time in days, the pinched ribs sensation lets up, and it doesn't hurt to breathe.

But then, instead of leaving the room, Samuel turns his hard gaze on me directly. "Your buddy made a good impression today. Much to my chagrin."

I struggle to find the right words to respond. "That's...uh...too bad," I finally say, trying to sound sympathetic.

Samuel tilts his head, studying me intently. "You don't need to hide your hand from me," he says with a knowing smirk. "It might not be obvious to the others how much he's been coached, but I see your hand in his vision."

A sense of guilt washes over me as I recall my role in Hunter's rise to power. "I don't think that's true," I reply, trying to keep my voice steady.

"It's a compliment, Ax," Samuel continues, seeming somehow taller. "Hunter's ideas have merit. They may be ambitious, but manageable. And they address almost every issue SNC currently faces. No wonder he's captured the vote."

The unexpected praise throws me. "Thank you. But I do understand that Hunter isn't for everyone."

Samuel lets out a small chuckle. "That's putting it kindly." Then his expression turns serious. "In the end, the board is only concerned with money. They'll overlook any flaws in their chosen leader if it means fattening their own pockets. In most situations, I would vote exactly the same."

I nod, knowing firsthand how cutthroat corporate politics can be.

He pauses, studying me for a moment before going on. "What interests me is *your* loyalty. After everything you've done to help cement Hunter's transition to the helm, I would expect him to reward you in some way. Yet, the plan he's proposed today—the one that sealed the deal for him—includes a reformation of the executive offices. Essentially reducing the power of every vice president currently employed."

No. That can't be how it sounds.

I take a deep breath before responding. "Reformation of the executive offices?" My tone is only barely calm.

"You didn't know? I suspected as much." Samuel's sympathy borders on patronizing. "Hunter suggested that we've grown too big to have all the CEO duties fall on one person. Admittedly, it's been a lot for me this past year, even with Arthur sharing the load. Hunter's proposal is to add three additional CEO positions to bear that load—one specifically for regional news outlets, another for national news, and the final for alternative media entertainment—not that I understand why we need a division for that last one. Hunter didn't extrapolate on his plans there."

I try to process this information while keeping my

emotions in check. The new division is for SHE. We'd discussed that, but nothing else in terms of reorganizing.

Why would he do that unless...?

No. I refuse to jump to conclusions without talking to Hunter first.

But then Samuel opens up the presentation document he's been holding and flips through the pages. "I expected your name to be floated for one of those spots. Seems only fair, when you've been his right hand man all this time, and yet he still has you listed as VP of Programming. You'll report directly to...let's see..." He stops flipping and squints at a diagram. "Craig Rasmussen pegged for your superior."

"Craig Rasmussen from TTC?" I repeat incredulously. That network has only been broadcasting nationally for a couple of years. The guy is an up-and-comer in the news world, but he brings nothing to the table that I haven't brought tenfold.

Is that why Hunter didn't run this by me? Because then he'd have to admit to my face that he's stabbing me in the back?

Try as I might to hide it, I'm sure my expression gives too much away.

"See for yourself." Samuel holds the presentation print-out toward me.

I will myself not to take it from him, but I can't help myself. Snatching it from Samuel's hand, I stare at the page he's left it open to. Sure enough, the employment hierarchy is depicted in illustration form, and I'm on the third level from the top.

What the actual fuck?

My throat tightens, anger slowly boiling beneath the surface.

"Sorry to be the bearer of...well, bad news. The pun is unintended. A little news man humor, if you will."

The flippant apology reminds me who I'm dealing with, and it puts a pin in my growing rage. "Why are you telling me all this?"

Samuel doesn't miss a beat. "Now that you're the man entrusted with caring for my daughter, I felt it was my obligation to make sure you were aware. Looking out for your future and all."

Looking out for my future, my ass.

He's pissed that Hunter's the man the board has chosen, and he can't help stirring shit in retaliation. He's not worried about Adly. He's worried about his legacy. I've known the Sebastians too long not to recognize their manipulation tactics.

"I appreciate that, sir." For the first time in days, he doesn't try to get me to call him Dad. The sarcasm in my tone must be evident.

"Anytime," he says, with equal coolness. He nods at the booklet still in my hand. "You can keep that."

I don't look at him as he slowly makes his way across the room to the door. I'm too busy staring at the printout. I flip through to the beginning and verify that Hunter is the author—he is. The table of contents shows most of his plan contains ideas I came up with. No credit to me, of course. Then I skim through the description of the new positions he's created. They're all jobs I could do with my eyes closed.

There has to be a reason that Hunter hasn't slotted me in

for one of them. Because he hasn't talked to me yet? Because he thought Craig Rasmussen might attract more of the vote?

But neither of those options makes sense. One of the plusses in Hunter's favor has always been that he has me in his court. He made it to the long consideration list because of his name, but I got him what he needed to be on the short list.

Even if Samuel's just trying to create drama by telling me, it's Hunter's presentation that fucks me over. There's no two ways about it.

And I'm not just pissed—I'm livid.

"It isn't the best move," I say, just as Samuel reaches the door. I wait until he turns to give me his attention to go on. "Reorganizing as soon as he gets in, I mean. It's a disaster waiting to happen."

Samuel's head bobs as he considers. "Go on."

I shouldn't. It's a conversation that could bite me in the ass later on. What I should do is cancel my meetings for the rest of the day, track Hunter down, and demand an explanation.

But shouldn't that be on him to come to me?

Good idea or not, I press on. "There has been conflict surrounding this position already. The new CEO would benefit from relying on current executives who have a strong rapport with employees to build unity. Alienating those who have poured their heart and soul into the company is just asking for an uphill battle."

"The board wants someone who will shake things up."

"There are more effective ways to do that."

Samuel shifts his weight from one hip to the other. "And what would you suggest?"

"It doesn't really matter what I would do." Because all of my ideas are already listed in the printout I'm holding, with Hunter's name on it.

Well. Not *all* of my ideas. Not the best one.

And who doesn't want to impress the boss? A man who has never cared a damn what I thought until now. A man who I've at times respected and feared and wanted so badly to acknowledge my work.

So when he says, "Please, indulge my curiosity," the words tumble out before I can second guess myself.

"SNC's numbers have dropped in two key demographics: youth and women. Every day we ignore them is a step closer to losing our status as a top news company in the U.S. That's where our focus should be. And instead of starting from scratch, we should consider purchasing a platform that already has a strong following and build from there."

"Like SHE network, I assume."

Warning bells sound in my head.

But Samuel's the one who brought up SHE. And I'm only floating an idea, not executing it. "If it's available...yes. SHE would be an excellent acquisition."

"Hm." Samuel stares at me with narrowed eyes as if seeing me in a new light. "It would bring the family back into the fold, too."

He's talking about Holt, I remind myself.

"Well, let's hope your influence still carries weight when your friend takes over," Samuel says, as one of my teammates comes up behind him, wanting entrance to the room but likely not wanting to inconvenience the boss.

Steele arrives behind him, and apparently has no such qualms. "Dad? Could you...?"

"Yes, of course." Samuel steps out of the way to let them in, and addresses me a final time. "Thank you for your thoughts, Ax. I'll let you get on with your meeting."

As soon as he leaves, regret hits me like a Mack truck.

Samuel wants dissension in his wake. He's probably already planning how he'll get the board to turn on Hunter, and I played right into his hand. Hunter's proposal might fuck me over, but it isn't a done deal. I'll be less likely to convince him to reverse course if he finds out I've blabbed about his secret plans.

But it's not Hunter I feel bad about. It's what I've done to my wife.

Whether I had the idea or not, SNC was always going to go after SHE eventually. But that doesn't have to be a move against Adly. In fact, the ideal solution would be to work *with* her, and as someone who understands this company as well as I do, I'm ashamed that I didn't stand up for her sooner.

Bad timing to realize it when my entire team and a fellow vice president are looking at me to get this meeting running.

I'm not letting that be my excuse. "Steele, can you get things started? I have something I need to do."

Without waiting for his reply, I jog out of the room and down the hall to my father-in-law's office. He's standing at his secretary's desk discussing his schedule when I get there.

"Samuel," I call out, still several yards away. When he doesn't respond, I try again, my voice louder. "Dad."

This time he looks up.

I trot over to him. "Sorry to interrupt," I say, breathless. "I had one more thing. Do you have a minute?"

Samuel glances at his watch. "I have seven. Come on in." He opens the door behind him and gestures for me to enter.

Once inside, he shuts the door behind us and starts toward his sitting area. "Would you like to take a seat?"

I shake my head, eager to get this off my chest. "This will be quick. I know the board has already made their decision, but if you really want to know what I'd do, it would be to pull from the pool of people who have already dedicated their entire careers to this network."

"I agree."

I try not to let his approval throw me off track. "It's logical. Why waste the talent you already have? Now, most of the members of the board are Sebastians. I get that they want to keep the family name at the helm, and it was a real blow when Holt didn't work out. But you have other children. You have another option right in front of your face."

"Steele isn't interested in—"

I cut him off, my voice sharp and determined. "I mean, Adly. Your daughter. My wife."

"Adly?" He seems taken aback, his eyebrows shooting up in surprise.

His reaction only spurs me on. "She knows this business backward and forward. Employees love her. She doesn't have drama associated with her, and no offense to you or any of your other relatives, but she's hands down the smartest person here."

Samuel's face twitches with annoyance at my boldness, but I'm not done.

"She's organized and strategic," I continue, "and what she lacks in experience she makes up for in vision. It's a real fucking tragedy if her name hasn't at least been seriously considered."

Samuel takes a breath. The kind of breath that says he's trying to decide how to answer politely. "It warms my heart to know my daughter has found someone so supportive that he can't help but overlook her weaknesses."

I narrow my eyes at him. If he was going for polite, he missed the mark. How dare he dismiss Adly's capabilities so easily? His own daughter?

"Her weaknesses?" I ask incredulously, unable to hide my frustration.

"She's young, Ax," Samuel replies condescendingly. "More importantly, she's a woman. A newly married woman in her reproductive prime. She needs to focus on growing a family, not leading a fifteen-billion-dollar corporation to record profits, which is very much what the board is looking for."

I clench my fists at my sides, fighting to keep my cool. "With all due respect," I say through gritted teeth. "You ran this company while you raised your family."

"We all know men and women have different roles in child rearing," he counters smugly. "Fathers can get away with quality not quantity. Kids need their mothers."

This isn't about gender roles, it's about Adly's capabilities, but I follow his lead. "Didn't their mother pass away when they were still young? I don't know who raised them if you were too busy at the office, but they seem to be doing just fine."

Samuel doesn't blink. "I should have included that mothers need their kids. As someone who has insight on our family secrets, I'm sure you're aware that Sonya's death was very much brought about from being separated from her firstborn."

As much as I want to argue back, I hold my tongue. I'm not about to discuss Hunter and his mother's suicide with Samuel, who obviously has a lot of resentment.

"Anyway," he continues. "You've proven my point. Her bond with him was so strong that she'd rather not be on this earth at all than be apart from him, despite having three other children who needed her care. You can't convince me that a bond like that wouldn't prove distracting during long work hours."

I'm disgusted with his reasoning. "That was one woman. One situation. It's not fair to attribute that to all women."

"I'm not," he snaps back. "I'm attributing it to that woman's daughter. *My* daughter. Whom I've known for plenty longer than you have, Ax."

I swallow hard. It's a fucking bitch of a destiny he's assigned to his one and only daughter. One that I can tell he's not going to abandon easily.

It explains a lot about Adly that I hadn't understood before. It hits me deep in my chest, making it hard to breathe. No wonder she's desperate to get out of here. Frankly, I'm surprised she hasn't run sooner.

"I do trust that you will take care of her," Samuel says in

a softer tone, when I don't refute his last appalling statement. "But in this instance, I'm glad that it's people who are less blinded by emotion that are making the decision."

"I think you're the one who might be blinded by emotion, sir," I say bitterly. "But I won't waste more of your time. It's evident that your mind is already made up."

I turn on my heel, but stop at the door, suddenly compelled to make a promise I have no business making. "One thing you're right about, Samuel—Adly *will* be taken care of. I assure you of that."

She deserves better than SNC, better than him. Better than all of us.

And if she can't have SHE, I'll find better for her, if it's the last thing I do.

CHAPTER
SEVENTEEN
ADLY

"Pull over here, please," Ax tells our driver.

I groan. "Where now?"

We've spent the entire Saturday shopping for furniture, and by shopping for furniture, I mean arguing about furniture.

And rugs.

And throw pillow accents.

And color schemes.

And closets, because apparently Ax is set on me clearing out the one in my yoga room turned Ax-room so he can use it for his own clothes. Which means I have to pare things down since every other closet in the apartment is stuffed.

He's also said I can't keep using the oven to store shoes, but that's a battle we've put off until another day.

I'm tired and beyond ready to be horizontal, and since I thought we'd finished ordering everything we needed and were done, I haven't been paying attention to our surroundings. My shoes are off, my feet are propped on the back of the seat in front of me, and my head is replaying chapter eleven from my current read.

There was banging on a public roof.

It's a real mystery how I was able to put it down to come out to do anything at all today. Needless to say, if I don't get back to my book real soon, there will be death threats involved.

Ax doesn't seem to understand that. "Just one more stop. It will be a quickie."

"Fuck." Pretending that my pussy girl didn't perk up at the mention of a quickie, I lean across Ax to see what's out his window and am confused to see we're at my favorite bookstore.

"This is the place, right?" he asks.

When I look back at him for more of an explanation, he's grinning like he just gave me an O for the record books. I'm not sure why. Because he remembered something I told him less than a week ago? Are men supposed to get points now for paying attention in conversations? Is this the bar?

Or maybe he's missed a very important detail. "It's closed."

He shakes his head, as though I'm frustrating and impatient when we both know I'm a delight. "Ye of little faith."

The driver parks. Ax tells him he'll text when we're ready to be picked up, then steps out of the car before turning back to grab my hand.

As soon as his skin touches mine, electricity sparks and tingles travel up my arm. It's intense, but I don't pull away, knowing Ax will make a big deal about it if I do.

Besides, it's not exactly a terrible feeling to hold his hand.

He keeps my hand in his when we stop in front of the dark storefront. "'Under the Cover,'" he reads from the signage. "Shouldn't *Cover* be plural?"

"No. It's a pun."

"Right. The pun is you're talking about covers in a bed and the covers on books."

"But a book only has one cover. So singular."

"But it's a store. And there are multiple books. So it's still covers."

"But you don't sell an idea to people in multiplicity. You sell it by dialing in on the one. *We have your next mattress!* Not *We have your next* mattresses. *Start your day with a caramel iced latte! Fall in love with what's under the cover!*"

He stares at me like I don't understand marketing.

I stare at him like I don't understand men. "Did you bring me here just so I could stare longingly into my favorite place while you disparage its name?"

"Does that seem like something I would do?" The smug smile has returned.

"I don't think you want me to answer that."

But midway through my sentence, his free hand reaches into his jeans pocket, pulls something small out, and holds it up for me like it's the holy grail.

Admittedly, it takes me a beat to focus on the item because every time I'm reminded that he's wearing jeans, I have to stare and drool all over again. It's a rare look for him, and I'm not generally a girl who gets hot and bothered by denim, but put Ax Morgan in a pair along with a snug T-shirt, and my vagina starts making plans.

It might be safe to say I'm due for a shag.

That's complicated since Ax's bed is being delivered in the morning, and he's officially moving in. I have no regrets about making the apartment a safe zone, but now I'm in a quandary because everyone at work likely assumes we've been fucking every time we've been behind closed doors. Chances are we were, but when they know we are, is that weird?

It's a little weird.

Not like Ax is my only option.

It's just been so long since I've even thought about hooking up with someone else, and now I'm a married woman. Booty calls are definitely weird when you're newly wearing someone else's last name.

Point being, my libido is distracting, and it takes several seconds to hush her down before I dial in on the object in Ax's hand. "You have a key?"

"I have a key."

He drops my hand so he can use both of his to wiggle said key into the lock on the front door, and I start to full-on panic. "Ax...what did you do?"

I suppose it's possible he could have a key somehow by legal means, but the likelihood feels low. Particularly, when he has to fight with the lock. The way he glances up and down the street as if afraid we might be caught isn't reassuring either.

Nor is his response. "Let's just say I know people."

"People who will make you a key to whatever building you want without asking questions kind of people?"

"Something like that." The latch catches then and Ax pushes the door open. "Come on in."

When I don't move, he shrugs. "Suit yourself."

The door closes, and he disappears into the dark.

I'm not eager to break the law, but I'm less eager to be left alone on the street while Ax does who knows what to my sacred place. Barely five seconds have passed when I push in after him.

Then, after locking the door behind me, I go in search. "Ax?" The place is very obviously empty besides the two of us, but I whisper-call all the same. "What are you doing? Ax?"

Suddenly, the overhead lights flicker on, filling the entire store with harsh fluorescent lighting. It doesn't matter that I've visited this place a hundred times before or that I'm currently having a panic attack about being here illegally—I still audibly gasp at the sight of All. The Books. The shelves are lined with romance novels, and a mural of Stevie Nicks holding a book adorns one wall. An art illustration hangs above the seating area, and there's even a cozy reading nook under the stairs leading up to the apartment above.

And did I mention all the books?

Each one filled with stories of meet cutes, push and pulls, and happily ever afters. Some have spice as well with unrealistically hot men saying phrases like "good girl" and "take the dick" and "lift up your hips, love" and "in public you're my princess, but in private you're my whore."

I am in literary paradise, surrounded by these fantastical tales and not another soul in sight. It's safe to say I've died and gone to heaven.

Until an alarm starts blaring, and Ax lets out a stream of

curse words from behind the curtain hiding the back of the store storage space.

"Shit! Fuck! Shit!" I rush to the front door, presuming this is our cue to get gone before the police show up. "I'm not waiting around, Ax. You go down, you go down alone!"

But then the alarm stops, and Ax emerges from behind the curtain. "Would you soothe your boobs, already? I mistyped the code the first time. All good now."

"You hacked into the security system too?" I ask, stepping away from the door, not because I'm soothed by his reassurance or because I'm cool with my impending arrest, but because there's a new blue alien romance sitting on the table near me, and I can't not pick it up and hold it with my grabby hands.

"I didn't hack into anything."

"Paid someone then." I flip through the pages, stopping in the middle, only to see a major spoiler in the first paragraph. "Goddammit." I tuck the book under my arm, not quite decided on stealing it per se...

There are three more under my arm by the time Ax makes his way to my side. "Here, can you...?" I hand him the stack. "Thank you. You were saying?"

I'm not sure he was saying anything. It was hard to hear him clearly over the sound of all the books calling me to *choose me, pick me, love me!* Case in point, I've added a why choose hockey romance and a pirate fantasy to the stack before I realize he's talking again.

"...write down all the titles you're taking, and she'll run it through on your credit card when she's open again."

I stare at him trying to process what he's saying. "What?"

"We didn't break in," he says, slowly and enunciated.

He'd said something about a woman though, and I attempt to add the pieces together. "Are you banging the manager?"

It's a leap, maybe, but it feels accurate to assume that Ax uses sex as a bargaining chip. Logical though it is, the thought makes my chest feel hollow.

"Where did you get that from what I said?" He sighs with impatience. "I had a conversation with her. Fully clothed. We made an arrangement. No sex was exchanged. My God, woman. What do you take me for?"

"I don't know. I'm surrounded by smut." I pick up a cock shaped bookmark from one of the displays and hold it up to prove my point. "It's not my fault where my mind goes."

His eyes darken and that wicked smile of his makes an appearance. "Say more about that…"

Heat flares through my body.

Heat that I ignore because I'm not wasting my fictional man time on a real man. "How about we play sexy librarian," I tell him, stealing my response from a popular meme. "You go across the room and be quiet while I read a book." Or ten.

With a special edition vampire mafia romance in hand, I shoo Ax away.

Either he takes the hint or he falls asleep somewhere because I don't see him again until I've gathered three more stacks of books to purchase, and have settled into the reading nook to read from a hardcover edition of the story that I'd had to set aside to go shopping today.

I have no idea how much time has passed—I'm often

time blind when reading—and I brace myself for his inevitable bitching.

Except the expression on his face is more wonder than exasperation. "I just read a book about a love affair with a woman and her front door."

"Oh! I've read that one. Original, isn't it?"

"That's one word for it." He surveys the chair I'm sitting on, and when he determines there isn't room to join me, he sinks to the floor next to me. "What are you reading?"

A dirty, rough, semi non-consensual spicy scene that was sublime.

I'm so aroused that I've literally swept my eyes toward Ax's cock three times now.

Not that I'm sharing that. "An angsty billionaire romance," I say instead. I absolutely love how authors imagine the lives of the rich. For the most part, they're off base. We're a lot more unhinged than they depict.

Sure he only asked to be polite, I don't expand. Besides, something more pressing has caught my attention. "Where are all the books I pulled?"

"Already cataloged and packed into sacks." Damn. I was so involved in my story, I hadn't noticed. "Angsty billionaire romance—what's it about?"

"You know. The usual. He uses his money to be an absolute alphahole and uses his cock to fix all their problems."

"Does that work?" Ax's eyes are pinned on me, waiting for me to say more.

"I mean, it's a big, powerful cock so..." I'm too turned on to talk about this without blushing. "You really want to hear this?"

"Are you kidding? Big, powerful cocks are my jam."

I giggle and blush some more. It's awkward explaining my interest in romance books to someone else, particularly the smutty parts, even when I'm fucking them on the regular.

Maybe *especially* when I'm fucking them on the regular.

At the very least, it feels dangerous.

But we're not at the apartment, and we are alone. It's possible that what feels dangerous is actually just exciting.

"Well." I swipe my tongue across my bottom lip. "The MMC—that stands for male main character—is in an argument with the FMC. That's the fe—"

"Female main character," he finishes. "I can follow reason, Addles."

A shiver runs through me at the pet name. "Right. So, anyway. They're fighting because he tried to give her a night club."

"A night club?"

"It's the place she works. He owns it, but he bought it because of her, and he wants her to run it, so he tells her it's hers."

"And she doesn't want it?" Ax's tone suggests he's really interested.

"That's not the point. She's pretty sure he's giving it to her for the wrong reasons. Because he thinks she's into the current manager, which she's not. Anymore. And he's jealous, and she overreacts and says she's going to quit, and he gets all alpha and says he bought it for her, and she's not living up to her potential, which rubs her the wrong way because of past family trauma, and so she tries to storm out, and then…" I trail off, the heat extending now from my face to my belly.

"And then…?"

It's hard to hide my face when he's sitting on the floor below me. I lower my head all the same. "And then he grabs her around the waist, forces her down to the ground, and fucks her rough. It's totally toxic and doesn't honor consent, but it's fiction, and she's into it, and so it's…um…"

"Hot," he finishes again.

There's intensity in his tone, and I force myself to meet his eyes. They're dark and hooded, and under his stare, my nipples pop like two spring buds. The air around us crackles with *what's next?* and the anticipation makes my pulse jittery, like I've had way too much coffee. Gravity seems to have shifted from a force pulling me to the ground to a force pulling me toward him.

With that mouth of his in my sight lines, I start to lean forward.

I don't make it more than a couple of inches because abruptly, Ax stands up. He brushes dust and floor junk from his ass then holds his hand out toward me.

My forehead wrinkles. Did I misread the vibe?

Irritated—disappointed, really—I ignore his hand and stand up on my own. We've probably been here for a couple of hours now. I guess it's time to go.

But when I'm on my feet, Ax makes no move to leave. "You should take it," he says.

Now I'm really confused. "Take what?"

"The job."

My stomach plummets. He knows about SHE? How? I've considered telling him myself, and figured I would as soon as the bid was in, which won't be for at least another week since the money isn't supposed to hit my account until next Friday.

But his wording is weird, and when I hesitate, he goes on. "I bought it for you, Adly. And you don't want it because…why? *Him*? That's fucked up if you think I'm not going to have a problem with that. He's standing in the way of your potential, and if you can't see that…"

He shakes his head, rage emanating off him. Rage that feels so real, it takes me a second to realize that he's turning my book into a scene.

Damn. I don't think I realized quite how good an actor Ax was.

Or maybe it's the use of my first name that makes it feel so authentic. Usually it's Ms. Sebastian, or lately, Mrs. Morgan, and the formality of the titles formed some sort of distance. I was never actually the person in the scene. I was always playing a part. He was always playing a part.

Right now, it doesn't feel like he's playing anything but himself.

It arouses and rouses me. Turns me on and turns me up, his anger igniting a fantasy anger of my own. "Fuck you, *my potential*. You're so manipulative. Pretending it's about giving me a gift when it's really about you."

"It *is* a gift. This is for *you*. He wins when you let him outshine you. Quit dimming your light for him. It's you who deserves the sky, Addy."

His words touch something deep inside me, and my eyes prick. The man holding me back isn't a former lover—it's my father. He wins, every time. There is no outshining him. There is no one who has ever suggested that I could.

What would it be like to have a man really believe those things about me?

Romantic, sure. Fucking terrifying, too.

Because even a man who wants the best for you can overstep. "You can't decide that for me," I tell him. Yell, at him, actually. "This is supposed to be a partnership. You didn't even ask what I wanted!"

He slams his fist against the wall, so hard that I jump. "Because I know you, Ad. I fucking know you."

"Apparently, you don't. Because I would never accept a position that I got by stepping on the back of someone else."

His eye twitches. "I wouldn't be so high and mighty about it if I were you. You might think you'd never betray someone to get to the top, but it's just as selfish to insist you get there all on your own."

Game or not, it's a fault that hits close to home. I would do everything on my own, if I could. I hate needing people. I don't want to give trust to someone who might burn me— and from what I've seen in my family, most everyone will try to burn you eventually. It's not selfish—it's self-protection.

But I'm playing a part so I don't have to be honest. "I don't do that."

"You don't?" He takes a step toward me. "You don't set boundaries and build walls and push away anyone who tries to get close?"

All I can do is shake my head.

"I don't think the problem here is a fucking promotion, Adly. The problem is that you won't let anybody love you."

It's like he's reached inside me, taken my heart in his hands, and squeezed.

I know he's talking to a character—not me. But how does he manage to display such sincerity in his features? How does he make the game feel like a personal attack?

And what the fuck is the mention of love? The games have always been sex only. *Scenes From a Porno* type of detachment. We don't pretend relationships or romance. We definitely don't pretend love.

It's certainly a leveling up in terms of stakes, which makes the sexual tension spike high, but the emotional aspect it adds is shocking.

It's too much. "I don't want this." Pushing past him, I say it again, louder. "I don't want this."

I barely take a few steps before his strong arms encircle my waist, pulling me tightly against his body. I feel the unmistakable hardness of his erection pressing against my backside, and I struggle to break free from his grasp. "Let me go, Ax," I gasp out.

"Never." His voice is playful, as if we are just engaging in another round of our usual game. But this time, something feels different. Panic rushes through me as I realize that we have no safe word, never needed one before. The fear and excitement intertwine into a red hot wave of want that threatens to consume me. I momentarily consider giving in to it, but the fear is equally powerful and I drive my elbow back into his side in retaliation.

"Fuck." He bends over from the pain, and I use the opportunity to slip out from under his arms and run.

But my feet betray me and I trip over nothing, falling to my knees.

Before I can stand up again, he's on top of me, pushing me down onto my stomach. The pressure of his cock against my ass is like a steel bar. "Why can't you just let me fucking take care of you?" he growls.

"You can't. You won't. You'll let me down." I claw at the floor frantically, unsure if I'm fighting him or myself. I swear I don't want this. I don't want to want him with such intensity. I don't want to let him in.

And yet, feeling him pinned above me, I know he's already tattooed on my insides and inked into my soul.

With one hand holding me down and the other exploring under my dress, he pushes the crotch panel of my panties aside and slips a long finger inside me.

"Damn, you're so wet." He groans as if my arousal has weakened him. As if I hold all the power. As if I am the one who has undone him, instead of the other way around. "Tell me you want more."

"No," I pant. But then, "Yes." In this moment, my desire overpowers any doubts or fears. I want all of him.

He responds by plunging two more fingers into my dripping pussy, and I swear my eyes roll back into my head from the pleasure. "Oh my God."

"See how good I can be to you?" He nibbles at my ear. "When you let me."

I shake my head wildly as an orgasm builds inside me like a balloon inflating.

He lifts his body and turns me onto my back, pushing my knee up to my chest so he doesn't have to remove his fingers from inside me.

"You're going to let me fuck you now." His face is so close to mine that I can feel his breath on my lips. I can't bring myself to look him in the eyes. "Look at me, Adly," he barks.

In that moment, he becomes the bossy, dominant Ax from the day he fucked me at the school, and my body instinctively submits as our eyes lock.

"You're going to let me fuck you now, aren't you?"

He needs to hear it from me, but even as he waits for my response, his fingers continue stroking that sensitive spot inside me, influencing my answer in a way that feels both thrilling and manipulative.

And in a split-second decision, I give in to him completely. "Yes," I whisper, unable to deny the pleasure that he is giving me.

But I'm also hardheaded, so I throw in a line from the original scene we're roleplaying. "It doesn't mean I'm not still mad."

A satisfied smile crosses his lips. "Mad looks good on you, Adly Morgan. I'm betting it feels even better." At rapid speed, he undoes his pants and gets his cock free.

My pussy feels empty from the loss of his fingers, but it's only seconds before he has my panties down, and then he fills me up again, this time with his cock.

I gasp as he pushes inside me, his thickness over-whelming me in the best way, and it makes me more mad than ever. He has no right to fit so perfectly inside me. No goddamn right.

My hands grip at his shoulders, nails digging into his T-shirt as I try to pull him deeper into me. He responds by thrusting harder, each movement sending waves of plea-sure through my body, making it harder and harder to hold on to my anger.

"See how easy it can be," he asks, his voice thick with lust. "When you just take what I give you."

"Yes," I moan, arching my back to meet his thrusts. "Give it to me."

I want to close my eyes, but I force myself to keep eye contact, savoring the feeling of him filling me, the sound of our bodies slapping together, the scent of his skin that I know so well. So much of this is familiar, and also completely new. Does he always study me so intently while he pushes into me? Is he always so aware of every one of my tells? Did I ever fool him when I faked not Os or did he always know?

The man who's rocking his hips against mine with such precision that my clit starts to buzz seems like he knows my body too well to ever have fallen for my tricks.

For some reason, that makes my eyes well up.

Or maybe it's the tender spot he's hitting right now that's the cause of the tears. I'm confused with pleasure, not sure who I'm playing anymore or if I'm finally not playing at all.

And all the while that he fucks me, he sticks to the scene. "Why can't you take everything I want to give like you take my cock? Is this the only form of attention you can accept?"

"I don't...I don't know." It's truer than I want to admit.

"Then I'll tell you—you were made to be fucked like this. Fucked by *me*, Adly. And I alone know what you need. No one else. If I tell you you're the fucking sun in the sky, then you're the sun in the sky. If I tell you that you deserve more, then you take more. You take what I give. You understand yet?"

Suddenly, the world seems to spin around me as I near the edge of orgasm. I can feel it building like a storm, threatening to take over my entire being.

"Ax," I whimper, my voice barely above a plea. It's the first time I can recall saying his name while he's been inside me, and the simple syllable on my lips feels both humbling and empowering. "I'm going to come."

He doesn't break his pace, continuing to fuck me with a fervor that mirrors my own. "Do it. Come all over my cock, baby. Squeeze me like you know I deserve."

His words push me over the edge and I erupt with an intensity that shakes me to my core. My body thrashes beneath him, my nails clutching at his skin as I scream his name. Ax is relentless, matching my pace with his own as he rams into me over and over in sync with my climax.

He releases with a long, low grunt, sweat dripping from his brow as his face contorts and transforms into an expression that makes me want to laugh and break all at once.

I manage not to laugh. I'm not sure I manage not to break.

When it's over, we lay there, catching our breath. The silence between us is heavy with unspoken words, unresolved feelings, and unanswered questions. We've both still got most of our clothes on, yet I feel more naked than I've ever been with him. Part of me wants to cover myself up—metaphorically—and run away. Vow to never let myself feel this exposed with him again.

It's on impulse that I open my mouth and confess instead. "I'm going to buy SHE. The network. With Holt and Alex. That's what I need the money for. That's why I needed you."

It's like a weight is taken from me when I tell him. The risk is still there. Bringing more people into the scheme means more chances for it to be blown, but I don't feel scared.

I feel safe.

Ax turns his head toward me. I hold my breath, shocked that I care so much about his approval.

When he smiles, I can breathe again. "You deserve it, Adly. You really do."

I'm sure he means it. His eyes look sincere.

But there's something weary in his tone, and for some reason I can't explain, out of every line he delivered in our scene, this is the one that feels hardest to believe.

pause on the way out of the yoga room—scratch that, Ax's room—to survey the latest items that the movers have brought up. Most everything has been delivered in sealed plastic totes, but some of his stuff is in crates with no lids.

I know I shouldn't.

But I'm not about to let an opportunity to snoop go by.

Transferring the clothing and hangers to balance on one arm, I use the other to move a stack of manila folders in one of the crates and uncover a pile of photos to pick through. There are several of Ax growing up. Most of which I know are him because I remember what he looked like in the periods they were taken. I'm guessing the younger ones are him too.

I'm studying a picture of a toddler with thick dark hair climbing onto an older woman's lap when Ax and the movers return with another load.

"Who's this?" I ask, holding it up for him to see.

"Me." He turns to the movers behind him. "You can put all those boxes on the other side of the bed."

"And your grandma, I'm guessing?" I've already put the photo down before he answers in the affirmative. I hold up another picture of a woman about my age with dark hair and a bright smile. "Is this your mom?"

He barely glances from the box he's ripping open. "Yep."

"She was gorgeous." Ax's parents were divorced soon after I was born, so I don't remember meeting his mother, if I ever did. I'm pretty sure he saw her regularly while growing up, but she lived in London, and he always flew to see her.

Then she died when he was twenty-one. There's a pamphlet from the funeral in the stack of photos that I don't ask about, as well as a clipping from an obituary. He took it hard, I remember that.

The next picture is a high school graduation notice of a teenager that resembles Ax's mother enough to assume she's a relative.

"Who's this?" I flash it toward him as he walks by.

Frowning, he snatches it out of my hand. "Would you stop going through my shit?"

He seems annoyed and distracted, but I don't sense real anger in his tone.

"I can't help it. It's right there." Under another crate and a bunch of random stuff, but totally right there.

He tosses the announcement back on the pile and picks up the crate. "What are you even doing in here?" He finds his answer when he arrives at the closet. "You still haven't cleared everything out?"

I lift up the clothing. "Hello! Doing it now."

"You were supposed to have it ready before I got here today so that we wouldn't be on top of each other. What happened to boundaries and safe space?"

I give a casual shrug. Obviously, when I was talking about boundaries and safe spaces, I was talking about me.

Also—less obvious, perhaps—I'm getting used to the idea of being on top of each other. In all the different ways that roommates can be on top of each other. Including the dirty ways.

Some of his improvised talk last night hit too close to home, and I realized the person he was playing to is not a person I want to be. I want to be able to open up to people.

I want to be able to trust Ax.

I don't yet. Not entirely, anyway, but hooking me up with a bookstore connection has earned him a lot of points.

I suppose he earns points for pivoting every time a wrench is thrown in our negotiations, too.

And for making pancakes from scratch.

And for saying I deserve SHE.

And for knowing Adly means heather and still having it tattooed on his arm. Or having it tattooed *because* he knew that? I've considered the possibility, as improbable as it seems.

I try not to focus on that tidbit too much, though. It's in a locked box in my brain that I only open up at night, when I'm alone in the dark, thinking things I shouldn't, along with the tidbit that he's honestly the best kiss I've had in years, if not ever.

But back to the obvious, there's no way I can tell Ax that I'm wiggling on my distrust issues. That would be too easy for everyone, and I'm only easy when there's an orgasm involved.

"Should have gotten a lock for your bedroom door," I tease. Though it's only pretend tease, because the truth is that I can see myself coming in and snooping more in the future.

Huh. Maybe I'm the asshole.

I ponder that as I take the armful of clothes to the other spare bedroom, the one I've transformed completely into a closet, and dump them on a chair to deal with later.

Then I stop in front of my mirror to straighten my pony-tail and pull up my T-shirt to check my ass in my leggings before I head back down the hall to his room.

"We wouldn't be stuck together if you hadn't snooped through the papers on my printer, so it's your fault that I'm…" I trail off when I round through his doorway and find he's not there.

But several new items are, including more totes. Cloth-ing, it seems, since they're labeled as *closet*. There's only another trip or two required before my things are completely out of his room, which I should finish up so I can get out of his hair.

Instead of finishing that task, I plop myself on his new bed—mattress still wrapped in plastic—and open one of the totes to peek inside. When else am I going to get a chance to see what a man like Ax hides in his closet?

Well, except for every day if he doesn't heed my advice about that lock.

The top tote is full of smaller boxes that are specifically

designed for moving accessories. Socks and ties and tie pins and cufflinks, all ordered in neat little rows that suggest he hired someone to pack everything instead of doing it himself. I run my fingers over an Italian blue silk jacquard tie that I've seen him wear a thousand times.

I'm not sure I've ever fully appreciated Ax's fashion sense. Unlike most of his traits, his taste is sophisticated. The other men in my life—Holt and Steele and Daddy, and even Hunter—shop top quality and luxury designers too, but their clothing is always sharp and in-line. Ax tends to keep his accents loud, with daisy patterned Burberry ties and bejeweled cuff links and suede leather loafers adorned with gold-tone stones.

Honestly, he's one of the only men I know who dresses well enough to be seen with me. Too bad we're rarely photographed together. I suppose I have a little under a year to change that.

Dissatisfied that no Ax secrets have been unveiled, I close the crate and move to the rustic wood box that looks like a cross between an antique chest and a nightstand.

At first glance, it looks like a pile of different colors of lace. I put my hand in and pull one of the pieces out. "Holiest of molies, what the fuck is…"

"Movers are paid and gone. Now…Goddammit, Adly."

I sense Ax headed my way, but I can't look up, too preoccupied with the realization of exactly what the fuck this box is—Ax's *trophy panties*.

"Jesus, Axhole. Can you be any more disgusting?"

It's not disgust that kicks me in the gut, though. This emotion is green and sharp and jealous, but before I start spiraling, something occurs to me, and I look back in the box and push around the underwear a bit before I'm sure.

Abruptly, the lid comes down. I barely get my fingers out before they're smashed.

"Get the fuck out of my shit," Ax says, tone pointed. There's a hint of panic to it, as well, which pairs well with my own rising alarm.

The thing is, I always assumed that he had a stash of women's panties stowed away somewhere. I've always tried not to think about it, for a myriad of reasons. Primarily because I didn't want to know about the other women who contributed to the collection, but also because I didn't want to consider that he was doing something much more nefarious with my lingerie.

The situation I'm faced with at current is not one I ever would have expected. "Those are all my panties."

"It's not like I don't wash them," he says, as if that's my main concern. "Eventually."

Ew.

Well…also kind of hot.

I shake that depraved thought from my head and focus on the much more urgent question. "But why are they only *my* panties? What about all the other women?"

When he doesn't respond, I try again, louder, more forceful. "What about the other women, Ax?"

I have never described Ax as sheepish, but that's the closest word I can find for the way he's looking at me now —or should I say, the way he's avoiding looking at me. "I don't collect other women's panties. Just yours."

I'm confused and maybe mad, mostly confused. "What…so you can keep tally?"

"No." He sounds disgusted by the prospect. "I just…this is *our* thing."

"We have a thing?"

"Don't we?"

Well, shit.

He doesn't stop me when I open the box again. Inside are dozens and dozens of, might I say, gorgeous panties. I treat myself when it comes to what's next to my skin, and that means I have god tier lingerie.

Lingerie that I never really minded letting him take because, number one, it gave me an excuse to buy more, but more importantly, because I liked that it was proof. Even when I thought Ax was dumping mine into a chest with a bunch of other women's underwear, I liked to think that the proof made it impossible for him to deny that we were hooking up.

Though, I'm the one who's always pretending nothing's happening, not him. Was this just me projecting? Expecting him to detach while I was the one detaching?

I think I *am* the asshole.

"Yeah. It's our thing." It's both easier and harder to admit than I would think, and once it's said, something dislodges in my chest. An iceberg of sorts, a piece broken from the chunk of ice around my heart, and all I can think is, how long before this all melts, and I start to drown?

It's terrifying.

Good thing I'm an excellent swimmer.

I find myself smiling. *He only keeps* my *panties.*

Ax perches on a tote next to the bed as I browse through the contents of the box once again. "Hey, you don't get

those back just because you found them. It's not like a treasure chest. I earned those."

My eyes catch on a pair of lacy boy shorts. They're mine,
but…"Ax. I never gave you these panties. These are
from…" I try to remember how long it's been since I
stopped wearing this style of underwear. They're cute as
fuck but always ride up my ass. It's been at least a decade.
High school? "God, I don't even know. How do you have
these?"

I hold them up to show him, only to have them snatched
away. "We don't need to talk about these."

"Oh, I think we do."

"Uh uh." He shoves them in the back pocket of his jeans.

I stare at him, waiting.

Eventually, he sighs. "They were left in the pool house
once. After you changed into your suit."

"Were they hidden under a stack of clothes?" I'm not
sure which pool house it was or when, but I know me. I'm
the kind of girl who folds my clothes at the gynecologist's
office and tucks my panties underneath so no one can see
them. I'm the same way at the gym and at the pool, even
when everything's going into a locker. There's no way I left
a pair out where they could be easily found.

Ax rubs his forehead with his thumb and index finger.
"Are you asking if I had to go searching for them? No
comment."

My eyes and mouth widen in horror.

Or…delight?

It's confusing inside the Adly hall of emotions at the
moment. All I know is, my heart is beating a mile a minute,
and my entire body feels warm. "When was this?"

He shakes his head as if he's not going to answer, but then begrudgingly admits, "The summer after I came back from Yale. So I was twenty-three? I think."

I do the math. My birthday is in the fall. "Oh my God. You stole a pair of panties from a seventeen-year-old? You're a child predator!"

Ax's dark complexion hides a lot, but I almost think he's blushing. "It was *one* child." Realizing that's not any better when I gasp, he reframes. "One *seventeen-year-old girl* who looked nothing like a child, I might add. And you might recall that nothing else happened between us."

Not for another fifteen years, anyway.

It's a lot of new information to catalog. Hard to believe information. Information that brings up new questions. Is Ax saying he had a crush on me? An attraction? Way back then?

It's my turn to shake my head. "Why were you always so mean to me?"

"When was I mean to you?"

"Growing up. You were always such a bully."

He shrugs and points his gaze at his shoes. "I don't know what you're talking about."

I laugh in disbelief. "Don't gaslight me."

His head snaps up, and along with it, his arms, which he throws in the air in frustration or surrender. "I don't know. Why are boys ever mean to girls, Adly?"

"If you're suggesting you were into me when I was seven, we're going to have to revisit the child predator conversation."

"I was mean to you when you were seven because you were fucking annoying."

"Well, that's when you were the meanest. When are *you* talking about?" Before he can answer, I remember which summer it was that he came back from Yale. "Wait! It was at Grandpa's Caribbean house."

I know I'm right when his shoulders slump. "You were such a giant dick. On the boat? When I was doing nothing but trying to read my book—"

"You were practically naked. Flaunting yourself."

"It's called sunbathing." I was in a swimsuit. And he kept pestering me. Throwing water on me. Then a blanket. Then ice. Then he'd mess with the music on my phone when my eyes were closed, and he put down everything I talked about and treated me like he was my babysitter.

Kinky when you add in the fact that he was probably sniffing my panties and whacking off in his cabin in between tormenting me.

It's Ax who remembers who else was there that summer. "You were all over that friend of Steele's."

His name comes back to me in a rush. "Miles."

"Miles."

"Miles Whitby."

"Fucking hate those Whitbys."

I haven't thought about him in over a decade. I had such a crush. "He was the first guy to ever go down on me." That summer, in fact.

"Fucking *hate* those Whitbys."

Things click into place, and I think I understand. "Ax... were you...jealous?"

Abruptly, he stands and shuts the panty treasure box, for a second time. "Trip down memory lane is over now."

It most definitely is not. Especially not now that I've

remembered something else. "Wasn't that the same summer you got that tattoo for your mom?" The cross wrapped in heather like my name.

"We're not talking about something that happened over fifteen years ago." He heads over to one of the crates, pretending like he's really into unpacking all of a sudden.

Seems more like he's avoiding the subject at hand.

I have no other choice but to call him out on it. "Bawk, bawk."

"Boundaries, Addles. That came out of your mouth, not mine."

"Bawwwwwk." I'm grinning like a madwoman as I open the panty chest a final time to throw in a pair that I'd dropped earlier.

This time, I notice something sticking out that I hadn't before. A small enough box to be easily missed. The kind of box that holds jewelry. A small necklace. Earrings. A ring.

Strange to keep something like that inside a chest of panties—specifically my panties—unless...

I dig it out of the chest and stand up, my heart thumping like I'm a Disney rabbit. "Ax, what's this?"

As soon as he sees it, he hangs his head. "Jesus, woman, you're such a pain in the fucking ass."

His annoyance seems overblown. "If you're going to leave a velvet box out for anyone to find, you've got to expect questions."

"I didn't leave it out for anyone to find."

Good point. "Well. I found it."

"Because you're a meddling little snoop." It's half teasing, half frustration. "Stay out of my fucking stuff." He maneuvers around the crates and holds his hand out.

As if I'm going to give him the box before I've even looked inside.

I pivot away from him. "I don't really think this is my fault, though. I was just trying to put all the panties away like you wanted."

Just as I lift the lid to peer inside, Ax swipes it from me. "Aha!"

The pout that falls on my face is only slightly put on. My disappointment is genuine. I really do want to see what's inside.

He swears under his breath, then runs a hand through his dark hair. "I suppose this is just as good a time as any to give it to you."

With my hand on my chest, I feign surprise. "It's for me?"

"I said I'd get you a ring."

"It totally slipped my mind." It hasn't slipped my mind for one second. The minute he said he'd buy one for me, my brain put it on repeat broadcast. It's been driving me crazy that he hasn't mentioned it again.

Because I'm a jewelry girl. Not for any other reason.

Okay, also because...I don't know. I've never been proposed to before. It's supposedly a big deal. "Aren't you supposed to be down on your knee?" I ask as he props the box in his palm.

"We're already married, sweetheart. I don't feel like I need to propose."

Then he's opening the box toward me, and honestly, it doesn't just feel like a big deal.

It feels like a fucking huge deal.

My hands are sweating so much I have to wipe them on

my shirt, and I swear to God another iceberg goes floating in my chest.

When I see the ring, my breathing stops.

First of all, there's the setting—it's platinum, I think, with a pavé band and two half-moon diamonds that flank the center stone.

Then there's the stone itself, which is giant. Five carats, if I had to guess. It's cushion shaped and flawless with perfect clarity. And best part of all? It's *pink*.

There's a lump in my throat and my hand shakes as Ax slips it on my ring finger. "Is it a diamond?"

"Padparadscha sapphire." He earns most of my respect for just pronouncing the Sanskrit word correctly.

He earns the rest when he says, "I wanted it to be something you could wear on another finger. You know...later."

Later. When we're divorced, and this is over, and I have my apartment to myself again, and I won't need an engagement ring because I'm no longer Mrs. Morgan.

"It's perfect," I say. "The fit. The color." I'm not sure why my eyes well up.

The embarrassing part is when a tear makes it down my cheek.

Ax reaches out with a single finger to wipe it from my face. "What are you getting all sobby about?"

"I'm not. Fuck you. I don't cry." I swipe another tear with the back of my hand. This could be it. This could be the only time a man puts a ring on my finger, and even if it's not the only time, I don't think there could ever be a ring or a moment—or a man—that would ever be better than this ring and this moment. This man.

"Oh my Lord, this is humiliating." I wipe the rest of the

tears and sniffle back any threatening to fall. "It's just really thoughtful, Ax. I'm not used to people thinking about me."

It's the truth. Not all of it, perhaps, but it's as much of the truth as I can admit without first having a deep conversation with my therapist.

Ax fiddles with the box like it's a fidget toy. "It was about me, remember? I'm the one who looks bad if you don't have a ring."

"Right. Definitely all about you." My tone says what he has to already know—it's a hard sell to claim he's selfish when this past hour has exposed so much evidence to refute it.

My body moves without my mind's consent, and I reach out to hug him. His surprise is evident, and it takes a solid few seconds before his arms come around me.

"Thank you," I say.

It's a bigger sentiment than two words can possibly express. He's done so much, agreed to so much, and I've mistrusted and doubted him at every turn.

Then all these new revelations coming to light...

As I slowly pull back, my gaze locks with his. My chin lifts with determination, and my mouth inches closer to his. Our lips brush, sending a jolt of lust through my veins. The heat between us intensifies.

But just as I lean in for a deeper kiss, Ax abruptly pulls away.

A rush of emotions flood through me—disappointment, frustration longing—making it hard to catch my breath. What is he thinking? Did I misread everything? Did I miss my moment with him years ago?

The moment hangs in the air, heavy with unspoken words and unfulfilled desires.

"I should finish..." He gestures to the room cluttered with crates and totes.

I try not to let my feelings get hurt as his attention returns to his task. "Yeah, I'll get out of your way."

"Finally," he teases under his breath, almost like an afterthought. A failed attempt to lighten the mood. Our once lively conversation now feels strained, as if there is something unsaid between us. Too much unsaid.

Or maybe too much *said*, just only by him.

I should have handled this all differently, though I'm not sure how. Should have said words back, but I don't know what they'd be, and I don't even know if they're words he'd want to hear.

What I do know is, it's not the time to try to figure it out now. We have boundaries. The apartment is a safe space.

I turn to leave, avoiding meeting his gaze as I make my way toward the door. The room feels smaller now, filled with tension and unfinished business.

I shut his door behind me when I leave. Then I press my back against the hallway wall, and try not to choke on emotion. It almost does me in until I hear his closet door opening behind me and remember that I still haven't finished clearing it out.

"Adly!" he shouts out.

Covering my mouth so that I don't let out a sudden burst of laughter, I tiptoe-run to my room. When he doesn't come after me, I remind myself it's for the best.

CHAPTER
NINETEEN
ADLY

'm giddy as I screenshot a picture of my fat bank account balance and send it to Holt. I've never seen so many zeroes that aren't behind another zero. It's all about to be collateral for a giant loan with many more zeroes, and that makes me feel like throwing up a bit, but right at this particular moment, I feel like a god.

Is this why my older cousins are so confident all the time?

I'd assumed it was because they all had balls, but maybe it's all the zeroes in their accounts.

It almost makes up for the hell that I'm currently enduring outside the fitting rooms at Mirabelle's. Normally, this boutique is one of my favorite places on earth. The shop owner, Mira, is a spunky, animated pixie type woman who somehow doesn't irritate the fuck out of me with her positivity and perma-cheer. In fact, she's one of the few people I actually like.

But there is no one that I like well enough to make me want to shop for bridal gowns. No one.

Which is probably why I never plan on walking down the aisle for real. Along with the I'll-never-trust-anyone-enough-to-want-to-share-my-life-with-them reason. Scary thing is that I think Holt once felt that way as well. My father, too, after my mother died.

But they're men and men are fickle. I'm definitely blaming that on their balls.

Thankfully, I've managed to avoid having to try anything on so far by playing the role of photographer. Still not sure how I got talked into coming in the first place, nor why I agreed to take a half-day off from work to do it. Innocent as Giulia seems, she's very persuasive.

At least there's champagne.

Unfortunately, I take a sip from my flute just as Giulia starts excitedly tapping my arm. "Here she comes, here she comes."

Barely managing not to choke, I look up to see Brystin emerge from the fitting room dressed in a strapless ivory gown with a side bow and beaded lace underskirt. Before I form any opinions, I lift my phone and snap a pic.

"You're gorgeous." It's not my favorite that she's tried on, but I don't want to rain on her parade if she's already decided it's The One.

"Stunning," Mira says, though she's said that about most of them. "It wouldn't even need much tailoring."

Giulia isn't so polite. "Where's the drama? There's no train. Is there a coat?" She crosses to Brystin and spins her around to look at the back. "The buttons don't line up."

"The bolero is detachable," Brystin says, which is

somehow an explanation that I'm not interested in understanding.

Especially not when I have a brand new message on my
phone from Holt.

> Fuck yeah. Want to get a pre-drink before
> leaving for Adeline?

I try not to groan out loud. It's only been five days since
Ax officially moved in, and I swear we haven't been home a
single day since. Fourth of July festivities tied us up both
Monday and Tuesday, and there was so much catch-up to
do at work the next two days that we both stayed late. I
don't even remember getting to my bedroom either night
before crashing.

I'd been looking forward to a quiet weekend at home—a
totally platonic, roommate kind of weekend, of course—but
Grandpa Irving invited my father's family to Adeline,
Holt's country house in Connecticut, for more family bond-
ing, and no one says no to Grandpa.

That was how Giulia got me here today, actually. By first
suggesting we all ride to Adeline together, and then adding
the trip to Mirabelle's after I said yes. Classic bait and
switch, and now Holt's tempting me with day drinking.

I type back my reply.

> Sure! Want to swing by the Village and pick
> me up?

> Wait. Shit. Forgot ur doing the bridal thing.
> I'm not your rescue man.

I hadn't mentioned where I was exactly because I wasn't

sure my brother knew that I was bridal shopping with his fiancée. Isn't everything gown-related supposed to be a big ass secret from the groom?

I decide to ask him flat out.

> Should you know where we are?

"You better not be texting your brother," Brystin says, as if she can see my cell screen from several feet away. "He's dying to be here with us."

Mira claps a hand to her chest. "That's so swoony."

"It's not swoony—it's egotistical and domineering. He thinks he's the only one who knows how to dress me." It doesn't really sound like Brystin's complaining, but dressing a woman walks the line of being kink, and I refuse to think about my brother in any situation that is even remotely sexual so I'm not touching that with a ten foot pole.

Instead, I defend my honor. "I have other people I talk to besides Holt," I lie.

…then am relieved when the text that comes in immediately after is from *Axhole*.

> Why the fuck aren't you at work?

I don't mean to grin but I can't help myself.

> Ah. You miss me.

We'd gone over today's plan on the drive home from work last night, when we were both exhausted. Our luggage for the weekend is already in the car. Giulia and Brystin and I will pick him up along with Holt and Daddy when we're done.

I send Ax a picture of Brystin in her bridal gown, in case he really has forgotten where I am and isn't just being a pain in the ass.

> Kill me now.

"It must be Ax," Giulia says.

No surprise, Mira gushes. "Is this the hubby?"

Giulia nods. "Isn't it obvious? Look at her glow."

I catch Brystin's eye, since she's the one person here that knows the truth about me and Ax's sham relationship. *I'm glowing?* I mouth.

She studies me, and then shrugs.

I turn to look at myself in one of the mirrors. Damn, I *am* glowing. "It's the lighting."

"Sure, the lighting," Mira says.

Dismissing her with a shake of my head, I turn my attention back to my phone to read Ax's response.

> You should have been in three hours ago, Mrs. Morgan.

Mentally, I pump my fist in the air. Sexting roleplay is the perfect way to make the time fly by. Plus I always have a weird adrenaline rush when he attaches his name to mine. Some ingrained patriarchal shit, I'm guessing.

> Three whole hours? I guess I lost track of time. Whoops.

As soon as I've sent the text, I switch over to the new message from Holt.

> I know everything. Ur taking pics, right? Sneak me some of my woman.

There's only one appropriate reply:

> You're an ass. The dress is supposed to be a surprise.

My irritation with Holt is immediately forgotten when Ax continues the roleplay.

> That flippant attitude isn't going to get you that bonus you're after.

> Please, no, sir. I need that money to pay for my mother's hospital bill.

> Then you'll have to figure out another way to earn it.

Earn it are maybe my two favorite words in kink speak. My thighs are already vibrating, which is maybe a sign that I should cut the fun right now, since I am still hanging out with my stepmom and soon to be sister-in-law, and can't easily slip away to make this more entertaining.

I probably should be more present anyway.

Lifting my head, I return to the conversation just in time to hear Mira say, "I'll pull some dresses for her in case she changes her mind."

Pretty sure I'm the *her* in this scenario. "I won't," I offer with as much cheer as I can muster.

But she's already left the room, and now I really need a distraction from the horror, so I quickly type Ax a reply.

> Do you have a suggestion? I'm willing to do anything.

Willing to do anything to get out of trying on a dress, too, if necessary.

"Adly? Want to help me out of this?" Brystin stares at me like she's trying to tell me something in code.

"Coming!" I slip my phone into my pocket and follow her into the dressing room, closing the door behind us.

She holds up her blonde hair so I can unbutton the back of her dress. "Are you dying?"

"Eh." I shake my head then realize she can't see me since I'm bent behind her. "Giulia hasn't been nearly as pushy as I thought she'd be. She's focused on you, thank God, since you're the one who's having a wedding."

"That might be my fault," she confesses. "I told her I didn't think you were interested in sharing your event with anyone else."

I peer around her so I can meet her eyes in the mirror. "You made me out to be a bridezilla?" I pretend to be aghast for all of five seconds before breaking out in a grin. "Right on."

Honestly, there's truth in it, but the other way around. It's not fair to make Brystin share her event, especially with someone who isn't really having one at all.

I'm sure it's that unfairness that's the cause of the pit in my stomach. Not because I'm jealous or anything.

A notification sounds from my phone, and I swear I get wet. I'm like Pavlov's dog, trained to respond to my master

who wants to do very bad things to me. It takes everything
in me not to abandon my task and check my phone.

Then Brystin asks, "Is that Holt?" and now it's like I
have permission.

I hope not, I think, as I pause to look. Disappointment
kicks in when I see my notification says it's from *assHolt.*
"He says, '*She'll knock my breath out in every dress. It's not fair
I don't get to see them all.*'"

I expect her to roll her eyes. Instead, she blushes.
"Really? Ah. I should marry him."

"You totally should. I'll tell him." I shoot back a text
with a similar sentiment.

> God, you're such a simp.

"By the way…" She trails out the last word, as though
she's afraid of how I might react to what she has to say
next.

"Yes…?"

She waits until she's stepped out of the dress before she
turns and faces me. "Giulia hinted that she's going to be all
up in bridal shit this weekend, and I don't think she just
means with me."

Holt and I had hoped to turn this family get together into
productivity and planned to sneak away to talk SHE. Ax isn't
going to get in the way, especially now that he knows what
we're up to, but if Giulia wants to play wedding planner, Holt
and I might as well throw our plans out the window. "Shit.
Maybe I can come down with food poisoning or something."

"No, don't do that. I know you need to meet. I'll see if

she wants to drive around and check out venues for me or something."

God, that sounds awful.

An unexpected rush of emotion comes over me.

Family has always been a thorny flower. There's a lot of beauty amongst the Sebastians, but we're also over-ambitious and self-centered and damaged. Any interaction with us, no matter how seemingly harmless, has the likelihood of pricking through to blood. Me included. I'm not immune to the baggage we all carry.

I've learned, though. Learned to have thick skin and a metal plate around my heart. Learned so well that distrust and skepticism are my go-to, so I'm not only surprised by Brystin's generous offer—after all, this plan leaves her to entertain my parents by herself, which is a nobility that deserves sainthood—but even more surprised that I actually believe her.

I swallow past the lump in my throat. "Thank you, Brystin. You're definitely my favorite older sister."

She gapes dramatically. "By only five months!"

We're both laughing when the door bursts open, and Mira brings in another dress for Brystin to try on. "I thought something a little unusual might be what you're after."

With Brystin preoccupied, I'm back to my phone and Holt's latest message.

Simply incredible, you mean?

I'm so annoyed, I mute his conversation, just as another

text comes in from Ax. My heart flip-flops before I even read it.

> Might be persuaded with a picture. I like pics with varied hues of pink. The kind tempting enough to lick.

Just to be a brat, I take a picture of my pink ring and send it to him.

His reply comes in fast.

> Now you just need to be doing something with that hand. Petting something maybe. Is there a kitty around?

"If you don't mind, I'm going to step out and..." I don't bother finishing the statement, slipping out the door before anyone can stop me.

Only to remember I'm not alone out here either.

Giulia gestures to a rack of dresses. "Mira left you some amazing options. Are you sure you don't want to try one?"

"Uh...sure." It's as good an excuse as any.

Grabbing the first one I see, I take it into the dressing room with me and hang it on the wall hook.

Then I get to work on my real mission—keeping *my boss* happy.

It takes only a handful of seconds to get my panties off. Adjusting my dress so that I can hold it and take a pic with the same hand takes a little longer. With my left hand, I reach down to pet my pussy, sure to get both the ring and the other pink good stuff in the shot.

I stay a few minutes longer to rub a quick one out, trying very hard to fantasize about *the boss who's taking advantage of me* and not the man who increasingly feels less like a roommate and more like someone who would horde my panties and give me a ring and take me to both a courthouse and a bookstore.

I definitely pretend it's not Ax's name I'm whispering when the orgasm hits.

"Do you need help in there?" Giulia asks, just as I'm catching my breath.

"I'm good!" But I run to the door to make sure it's locked before putting my panties back on.

I don't know how it's possible to still be turned on when a new notification comes in, but I am.

Except the message isn't from Ax. It's from Holt in the group chat we have with Alex. Fucker probably sensed I muted him when I left him on read. I make sure to mute this one too before reading the text.

> Money has landed. Should have approval on the loan amount by morning, and I can submit the bid. What's your final number?

We'd been floating a few different bid options, all with enough variation that I can't remember which one I prefer off the top of my head. After a few clicks, I have the email open with the alternatives. For ease, I screenshot the one I like.

Before I can send it, I hear Giulia gasp on the other side of the door. "Oh, Brystin!"

"I know, right?" Mira says with equal awe in her tone.

"What? Know what?" As much as I've complained about being here, I actually do care about Brystin. If she's found The Dress, I want to be one of the firsts to know.

Especially since I'll be able to hold it over Holt's head.

"Get out here and tell me what you think," Brystin says.

Quickly, I send the screenshot of the bid, pocket my phone, and come out of the fitting room to find Brystin looking like a goddess in a champagne gold strapless gown with Indian inspired embroidery all the way down the back, extending to the end of the short train.

It's fresh and new and untraditional, and I've never seen her look more exquisite.

"This is it," I say, surprised how raw my voice sounds.

"This is it," Brystin repeats.

I snap a few pics from different angles and promise to send them all to her while Giulia chatters on about what shoes she should wear and what kind of veil.

"Did the dress not work out?" Mira asks me.

"Oh." I try to come up with a reason that I took a gown with me into the fitting room and didn't bother to try it on.

My expression must expose more than I realize.

"It's okay," Mira says. "When you're ready, I'll be here."

Yeah, that will be never.

"Thank you," I say, and leave it at that, ignoring the tightness in my ribs and the way my gut feels like it's pulling with weight.

The ding on my phone snaps me out of my melancholy, and I open it up with excitement, remembering I still have a pussy pic to send.

I'm surprised when the newest message is again from Ax when I haven't replied to his last one yet.

I'm afraid I don't take cash bribes.

Confused, I scroll up and discover I'd sent the screen-shot with the bid to him instead of the group. If he hadn't known about SHE before, he would now since there is enough incriminating information in the image to figure it out.

Strangely, I don't feel panicked about the mistake. Does this mean I'm starting to trust Ax?

Maybe in this one area, anyway.

I type out a fast reply.

> Whoops. Wrong blackmail thread.

Then, after carefully checking several times to be sure I'm in the right thread, I send Ax the pussy pic and the bid to the group. Imagine sending *that* to the wrong chat.

Alex and Holt have already submitted their preferred numbers. Seems we're all on the same page, and for maybe the first time, I believe this deal might actually happen.

It feels good.

Almost as good as Ax's reply feels.

> I need you back in the office, Mrs. Morgan, right the fuck now.

> Are you having a problem that you can't handle?

> Do I look like someone with a problem?

This text is immediately followed by a picture of him sitting in an office chair with his hand wrapped around his exposed and very erect cock.

My pussy clenches with envy.

Wait a minute…is that my office?

I'm about to scroll in and check it out, but I'm distracted when Brystin calls my name. "Adly…it's perfect."

When I look up, she's focused on Mira, who's brought the gown I didn't try on from the fitting room and is currently hanging it back on the rack. The gown I never really looked at until now.

And…wow.

Really. *Wow.*

I cross to it to study it closer. It's another untraditional piece. A simple A–line with 3D flower embroidery and appliqués and a bustier style corset and flowy tulle skirt.

The best part? It's pink. Not all-out Pepto-Bismol kind of pink—more blush. It's fairytale and overly feminine and stupid romantic, and I'm entranced.

The thing is, Brystin's wrong. It's not perfect, because there can be no perfect dress for an event that will never happen, no way, no how.

But if I were a character, say, in a romance novel, and if I were able to overcome my flaws and my doubts and could fall even a little bit in love with someone…

If I could believe that everyone deserves a happily ever after, even a jaded Sebastian, then yes. This would be the perfect dress.

I finger the lace tulle and imagine what earrings I'd wear with it and how I'd do my hair. I know exactly what shoes I'd pair with it too. They're buried in a box in my extra closet/room; I've been waiting for a reason to wear them. There could never be a reason that isn't more fitting than this dress.

"Are you sure you don't want to try it on?" Giulia asks.

I drop the skirt from my hand. "Yeah. I'm sure."

Because I live in the real world, and my destiny is to run my own network—which I'm on the verge of finally buying —not being a bride.

If I could be both, though…wouldn't that truly be the fantasy?

IT TAKES a while to get Brystin's dress measured for tailoring. Then Giulia spends nearly another half an hour in hushed conversation with Mira, probably conspiring when to get me to come back in. We only have time to grab smoothies to go for a late lunch before we have to meet the men at the office.

Then there's weekend traffic as we leave the city.

By the time make the hour-and-a-half drive up to Adeline, everyone's already there and seated outside for dinner.

And by everyone, I mean all of Dad's branch of the family—minus my stepsister Lina who stayed in town with Reid, who had to work late—plus Ax's dad and Hunter. The last time Grandpa tried to combine our families for an event was Christmas, and Hunter had to be tricked into that. When he found out, he barely made it half an hour before he bailed, so his appearance here is odd, to say the least.

And Ax's father and mine are not friendly. Why he's here is an even stranger mystery.

"Did you know—?" I start to ask Ax about it and don't have to say any more for him to understand.

"That my father was coming? Not a clue." He gives his dad a tight smile.

When my eyes land on Hunter's smirk, I give him the bird, in case he's forgotten how I feel about him. Then I lean toward Holt to whisper, "Why is he here?"

He looks to Brystin, who shakes her head, before he shrugs.

I probably missed some detail in all the chaos of the week. Maybe Dad's celebrating his upcoming second retirement, and he's formally passing the reins down to Hunter. It's not a situation I can fathom, but Grandpa makes unfathomable things happen. Why Kevin Morgan is here, though, still makes no sense.

Whatever's going on, all eyes seem to be on us as we take our seats in the open spots next to Grandpa at the head table.

Giulia makes our excuses for us. "So sorry we're late. We got caught up at the bridal shop."

"Did you find anything?" Grandpa asks.

Since this is a question for Brystin, I take the opportunity to whisper to Ax, "It's weird that Hunter's here, and you're sitting by me. Good thing he has your father, I suppose."

Come to think of it, I haven't noticed Ax around Hunter at all as of late. I hope our marriage hasn't put too much strain on their friendship—for Ax's sake. I care fuck all if Hunter's brooding.

"Eh..." Ax begins, but stops when he realizes that Grandpa is snapping his fingers in our direction.

"I'm talking to you, girl," Grandpa says. "Did you find a gown?"

"Oh…" Everyone's eyes are definitely on me. Oh, God. Is this why Grandpa gathered us this weekend? Because I'm the newlywed? And Hunter's here because he's Ax's best friend?

I feel like crawling under the table since it's a lot of attention given under false pretenses. Best to just acknowledge it and then turn the attention elsewhere. "I didn't want to make any decisions when the day is still so far away. This should be Brystin's time to shine."

"Ah, ah, ah, not so very far away, it turns out. It's this weekend." My stomach is already dropping before Grandpa continues. "Surprise! We're throwing you a wedding!"

Fuck.

I should have tried on the dress.

CHAPTER
TWENTY
AX

"Excuse me, what?" Adly's voice sounds steady enough, but the white-knuckled grip on her salad fork and the sudden loss of color in her cheeks gives away her panic.

"We're here for your wedding," Grandpa says. Slowly and with articulation, as though she's the elderly one who might be on the verge of hearing loss and declined cognition, instead of the other way around.

It might not be fair to suggest Irving Sebastian isn't as quick as he's ever been, despite being a nonagenarian, but this particular scheme of his really has me questioning that notion.

Adly takes an immediate sip of wine, as soon as the server hands it to her, and clears a laugh from her throat. "Good one, Grandpa. You almost had me there."

I kind of don't think it's a joke.

Though I've been avoiding Hunter since running into

him at SNC, I throw him a questioning glance. His shrug says he's just as clueless as I am.

Irving straightens his back, a physical reminder of his role as patriarch. "I'm dead ass serious, my girl. Planning a wedding will never be your priority. I get it. This is my way of helping you out."

"*Our way*, Dad," Samuel says, directly across from us. "You couldn't have pulled this off without me and Giulia."

I've never shot eye darts at such a nice woman before. First time for everything, I suppose.

"Don't forget Kevin," she adds, twisting her neck to exchange glances with my father.

"He gave us lots of valuable input."

Fuck, of course he's in on it. He's so determined that I take advantage of this union that he can't help interfering.

I send a mental apology to Adly for the man I share blood with, but she's focused solely on the family in front of her. "This is...so...uh..." She seems to be struggling for kind words.

"Sweet," I fill in.

She grabs onto the word and nods profusely. "Sweet. Yes! Weird. Weirdly sweet gesture, but—"

"But nothing," Irving says. "Everyone else arrives tomorrow. Consider this the rehearsal dinner. Hurry up and eat because we leave in ninety minutes for the church run-through."

Next to me, Steele whispers to his girlfriend. "Isn't the rehearsal usually before the dinner?"

Simone answers around a bite of a honey brown bread roll. "Who the fuck cares as long as dinner is free?"

On the other side of me, Adly seems to be having trouble breathing.

I truly have no skin in this. Do I want to put on a monkey suit and read from a script while all of my closest friends and colleagues watch me pretend to devote my life to one woman? Honestly, I've done far more deceitful things to far less deserving people.

Admittedly, it's not one of the recurring fantasies I've had about Adly. There have been plenty over the years, many that we've acted out a time or two. But even the ones I haven't shared with her—the ones that aren't wholly sexual in nature, the rated PG ones where I'm holding her tight, and she's fully present, and nothing between us is a lie—even those fantasies are a far cry from what Irving Sebastian is putting forward now.

Although...now that I've let the idea enter my mind, there are a lot of different versions of this situation that might be fun to enact...

Not helpful at the moment, wise ass.

But who cares what I want or don't want. I'm certain this is the last thing that *Adly* wants, and for all the hoops she's had to jump through in order to try to buy a company that she'll never be allowed to purchase, I think it's time for me to put my foot down.

In a way that doesn't alienate the richest man on earth, of course.

Clearing my throat, I raise my chin toward Irving. "I hate to be a wrench in this very thoughtful idea, but my mother was a devout Catholic. Adly and I are planning to have a priest preside over our nuptials in honor."

It's only partially lip service. If I were to ever marry for real, this is exactly how I'd bring my mother into it. It would piss my father off too, which is always fun.

Irving turns his head toward my father, and tsks. "It's like he doesn't trust me to do my research." Then he turns back to me. "Father John will meet us at the church tonight."

So this was my Dad's contribution. He's fairly anti-religious himself, but he knows I've been drawn to my mother's traditions.

His ignorance, however, is showing.

"Unfortunately, Catholic marriage preparation takes six months to complete." A fact I only know from being a teen when my mom remarried.

Samuel stifles a smile, but Irving laughs outright. "The kid is familiar with the concept of money, isn't he?"

It's been a while since I've felt this stupid in front of someone that matters.

Fortunately, Adly understands the concept of religious integrity. "I think something's lost in the honoring of his mother's faith if the priest presiding is crooked, Grandpa."

Irving snaps to answer, "Just like there's something lost in the spirit of my generosity when certain grandchildren choose not to honor the rules surrounding the gifts I've bestowed upon them."

Shit.

Fuck.

My stomach drops. I imagine Adly's has dropped so far that I wouldn't be surprised to find a crater-sized hole underneath her chair.

Diagonally across from us, Holt puts a hand up to his

mouth to hide his lips, and mouths what the rest of us are thinking, *"He knows."*

You think, dumbass?

It would be an absolute riot if anyone else were sitting in the hot seat but her.

It had always been a possibility that Irving knew our marriage was a farce—how could it not be? But I'd kind of figured if he hadn't called her out on it before now that he was happy to live in willful ignorance.

I'd somehow forgotten that the Sebastians like to do everything big. Including their reprimands.

Under the table, I put a palm on her thigh, hoping my touch conveys everything I need her to know right now. *Whatever Irving needs, whatever will make this right, I'm here. We got this.*

She covers my hand with hers.

My heart feels like I just did a line of coke, and while I don't really care to examine all the reasons, I'm pretty positive it isn't just because she's squeezing for dear life.

She glances at me and her expression says she knows I'm with her. That we're together in this.

That we're *together.*

Then she turns back to Irving. "Uh, Grandpa, I'm—"

Before she can get her apology/explanation/excuse even started, he cuts her off with his warmest smile. "Luckily, the only thing I want in return is to be seated in the front row when my intelligent, talented, accomplished, beautiful, and first granddaughter walks down the aisle." He puts his hand on hers—the one that's still tightly gripping her fork. "I'm not gonna live forever, honey. I'd hate to see you wait so long that we miss it."

We *miss it.*

I'm not sure what the point is exactly in his word choice. I'm also not sure if this means he thinks we're actually in love, or if he thinks we should be in love, or if he even cares whether or not Adly marries someone she loves. Did he always intend to use her trust fund access as an elaborate matchmaking scheme? Or is he simply in this for the twisted entertainment?

One thing I've learned about the richest of the rich—it seems to come with a fair bit of eccentricity.

But as long as Adly's off the hook, that's all I care about.

"Thank you," she says to Irving, her voice tight.

When she looks at me again, her eyes are watery. She might not be asking for my permission, but I give it anyway. "Let's have a wedding."

After that, things happen fast.

"I bought the dress," Giulia tells Adly, which seems to lessen the knot in my wife's shoulders by a tenth of a degree. "Mira's using your previous measurements to have it altered tonight. Reid and Lina will pick it up and bring it in the morning."

"I need shoes too," Adly says. "I have the perfect pair, in my closet. And jewelry. My mom's earrings—"

"Tell me where. Reid and Lina can get those too."

Adly looks like she might kiss her stepmom—wait, is that hot?

I shake the image from my head and jump in to help with the organizing. "I'll tell him. I need him to get things for me too."

"The Alexander McQueen reverse tuxedo," Adly

suggests. "It would be perfect with my dress. Black dress shirt. Skinny white tie."

I ignore how good it feels to have my clothes both appreciated and remembered by the woman that I...well, by Adly, and pull out my phone to start a text.

"What about rings?" she asks.

"Kevin has them," Giulia says, and I stop typing.

There's only one set of rings my father would bring. The pair he's kept in a safe since my parents' divorce. He's the kind of ass who didn't let my mother keep her own ring after they parted, claiming it was worth too much and shouldn't be separated from the set, and promised to hold it for my marriage, despite the thousands of times I've told him it wasn't happening.

I've never mentioned it to Adly, but somehow she figures it out. "No...you don't need to, Ax. That's too much. They're too important to you."

It *should* be too much. It should feel like going too far. Boundaries and all that.

But that isn't how I feel, surprisingly. Besides the fact that I'm pretty sure it's already a done deal, my parents' set is the natural option. "That's why it should be them. Because they're important." Because the woman you marry is supposed to be important.

And she *is* important. Important to me, in a bunch of ways I can't express.

The woman in question stares at me as if she can hear my inner monologue, and for a fraction of a second, I worry that this is what's too much. That all the feelings I never examine are starting to leak out of the dark recess inside me where I keep them contained, and that they are too big and too much and that they'll do us both in.

But she squeezes my hand again and nods, and when I take my next breath, it's the deepest one I've managed in ages.

"Wedding party—" Giulia says next, like she's going down a checklist in her mind.

"Lina, Steele, and Holt," Adly says without blinking.

Then they both stare at me. "Uh…"

"I figured you'd want Hunter," Giulia prompts, which explains why Hunter is invited. "Is there anyone else?"

It's a strange thing narrowing down the important people around you to the few that mean the most. Regrets about my own familial relations swirl in my stomach, despite the mental reminder that this wedding is only for show. Hunter is currently a big question mark in my life, but he should be beside me. And…

"Alex," I say, honestly. Our relationship is complicated, but he's been almost as much of a constant in my life as Hunter. "But he's obviously out since he's on tour with Riah."

Giulia nods her head like it's already covered. "They'll both be here tomorrow. We'll have someone stand in for tonight."

Well, that will be fun since Hunter's not speaking to Alex at the moment.

As long as we're playing family reunion… "Might as well have Reid up there as the third," I say.

Adly scrunches her nose in an adorable show of reluctance before shrugging. "What's a Sebastian wedding without a little drama?"

"Look at us being on brand." Truly, if this is what Grandpa Irving wants, then this is what Grandpa Irving should get. A Sebastian gathering complete with warts and rivalries and all.

Forty-five minutes later, the menu, music, and reception plans have been discussed and checked off Giulia's list. It's all already been arranged, but Giulia seems determined to get our input and modify wherever she can to make it *Adly's dream*.

I swear I can hear Addles' eye roll every time the phrase is muttered, though she's done an excellent job of appearing enthused at every turn.

Maybe it's even sincere.

Personally, this whole wedding thing originally sounded like a bit of a drag, but the more we talk about it, the more it seems potentially fun.

However it turns out, it's no doubt going to be exhausting. We'll need our fuel to get through the next two days. While I scarfed down the beef tenderloin like I've been raised in a barn, Adly has hardly touched her food, and plates are already being cleared for dessert, so when Grandpa announces that there's only twenty minutes before we leave for the church, I excuse myself from the table so I can corner a waiter and ask them for a portable snack of some kind for Adly. With the morning spent shopping, I'm sure she hasn't had a chance to really eat all day.

In short order, I'm loaded up with a bag of Adly's favorite munchies and turned around to head back to the table, only to find myself face to face with Hunter.

Let the drama begin.

Hunter claps me on the back like there's no bad blood

between us. "This is crazy, Ax. You in front of an altar—I wouldn't believe it if I wasn't here to witness it myself." He lowers his voice. "And all for fucking show. Jesus, my family's a circus. I don't know how you can stand us."

"Glad you can be entertained at our expense." It's the first time I've ever talked about Adly as part of my *we* directly to Hunter's face.

Maybe it's the first time I've ever thought of her as the one on my side, and him on another. It's like there's something bigger going on, something changing between all of us. I feel like I've been a random ball on a pool table for so long, happy to be knocked around by whoever was behind the cue, and now...

Now I'm ready for something different.

It must show in my tone. "I'm not behind this. You realize that, right?"

"Don't act like you're just along for the ride, my friend. You and I both know none of this would be necessary if you hadn't gotten Bob Peterson to raise the price, forcing Adly to need her trust fund."

"How the hell was I supposed to know you were going to step in and play knight in shining armor?" He takes a breath and comes back calmer. "We've been over this. What's your deal with me tonight?"

"What's my deal?" I fight not to let out a maniacal laugh. "My deal is that I saw your presentation for the SNC board. Craig Rasmussen? As my superior?"

Hunter is a smart, manipulative man—I'll never deny it —but he's not quick on his feet like Holt or even me. He's the kind of guy who has to brood a lot before he gets to his answers, but then they're always so fucking good, no one's off-the-cuff can ever compete.

It's why I'm expecting him to hem and haw and dance a bit around this confrontation.

Instead he surprises me with a direct comeback. "Because I had no time to talk to you first. You were off playing *husband* when I realized that I didn't have an answer to the board's management load. So I came up with the triple CEOS, and of course I pegged you for any of the three spots—and I did float your name in my presentation —but I didn't want to tie you to a position that you might have no interest in. Haven't you told me a million times you're happy exactly where you are?"

I'm about to swing back with a rebuttal until it hits me that I don't have one. "Okay. I have said that."

He holds his arms open like *Well?*

Then he takes a step toward me, closing the distance so we can be sure we're talking privately. "Do you really think I could ever do this without you? The board knows you're my secret weapon. You're my right hand guy. I've never made that a secret. Whatever you want, it's yours. Want to change the hierarchy of the CEOS? Let's do it. They'll all report to you. Whatever level of command you want to take, you decide. You're my brother, Axelrod. Fuck DNA. You're the only person I trust to always have my back, and you better believe I've got yours."

Could it all be just a bunch of words?

Sure.

But logic and history doesn't give me any reason to doubt him. Samuel was the one who told me I had been overlooked, but with how much he hates Hunter, he had every reason to stretch the truth, if not outright lie.

And I *haven't* been ambitious. My dad will be the first to say it, and it's true. Partly because I thought I'd hit the ceiling, but both Adly and Hunter are teaching me that there are ways to change where the ceiling is. A year ago, I'm not sure I would have been interested in the extra work, but now? Maybe I'm changing because the idea of building something new at SNC with Hunter is suddenly exciting.

That's when I remember what I did.

"Fuck, Hunter. I'm sorry." I run a hand through my hair, bracing myself for this confession. "I overreacted when I heard, and instead of broaching it with you, I got pissed off and spilled the idea about purchasing a smaller network to Samuel. I spoke out of turn, man, and there's no excuse."

Hunter's lips twist in a disbelieving smirk. "Why would you apologize for sharing an idea that was yours in the first place?"

It's not a comforting reminder that the proposal that will fuck Adly's plans came from me, but that isn't his point. "That didn't give me the right."

"Sure it did. You paved the way."

"I stole your thunder."

"It was *our* thunder." He lays a hand on my shoulder. "Like I said, everyone knows you're my guy. I wouldn't have been invited tonight, if anyone thought differently."

"All right." I nod, convincing myself. "All right. Yeah. Okay. Then we're good."

"We're good." He squeezes my shoulder before dropping his arm. "How did he react to the idea, anyway? Samuel?"

With that one question, it's like the clouds part and an opportunity lands in front of me—I could change everything for Adly. Right here, right now, I can deliver the words that might make the entire idea of buying SHE go away for now, if not forever.

But it means flubbing the truth.

It means choosing her over him.

Hunter's my fucking family. What about bros before hoes? What even is Adly to me?

Before I can stop myself, the words are out of my mouth. "He didn't seem that hot on it, actually. Maybe thought it was too much to undertake right off the bat?"

"Really?" Hunter's jaw moves back and forth while he thinks. "Sam and I don't see eye to eye most of the time, I guess. Kind of thought he'd be for this one though, because everyone knows how much he hates the fact that Holt is at SHE instead of SNC."

I shrug, already feeling the pit form in my stomach as I realize how easily this could go sideways. Hunter could try to win favor with the rest of the board. He could even try to convince Samuel to change his mind. So many chances for this to blow up in my face.

It's also the one chance Adly has.

"Maybe Sam's softening in his old age," I say. "Look— he helped throw a wedding. It's possible he doesn't really want to fuck things up for Holt. He might have a point, too. Get the executive team straightened out first and revisit acquiring another company next year." Hopefully, one that isn't already helmed by a Sebastian.

It's a tough pill for Hunter to swallow when he has so much animosity toward both Holt and Alex right now, but he seems to really consider it. "It might hurt more taking it away after they've already been running it, too."

"Exactly."

"Though I doubt that they'll leave any openings for us to purchase it later." No, they definitely won't. All three of them have been groomed by the best. "Do you know what bank they're going through for the loan?"

I start to say no and remember that's a lie. Earlier, Adly accidentally sent me the bid, which I'd already decided to pretend I never saw, but it also had the loan officer's information listed. If I passed it on to Hunter, he could potentially bribe the bank into fucking with the acquisition or setting up the loan so that it can be bought out at a later time.

"I don't," I lie. The thing is, buying out SHE is still the best way I know for SNC to expand their demographic. It's not just Hunter I'm deceiving, but the entire company that I've devoted my life to. It's a truth that makes my next words the biggest betrayal of all. "You might have to decide what's more important—elevating SNC to the next level or ruining them."

"Is there a difference?" But there's a wariness in his eyes that makes me think I could potentially keep steering him around this. "Yeah. That's something I'll have to think about."

"But you will? Think about it?"

"Of course, I will."

Admittedly, the taste in my mouth is bitter, but my shoulders feel looser than they have in weeks, and when I gaze past him and see Adly beckoning to me, the bitterness starts to dissolve.

Hunter turns to follow my sightline. "Ah. Looks like you're being summoned. I'll see you at the church."

As soon as I'm standing next to Adly again, my entire disposition feels lighter. The tables have been cleared and people have grouped into conversation huddles, but she's by herself holding two shots of what I would guess is whiskey.

Not going to lie, the offer of alcohol might be what's helping the mood.

She hands one of the glasses to me. "This is a lot, I know. I figured we need another round of negotiations."

"Right, right." Except I can't seem to think of a single thing to ask for.

I mean there are things I want. Things like a lift of the ban on sex in the apartment and maybe once when we fuck we don't have to play like we're someone else.

And kissing. God, I'd love to kiss her again.

But I'm not convinced that any of those things would mean what I want them to mean if they were attained through bargaining. Trying to figure out exactly what I want them to mean is a whole other can of worms.

So I simply say, "I think I'm good."

"You're good? With all this chaos?"

I scan my eyes over the others. It doesn't really feel so much like chaos as it feels like...family. "Yeah. I'm good."

"Huh. Me too." A small smile creeps across her face, causing her eyes to light up like a sudden burst of sunshine. But there's something more in those eyes—a spark of recognition or understanding, as if she's truly seeing me for the first time, or in a new light.

The feeling that washes over me is indescribable. It's like

I've grown a few inches taller and transformed into the best version of myself. It's empowering and humbling at the same time.

But despite my initial resistance, I can't deny the fact that this woman has some sort of hold over me. Every fiber of my being resists the idea, but deep down I know it's true —I'm completely and utterly captivated by her. And I'm not sure I could fight it even if I wanted to.

She lifts her glass to clink against mine. "*Salute.*"

"*Salute,*" I reply, my voice nonchalant and casual as if this clink of glasses is just like any other. As if I am the same man who eagerly volunteered to play the role of her husband, purely for my own twisted amusement.

But deep down, I know the truth—that I can never resist messing around with her, that I crave being the only one who has that power over her. And anyone who tries to take my place will be met with my wrath.

Is this what it feels like to fall in love?

As I grapple with the possibility, a knot forms in my stomach and I feel a sense of unease wash over me. Thankfully, the smooth burn of whiskey slides down my throat, soothing me from the impact of this twisted truth.

Just as Giulia comes over to herd us toward the cars, I take Adly's empty glass with the intention of finding someone to take them to the kitchen.

It wouldn't hurt to have some time alone to gather my thoughts as well.

But before I can make a move, Adly sprints back toward me, her breath coming out in short gasps. She grabs me forcefully by the lapels and looks up at me with intensity.

"No other women," she says firmly.

My mind races to figure out what she means before it clicks: the one thing I've been wanting her to ask for all along—my promise that I will be faithful to her during our marriage.

It may have been a difficult ask for me in the past, now all I want is to be with Adly and only Adly.

"No other women," she repeats, a desperate demand.

My hands settle at her waist. "Ah Addles, it was always only going to be you."

Eyes shining, she nods.

And then she pulls me toward her, and she kisses me.

I'm surprised, but it's quickly overwhelmed by want. My lips eagerly press against hers, and my tongue boldly explores every inch of her mouth, claiming it as mine.

She lets out a soft moan, which I devour eagerly, wishing we could stay like this forever. Wishing we didn't have obligations and people waiting and a whole show to put on.

But as abbreviated as the kiss has to be, there's one thing I'm sure of when we're forced to pull apart—I made the right choice, steering Hunter away from SHE.

And Adly isn't just some woman that I chose over my best friend—she's my wife.

CHAPTER
TWENTY-ONE
ADLY

St. Mary's is only ten minutes from Adeline.

The ride goes by in a flash because the whole time all I can think about is Ax. My lips still sting from our kiss. The words he whispered rattle in my head. *Addles, it was always only going to be you.*

How can one sentence both excite and calm me all at once?

I shouldn't be so susceptible to his charm. I shouldn't smile to myself every time I hear his name. I shouldn't be preparing to stand in front of my entire family to declare a lifelong commitment when I already know we're slated for divorce.

I shouldn't keep wondering if that's really how this marriage has to end.

But then we've arrived, and I'm thrown into logistics so the noise of my thoughts is easier to ignore.

As it turns out, I've passed St. Mary's a million times without a second glance, which is a shame considering how adorable it is. The small stone building was erected around the turn of the twentieth century and will be the star of all the pictures that I'm sure Giulia will expect us to sit through tomorrow.

As soon as we walk through the church's doors, we're in the nave. Then it's sixty feet down the main marble aisle, past wooden pews that seat three hundred, to the two short steps that lead to the altar. Organ pipes provide the background for a light blue and gold adorned Virgin Mary statue perched on top of the tabernacle.

To me, it looks pretty much like every other church I've ever had reason to visit, but it might as well be Notre Dame for how pleased I am when Ax scans the scene and gives an affirming nod.

That's about all the communication I have with him before Giulia herds us to our places and gives us very specific instructions to *be quiet and pay attention.*

It's impressive how quickly she gets such a privileged group of assholes to snap into line. Giulia Romano Sebastian in the role of matriarch is the family blessing that neither me nor my siblings saw coming. It's a nice change of pace to have a happy surprise for once.

I tell myself not to get used to it.

The rehearsal takes less time to run through than it did to herd all of us into cars to get here.

Actually, rehearsal might be a strong word for what is essentially talking through the program. When we've all arrived, Father John—dressed in a polo and khakis with no sign of priest about him—paces back and forth in front of the altar and spouts the format into his handheld microphone, even though most of us are gathered right in front of him.

He's warm and efficient with a collection of dad jokes that could give Lina a run for her money. His instructions are clear though canned, and I have the real sense that his entire spiel is recycled for every wedding he presides over. Not only does it work, but it's smooth.

Everyone gets a chance to practice both their entrance and where to stand. Beyond that it's, *"So and so will do a reading here. I'll say a blessing here. The music will start playing here. The couple will repeat after me here."*

As soon as I learn there's a church wedding coordinator that will give us all our cues—and that Giulia will make sure none are missed—I stop trying to memorize any of the instructions and just concentrate on trying to get my stomach to calm down.

The snacks Ax brought help immensely.

The whiskey I downed on a near empty stomach, not so much.

Thankfully, Ax is busy making notes in his phone when I walk down the aisle. I'm pretty sure I would have thrown up if he were looking at me. Every time I glance at him, my insides feel like they've gone full locust swarm. It's kind of like having butterflies but multiply them by a thousand and add liquor and dread.

I'm not sure if I'm nervous because I've lost total control of this entire scam or if it's because I've been called out by Grandpa and am now obliged to make sure the whole event goes off without a hitch and keeps him happy.

Or maybe it's something else entirely that has me dazed

and seasick. Something I don't have the bandwidth or the courage to try to analyze.

Whatever the cause, my turmoil must read on my face because as soon as we're dismissed and everyone starts toward the parking lot, Holt holds me back from the exodus with a hand on my shoulder. "I had no idea. I swear. When Giulia said Grandpa wanted to do something for you, I thought it was going to be dinner. Nothing else."

I'm not even mad at him, but it's a ridiculous defense. "Do you *know* our family?"

"Do *you*?"

In other words, his hands were tied. I get that as well as anyone. Sebastians are stubborn, every goddamn one of us, because we learned it from Grandpa Irving. There is no stopping any train he puts in motion. There's just holding onto the seat back in front of you and bracing for fast curves.

But I like the concern, and I'm not ready to put a stop to it. "You could have at least given me a heads-up." I don't admit that Brystin already did back at the bridal shop.

"You're right. I could have. I *should* have."

I just shrug and peer past his shoulder, watching the doors shut behind Steele and Simone. I'm pretty sure we're the only people in the church now besides whoever is locking up.

Holt tries again to make things better. "At this point, all I can do is ask how you're holding up." The look I give him expresses more than I could with two spiked middle fingers. "Yeah, stupid question. What do you want me to do?"

As much as I like him groveling, there isn't anything he

can do, and honestly, it's a little annoying that he thinks there is. "It's fine. I mean, isn't it? It's one weekend of parading around for the family in exchange for a chance at something so much bigger."

"It really is so much bigger, AJ," he says, reverting to the nickname he had for me when we were little. "There are opportunities that I could never have imagined out here. Different ways to do business that aren't only focused on SNC's bottom line. We actually care about the news more than our profits. What we do at SHE matters."

He moves so he's standing right in front of me. "Look, I know it's a major reframe of mind. We were taught that loyalty to the Sebastian brand was the be-all, end-all growing up. I don't know about you, but I was afraid of the world outside of that for so long. It felt like…" He gestures to the nave around us. "It felt like leaving a religion."

"And now you're going to hell and will burn for all eternity."

"Well…" He lets out a strangled laugh. "Funny how hell feels a lot like freedom."

I've been told all my life I was already free. Money awards a lot of privilege, after all.

So how did I live so long not realizing there was a cage around me?

Once upon a time, I honestly believed I could one day convince Dad that I deserved another position outside of human resources. Then I thought that SNC's patriarchal organization methods would retire along with the men behind them. Then I thought my trust fund would fix every-thing—and I still do—except now, freedom's on the horizon, but instead of feeling like I can finally unfurl my wings and soar, I keep glancing down at the pink stone on my finger wondering if independence isn't just another word for lonely.

"I appreciate this, Holt." There's an unspoken *but* at the end of the statement—a whole bunch of them, actually— and the word that follows every one is Ax.

But Ax is lying for me too.

But Ax doesn't get a reward.

But Ax isn't a religion that I want to leave.

That's the confusing part of all of this—Ax.

"I think I need some alone time," I tell Holt, and not the I'm-reading-a-really-spicy-scene kind of alone time that I usually need when I shoo him away. I need the kind of alone time that lets me get my thoughts in order. The kind of alone time that isn't possible back at Adeline, because even without being thrust into the spotlight this weekend, being around the family is always suffocating.

He nods emphatically like he understands all too well. "Why don't you hang here for a while? It looks like pretty much everyone's left. Giulia has the key and instructions for closing everything up. You can text when you want me to send the car, and I'll be sure the driver takes care of locking up then."

"Giulia has *a key*? How big of a donation did we make?"

"Let's just say St. Mary's is finally going to get to build the community center they've been wanting."

At least the money's going to a good cause. "Thank you Mr. and Mrs. Samuel Sebastian."

"Thank you Mr. and Mrs. Axel Morgan, you mean. Pretty sure the plaque will be in your names."

"There's going to be a plaque?" All for a marriage that

isn't designed to last. "I'm definitely burning in hell with you for this one."

"Think less about..." Holt reconsiders his words. "You know what? Just think less. It'll help way more than you can know."

When he's gone, I sink into a pew and do exactly the opposite and think a whole lot about the man I shouldn't be thinking about at all. Strange thing to say about my husband, but now that Grandpa Irving has admitted he knows this marriage is about the money, I would feel relieved if it weren't for Ax. It would be one thing if everything between us were fake, but some of it is very much real.

The question is, where does the "real" end and the pretending begin?

It doesn't help that we were sexually involved before all this fake marriage stuff started. It super doesn't help that we haven't put the kibosh on that, because now I'm scrambling to define what we are and what we're not.

We're coworkers with benefits, but not for much longer.

We're roommates without benefits, but that's been complicated, and it's only been a week.

We're currently married under the eyes of the law.

We're about to be married under the eyes of God and Grandpa, and it feels like utter blasphemy because....

We aren't anything else.

Those facts should be the end of it.

Except that none of those facts address how I feel, and defining that is the most complicated part of all of this because I feel a lot of things at once. Gratitude, attraction, ease. Admiration. I'm even, dare I say, starting to feel like I could trust him.

And I want him in my life.

It doesn't mean I'm ready to make vows to him, but I'm also not sure I can stand in front of everyone and profess my commitment to him and not mean it.

On the flip side, will I be able to hear those words come out of his mouth and not turn them into more?

Considering the way my heart races at the mere thought, I think the answer might be no.

I'm content to spend the next hour descending into agony over it but the old-building sounds of the church are much more apparent without people absorbing the noise. Every new creak spooks me out of my rumination, and eventually I'm rattled out of my pew to the back of the church to lock the big wooden doors.

Once they're secured, I realize I'm not alone.

There's movement in the small votive chapel nearby. Father John, I suspect, or possibly the wedding planner who was so upstaged by Giulia, I've yet to learn her name.

But the man who walks out a few seconds later is none other than Ax.

He's still in his suit from work—a blue Emporio Armani —but he's long lost the jacket and tie. His white dress shirt is unbuttoned at the collar and untucked from his pants. His usual stiff-styled hair has had his hands through it so many times, the shape has been lost, and his beard needs to be trimmed.

Ruffled as he is, there's no one else that I love looking at like I love looking at him.

Apparently, my lady puss agrees. I swear I can feel the

thrum of my pulse in my thighs and my clit is vibrating like it's an alarm going off.

On impulse, without fully considering where we are or what's appropriate, I offer up a scenario. "I'm sorry it's late, Father, but I was hoping you had time to hear one more confession."

As soon as I've said it, I realize it's blatant sacrilege to roleplay priest, especially in a church, but neither Ax nor the growing bulge in his pants seem offended. "I wouldn't dream of letting you walk down the aisle tomorrow with your heart not pure. Right this way."

He leads me across the nave to the vestibule, home of an old-fashioned wooden confessional box. I'd seen it earlier, noting the sign next to it that declared the box out of official use, as now the church does their reconciliation in another room where the penitent can choose to use a screen or confess face-to-face. The original structure has been left for décor and history, but it's not roped off and there's nothing saying not to touch.

The structure has a center compartment that I assume is for the priest, and a booth on either side. Father Ax opens one of the booth doors for me, and I step inside. It's a tight space with a wooden bench on the back wall. Or maybe it's a shelf for leaning on while kneeling. My knowledge about confessionals extends to what I've learned on television, and I feel like I remember seeing people do both.

Since I'm a princess and the floor is hard, I choose to sit. It's so small in the booth that once I'm sitting, my knees are only inches away from the door.

Cramped as it is, there's an immediate quiet that comes

over me. I feel shut off from the world, but protected. Like I'm in a cocoon.

Well, a cocoon if it had a window in it.

It's not actually a window, as there's no glass. Instead there's a lattice partition on the wall that's shared with the priest's compartment. The holes in the lattice are big enough that I can tell that it's Ax settling in next to me, but it somehow still gives privacy.

"Good evening, child," Father Ax says through the screen. "Tell me what's on your mind."

"Forgive me, Father, for I have sinned." There's an immediate rush of endorphins every time I sink into a new character with Ax. It's an opportunity to create a whole other life and personality, but it's also a place just to have fun and say the trite lines that are associated with certain roles. "This is my first confession, I'm afraid."

"No need to be ashamed. You're here now." Ax's priest voice is so spot on. Soothing and authoritative all at once. "What's troubling your spirit this evening?"

A shiver runs through me, and I'm full-blown aroused. After so long playing with him, my body is conditioned. It's like there's a switch that flips in my head as soon as we're in scene, and my nipples instantly pucker, and my panties dampen.

I press my legs tightly together to settle the hum between them. "I'm getting married tomorrow, Father, as you know. I'm afraid that…"

It's then that I pause.

Being here like this, with only a thin partition between us, I suddenly feel like I could say anything. Tell him everything. Confess everything in my heart, like how confusing it is to realize I might have feelings for the man I'm already married to. Falling for my husband is a trope that plays out much better in fiction. In real life, it's complicated by family politics and personal trauma and deep-rooted trust issues.

If there were ever a safe space to discuss it, this would be it.

But is it fair to throw my anxiety on him when we have the biggest performance of our scam tomorrow afternoon?

Also for consideration, is it fair to start a scene under the pretense of seduction only to turn it into an ill-timed heart-to-heart?

In the end, it's the persistence of my libido and Holt's words that guide me. *Think less.*

So I stop thinking all together and let my pussy come out to play. "I'm afraid that I don't know how to please my husband."

"Oh. A concerning problem indeed." His bench creaks, as if he's readjusting himself. "But you came to the right place. I'm certain I can help. Has he complained about your abilities in the past or is this insecurity unfounded?"

I pitch my voice high and innocent. "I don't know, Father. I haven't ever…been with a man at all."

Another creak of his bench. He clears his throat. "I see."

"Was that wrong, Father? I wanted to save myself for only him, but now I'm worried I'll be so inexperienced that he won't want to be with me."

"Trust me, child. Even if he has to teach you everything, I'm sure he'll still find pleasure from the experience. Some men actually prefer it. Your innocence is a thoughtful gift, but I understand your anxiety. I'm sure you understand what happens between a husband and wife on their wedding night?"

"Some? Not much, I'm afraid."

"Let me ask you this—have you ever given yourself pleasure?"

I feign horror. "Never!"

"I'm guessing you've been told that touching yourself is sinful, but in this case, it's quite appropriate. Your husband won't find relations satisfying if your body doesn't know how to respond to his touch."

"Oh." I pretend to think over the implications of his statement. "So I should practice? I wouldn't even know how to start. Could you tell me what to do, Father?"

His voice is a whisper in the dimly lit room. "For starters, you must find the most sensitive part of your nether regions. It's called the clitoris, my dear, and it's a small, but powerful bundle of nerves that can bring you immense pleasure if stimulated properly."

He instructs me to slip my fingers into my panties, and I can tell he's watching through the holes in the lattice with a mix of anticipation and desire. My breath hitches as I reach down, and my fingers tremble before they finally part the damp fabric from my skin.

When my fingers find the tiny nub, I gasp, and begin to explore it gently, as if it's a forbidden fruit.

Father Ax watches, his eyes filled with unspoken desire. "That's it," he murmurs, his tone a mixture of approval and hunger. "Keep going. Sometimes, you might want to vary the pressure of your touch, take it a little harder, a little softer, but always remember that this is your most precious part, and you must treat it with reverence."

He goes on to describe small, fluid motions, how to "cup the most intimate of my feminine folds," how to "tease the delicate skin of my lips" and to "tenderly trace the contours of my femininity." Any other time, I would laugh at his overly poetic language, but there's something sacred in the way he speaks so softly and tenderly, as if he were consecrating the act, and the subtle throbbing between my thighs turns into an urgent need.

My clit is swollen and sensitive when he asks, "How does it feel?"

"Like it's not enough," I tell him honestly. "Like I'm empty."

"Because your pussy wants to be filled. This means you're doing it right. Now we need to find out if you're ready. Move your fingers lower, through the slit of your lips to the hole below. Can you find it?"

"My panties are in the way." I'm already in the process of removing them when he tells me to take them off and give them over.

I thread the thin silk material through the lattice, and when Ax pulls it out on the other side, he lifts the crotch panel to his nose and sniffs. "It does smell like you are aroused, my child. You need to stick your fingers inside to see if it's enough."

I trace the opening of my pussy. It clenches in response, beckoning to be filled, but I know from experience that my fingers are not what she wants. "I can't do it, Father. I'm too scared. Please. Can't you come and help me?"

"It's not appropriate," he says, pretending to think it over. "If I come over there, no one can ever know."

"I'll never tell a soul."

I hear his door open and close. Then my door opens. Light spills in, and Ax devours me with his eyes before he shuts the door behind him. It was already cramped before. Now there's nowhere for him to be except between my legs. I spread them further apart, bracing a foot on each wall.

Ax sinks to his knees in front of me. "Keep rubbing yourself," he instructs. "Before I can touch you with these hands, I need to be sure you're clean."

He hesitates for the barest moment, taking in my trembling form before him.

Then he leans forward and licks me.

I cry out at the sudden sensation, my fingers still moving against my clit. His tongue is warm and wet, gliding over my folds with a slow and deliberate pace.

I can feel his breath on me, his lips lightly brushing against my skin as he continues to tease me with his tongue. I moan, unable to contain the pleasure that's building inside of me.

Ax pulls back for a moment, looking up at me with dark eyes before diving back in. His tongue swirls around my clit, sending shocks of pleasure through my body.

"I'm so turned on," I confess between ragged breaths.

"That's good," Ax murmurs against me. "Let go."

He continues to lick and suck at my clit, his hands gripping onto my hips to keep me steady as I lose myself in the pleasure he's giving me. My climax comes running through me, waves of intense pleasure crashing over me until I'm left panting and spent.

Ax pulls away from me, wiping his mouth with the back of his hand. "That was an orgasm," he says. "Not only should that make you feel pleasure, it also helps tell your husband that he's treating you the way you deserve to be treated. You should never hide your orgasms from him. Do you understand?"

I'm still too caught up in the throes of ecstasy to be bothered by the teasing about my past tendency to hide my Os. "Yes, Father."

"Good. You did well. Now I can test your pussy to see if it's capable of taking a man."

Slowly, he slides two fingers inside of me. My body immediately responds, clenching around him as he starts to move in and out.

"Does it hurt?" Ax asks softly, his fingers never stopping their movements.

"It feels so good," I moan, closing my eyes and reveling in the sensations coursing through me, wishing it were more. Wishing it were another part of his body fucking me.

He saws in and out of me, with three fingers now. "You're loosening up, but you're still so tight."

"Is that a problem?"

"It could be. Your husband seems like the kind of man who has a huge cock. There's a possibility that he'll tear you apart."

"That's terrible. I wouldn't want to ruin my wedding night. What can we do, Father?"

"The only thing to do is break your pussy in. I know you were saving yourself for your husband, though..."

He stands, and for a fraction of a second, the panic that he's leaving me wanting is real. "No! Please, Father. You have to help me. I need to know if I can take it. I want to be the best wife for him."

He pretends to consider.

Then he lifts the hem of his shirt and unbuckles his belt. "Looks like I'm going to have to make the sacrifice."

When his cock is out, he bends and lifts me up. I wrap my legs around him, and he braces my back against the wall then drives into me with a swift thrust.

My eyes widen at the sudden invasion as Father Ax thrusts his thick shaft inside me, stretching me further than his fingers ever could.

He bites his lower lip, watching my reaction as he continues to move, asserting his dominance over my body. I realize how desperate I am for this, craving the feel of something real inside me, craving the feel of him.

The pace quickens, his hips pounding against me as I cry out in a mix of agony and pleasure.

"You can take it, can't you?" he growls, his eyes locked on mine. "You're ready for him. He's going to fill you up. He's going to get so deep inside you, you'll never want him to leave."

It's hard to hold his gaze, even in the dim light, but I try. Each thrust sends waves of electricity through my core, but the hunger his words awaken within me is one that I didn't think was possible. I know they're just sex words, but I also think they might be more than that. A promise. A vow.

A wish.

A fantasy.

I nod, hoping he thinks the tears streaming down my face have to do with the intensity of the experience and not because I'm afraid that I won't be able to take it. That I'm too distrustful and too guarded. That he'll be right there, desperately trying to root himself inside me, and all he'll find is fallow ground.

I don't want to be fallow ground.

I don't want to not be able to let him in.

But even his gaze is too intense, and much as I try, I can't hold it.

So I wrap my legs tight around his waist, and bury my face in his neck as I cling onto him for support. "I can take it," I tell him.

Silently, I pray it's not a lie.

CHAPTER
TWENTY-TWO
ADLY

Back at Adeline, I panic that the sleeping arrangements will put Ax and I in the same room.

When I discover that Giulia is insistent that the groom can't see the bride until the wedding, my panic doubles. It was bad enough thinking I'd have to sidestep my feelings and concerns while sharing a bed with Ax, but being alone with my thoughts is a thousand times worse.

In the morning, after tossing and turning most of the night, I wake up in a cold sweat of dread. This wedding cannot happen until I talk to Ax.

After dressing in a T-shirt and sweats, I head down at the usual breakfast meal time and discover a full-on brunch happening in my honor outside on the patio. Several round tables have been set up, each with a centerpiece of pale pink begonias, along with a full buffet.

All the women who had been at dinner last night are

here, along with several more family members, coworkers, and friends.

There's a head table with a floral decorated seat of honor waiting for me, but I don't make it there before Lina pounces on me.

Literally pounces.

She runs toward me, and I think she's going in for a hug, so I throw my arms around her, but instead of returning the embrace, she reaches up and sets something on my head.

Immediately, she launches into a typical Lina monologue. "Today's your fairytale day, so of course you have to wear a tiara. It's the one my mother wore on her wedding day—I had to fight her to be the one to give it to you. Not for keeps, obviously. Or maybe not obviously, but she thought it could be your something borrowed. Or not! No pressure to wear it during the ceremony, but until then, you can princess all you want and no one can give you shit because you're wearing the crown."

I want to be irritated—this wedding stuff is going a little far and all—but it's a crown. A gorgeous piece too, but more importantly, a crown. I could never be angry at a crown.

Cautiously, I lift my hands to adjust the piece to make it more comfortable as Lina steps aside and reveals another person waiting to bombard me. "She is not a princess," Zully corrects. "She's a motherfucking queen."

Legitimate excitement surges through me as I embrace one of the coolest humans I've ever had the pleasure to know. "What are you doing here?"

She's supposed to be with Alex and his girlfriend, Riah,

who's currently on tour for her latest album. As soon as she's home, though, or possibly sooner depending on timing, I'm developing a show for Zully on SHE. The woman is insanely charismatic and has an endless backlist of gripping life stories, plus her beauty routines and makeup designs are fresh and unique. I'm dying to give her a vehicle to demonstrate techniques while entertaining the audience with a mixture of commentary on current events and biographical tales. I'm sure it will be a hit.

Let's be honest—I want the show for myself.

"I'm here for your wedding, duh. And to do your look today, if you're interested."

"Yes. Yes. I'm interested. Do you even have to ask?" I pull away to stare at her. "But what about the tour? Do we need to be done early so you can meet up with Riah somewhere?"

But then Zully steps aside and reveals Riah behind her.

"Jesus fuck," I blurt. "You're here too?"

She waits until we're done hugging to explain. "Your Grandpa Irving rescheduled tonight's concert. Refunded all the tickets and paid the fees to move the show to another night."

"He...what?" The math is too crazy to conceive of in my head. "That had to cost millions."

She nods, knowingly. "Seems he really wants this day to be special for you. Imagine my surprise getting the invite when just two months ago you implied your relationship with Ax was just a 'hate-kink' or the result of 'daddy issues.'"

Incredibly, Riah is the only person who has ever caught me messing around with Ax. It was at Grandpa Irving's birthday party, and I might have been so eager to finally tell someone about our weird ass hookup situation that I developed a little diarrhea of the mouth.

"Yeah, uh. A lot can change in a couple of months. Wasn't that the same day that Hunter proposed to you, but word is now you're dating Alex?" It's evident I'm teasing her back.

"How about I'm not judging if you're not?"

We laugh, and then it's on to the next guest.

It's nonstop like that for the better part of an hour before someone hands me a mimosa. It's another half hour before I snag a dry Belgian waffle to munch on in between girl talk. It's another half hour after that before I realize that there are no men are present.

I've lost track of time altogether when I'm finally able to catch Brystin's attention. "Do you know where Ax is?"

"The men took him offsite for his brunch. A gentlemen's club, if I had to guess."

Then there's someone else who wants to talk to me, and honestly, if my stomach wasn't tied up in a thousand knots, this would be exactly the kind of bridal brunch I'd have, if I were to ever have one for real. Just, I'd arrange a scepter too. Hello, queen for a day? Yes, ma'am.

While I do think I manage to hide the raging storm of nerves inside from all my guests, I'm stupid relieved when it's time to go upstairs and get ready, thinking I'll finally get a second to try to reach Ax.

Unfortunately, I'm not alone.

Lina heads up with me, chattering the entire time about the dress, which has already been delivered to my room, apparently, as well as my shoes and the jewelry I requested.

Brystin and Zully follow close behind, discussing ideas for how to style my bridal look.

As soon as we're in the bedroom, I dive for my phone, and start typing out a text to Ax.

> When the fuck will you be back? Need to talk.

Before I can press send, my cell is swiped from my hand. "You're texting Ax?" Giulia looks horrified. "You can't communicate with him at all! Are you trying to bring bad luck on your union?"

Actually, "Mom", I'm trying to prevent a catastrophe that will be impossible to come back from.

"We're already married," I remind her, as patiently as I can. "And I really have to talk to him."

"It doesn't count until you're married in a church." Hilarious since she was married at Panache. "This is just the nerves getting to you. Let's try the dress on to make sure we have time for any last minute tailoring."

Then she takes my phone with her when she leaves the room to go check on the men's return, promising to be back in a jiffy to see the dress.

I turn to find Brystin and Lina standing with said dress in their hands, ready to pull it over my head as soon as I'm ready.

With cortisol levels in my body rising to an all-time high, my brain is too dazed to argue, and a few minutes later, I'm standing in front of the mirror wearing the most fairytale-like dress I've ever worn. The A-line's blush color compliments my skin like it was made for me. The corset top does its job without being too uncomfortable, so well in fact, that I don't need a bra. The tulle and hand-embroidered flowers are the cherry on top. The little girl version of myself couldn't have imagined anything more glorious.

Zully comes to stand behind me and gasps. "It's stunning."

"Literal perfection," Brystin says.

"Your tits. Are incredible." This from Lina, who rarely has a shortage of words, but is too choked up to manage anything else.

"The tiara even works," Giulia says, magically reappearing. "If you like it, I mean. No offense if you prefer not to wear it." She tugs at my dress as she circles around me, looking for any place that needs adjusting, and finding none.

Like Brystin said, it's perfect. I'm a picture perfect bride.

And all I can think over and over in my head is *it's a lie, it's a lie, it's a lie.*

I don't know that it matters much to any of my family. We're known for scandal and arranged relationships and extravagant celebrations for the minorest of events, but there is absolutely no way I can walk down the aisle, looking like this—feeling like this—without a chance to talk to Ax first.

The panic that's been building since last night finally reaches its boiling point, and there is nothing I can do but explode. "Out! Out. Everybody out!"

While the most important women in my life stare at me wide-eyed, I start clawing at the corset ties. "And I need this off. Can someone help me take this off?"

"Which is it?" Lina whispers to no one in particular. "Do we leave or do we…?"

As always, Giulia takes charge. "Okay, you heard her. The bride needs some time to herself." She nods to Brystin who starts untying the corset. "We're ahead of schedule. This is fine."

I pivot my head toward her, careful not to interrupt Brystin's work because I need this dress off like it's poison ivy. "Fifteen minutes should be good. I just have to catch my breath."

"Totally understandable," Giulia affirms.

"I'll leave the curling iron on so it's all ready to go," Zully says. "Take your time."

As soon as the dress is undone, they start filing out, one by one. Brystin is last, pausing to lay the dress out on the bed before she goes.

I catch her before she shuts the door, realizing I still don't have my phone. "Is Ax back now?"

"He should be. Holt texted a bit ago that they were just pulling up."

I consider asking her for her phone, but of course I don't have Ax's phone number memorized, and I'm not sure that she has it in her contacts.

I'm also not a hundred percent positive that she isn't on board with Giulia with the rules about today, so I decide to play it safe and let her go.

As soon as she's gone, though, I throw a robe on, walk out to the balcony, and carefully climb over the railing and shimmy down the trellis to the private patio below me. It's not Ax's room, but it's the next best thing—my brother's.

Perhaps it's not the safest venture, but there's a hedge of bushes that will catch me if I fall. Still, I hold my breath the whole time, afraid that one of the many guests milling around the backyard will happen to look up, see me, and report me to Giulia as a runaway bride.

Or worse, to Grandpa Irving.

But God must be on my side, despite what I did in his church the night before, and no one seems to notice my escape. Once I'm safely on the patio, I have the option of slipping out the secret way to the garden. Again, I worry about being seen, so I choose the other route, which is through Holt's bedroom.

I start to twist the handle to the door—moron left it unlocked—and change my mind when it occurs to me I could walk in on him doing things I never want to see. In the end, I suck it up and knock.

He answers almost immediately, dressed only in tuxedo pants and suspenders, like a nerd. Big brother that he is, he goes directly to concern mode. Concern first for me—yay—before turning to capitalist mode. "What's wrong? What happened? Are you okay? Did you just shimmy down the lattice? I don't think insurance covers injuries due to poor decisions."

"Good thing I'm fine then, isn't it?" AssHolt doesn't bother inviting me in, that fucker.

Which is fine. I don't need to be inside. "I need Ax. Can you get me Ax?"

"You aren't supposed to see each other—"

"Fuck the fuck off, okay? Scam wedding, remember? I'm telling you, if you want our deal to go through, can you just fucking get him?" Spotting an ashtray on the wall ledge, I think I know why the door was unlocked. Holt was out here recently. "Is that a joint? I need that."

I cross to it the ledge and pick up the spliff.

Only to immediately have it snatched from my hand by Brystin. Damn, she came out of nowhere. Holt, on the other hand, is nowhere to be seen.

"You do not want to be fucked up for today, Adly. Trust me," Brystin says.

Then it must occur to her that I tricked everyone into leaving my room only to sneak a getaway. "Why didn't you just tell me to get Ax for you? I could have snuck him to your room in a way that was much safer."

"I'm fine, okay?" I mean, I'm not fine. "I just need to talk to Ax. Like really seriously need to talk to him, and I didn't know if you were going to give me trouble about it so this was my backup plan."

"Sure. Holt is getting him." She props herself on the wall. "Is there anything you want to talk about in the meantime? I can be a real good listener."

"No, I don't. I'm sorry. I only need Ax." I feel like a broken record, but I'm not budging. Maybe I'm not the most ethical person—I faked a marriage just to get my trust fund, after all—but I do have morals, and I can't do this without some clarification. Not to Ax.

"All right. Okay. No need to be sorry. You're just filling the role of bridezilla. It's cool."

If I wasn't so tense, I'd laugh.

But then it doesn't matter because the door starts to open, and I hear Holt saying, "She's out here," just in time for me to turn my back toward him and duck my head.

"He can't see me!" I might not believe in the bad luck that accompanies breaking the tradition, but just in case.

"Do you want me to stay in here?" Ax's gruff voice is

the first calming thing I've encountered all day. "Are you okay? What do you need?"

"I just need to talk. You can come out, but don't look at me, okay?"

There's a few footsteps, then they pause. "That's weird. I don't know where you are."

"We can stand back to back." Not sure if we're alone or not, I call out to the others. "Brystin? Holt?"

"She's right over here," Brystin says, and she must be guiding Ax because a second later, I feel the solid warmth of his back against mine.

Half of my tension melts from my body right then.

"We'll leave you," she says, her voice traveling as she moves inside. "Holt! Give them some privacy."

I hear the door shut, and finally, we're alone.

"What's up, Addles?" There's an edge of concern in Ax's tone, but it verges on playful, and somehow that takes the tension down a notch. It helps that his breathing is steady and even against my back. My own breaths sync with his, and for the first time all day, my pulse doesn't feel erratic.

Now that I'm finally here with him, it occurs to me that I spent so much of the last twelve plus hours spinning and very little of it thinking about what I wanted to say.

It means I'm going to have to wing it.

"I'm worried..." It's the wrong word. I try again. "I'm *bothered* about the ceremony." As soon as it's out, I know that's not the right explanation either. That he won't understand. So I try to clarify before he does. "I don't think it's right to say those things."

"Okay. Like, which part? The vows?"

"Yes. The vows." I hadn't narrowed it down in my mind, but that's exactly it.

Except I'm not sure if he understands that it isn't my family I'm concerned about, or anybody else that will be there today, so once again, I clarify. "I don't think it's right to say those things *to you*."

"Oh."

It's impossible to read his mind in that single syllable, and instinctively, I start to turn around before catching myself. "I'm not being clear."

His response is right on my heels. "I'm not going to hold you to any promises or—"

He's so far off base that I have to cut him off. "No, it's not..." I force myself to take a beat and formulate my thoughts. "It's confusing, I think."

"Confusing?"

"The thing is..." *The thing is...*

The thing is that I find myself surprised. The sorts of words spoken between a bride and a groom have never held much meaning to me. The vows that have been exchanged between so many of my family members have never been taken seriously by anyone. I learned early in life that the whole marriage is a sacrament thing is a sham. It's why I've never subscribed to the tradition.

But with Ax, I'm scared.

Because pledging a life of honor, fidelity, and devotion to Ax doesn't feel so bananas. Not right now, necessarily, not declared for the first time in front of a church full of people, but alone and in the future, yeah. I can see it. Possibly the near future.

But saying words too early that I might very well mean

someday—someday soon, even—seems like a surefire way to ruin the best thing I never knew I could want, let alone have.

And that terrifies the shit out of me.

Sebastians aren't supposed to be scared.

I lean more weight against Ax and sigh. "Have you ever been stupid afraid of something? Like you know there isn't any reason to be scared. The logic isn't there. It's ridiculous. Embarrassing. It's not like you're facing a lion or a bear. You'll land on your feet no matter what happens, and yet..."

I trail off, pretty sure I've never been more pathetic.

"...Yet the fear is so big, you're paralyzed," Ax says, finishing the thought for me. "Yeah. I've been that scared."

I let out a legit laugh. "Funny."

"Why funny?" The way his back moves against mine suggests he started to turn around and stopped himself. "You think I don't spook?"

"No, I don't. Not about stupid shit. Your entire persona is *tough guy.*"

"Like your entire persona isn't *untouchable.*"

Well, that's true.

His hand brushes against my hand. Accidentally, I think at first, until after making contact, he laces his fingers through mine. I'm already holding the other hand out for him to find when he goes searching for it so we're gripping each other on both sides now.

"Want to hear about stupid scared? I'll tell you about stupid scared." The next time he speaks, his voice is raw. "It's been eighteen years since my mother died. She died in childbirth—did you know that? Did you know the baby lived? Bianca is her name."

I suck in an astonished breath. I'd known his mother had been pregnant, but the story had been that both had passed away from complications.

Ax doesn't wait for more of a response. "Eighteen years later, my sister is finally old enough to decide for herself if she wants anything to do with my side of the family. If her father had his wish, she wouldn't even know I exist, but apparently she did some digging on her own. She reached out earlier this year on her birthday with an email to the office. Then again on the date of my mother's birthday. She sent cards to every address she could find for me for her high school graduation." So that was the girl in the notice I found when he was moving in. "And I've been too chicken-shit to answer a single one."

"Ax, no!" It's not just an admonishment, though I'm sure it comes out like that. More though, I'm gutted for him. Considering how much he loved his mother, I can only imagine how devastating it was for him to be cut off from the last living part of her.

Then to be unable to connect to her now—even if the reason is just his own fear…

It's a real good thing that he's anchoring me on both sides, because I'm desperate to turn around and take him into my arms.

"Stupid right?"

"No! Not stupid," I say, rushing to comfort him. "It's natural to be scared."

Then I remember that I hate platitudes.

"Well. I mean, it *is* natural to be scared. Sometimes that

fear even protects you from danger, but if it's preventing you from happiness, then it's kind of stupid if you let it keep you paralyzed. It's okay for a while. But eventually, you have to be scared and push through anyway."

In the classic trope where the character figures out her shit for herself, I realize that I need to take my own advice and push through. It doesn't mean I've changed my mind about today's ceremony, because it is still confusing to commit myself to him in public before ever discussing a real relationship, but I'm suddenly very aware that I have to decide to let Ax in. Scary as it is, terrified as I am, I can't just keep hoping it goes away or try to dance around the fear by pretending I'm someone else every time I'm with him. After this long with him, the fear would have gone away already if it was going to do that on its own.

It's not going away. I'm still scared.

And I have to push through it and love him anyway.

"Easier said than done," Ax says, echoing the thought going through my mind at the moment. It takes me a second to remember he's still talking about his sister.

His *secret* sister.

"Ax, meeting a new sibling is a big fucking deal. There's nothing easy about it."

"I could say the same thing to you about today. Your grandfather has put a lot of pressure on you for this to go perfectly."

It's obvious he still doesn't understand where my head is—or my heart—and he won't until I can truly tell him, but my doubts that this might not be the best moment are validated when there's a quick knock on the patio door followed by the sound of it opening.

"I'm not trying to be an ass, but I thought you should know that Giulia has discovered you're both not where you're supposed to be, and I'm not sure how long Brystin can keep her from freaking out about it." It's obvious from Holt's tone that Giulia is already freaking out.

Or maybe it's just obvious because I know my stepmother well enough by now.

"Got it," Ax says. "Two more minutes. That's all I need."

"All righty." Holt sounds like he'd rather we just step into line and go to our places right the fuck now, but luckily those two words are followed by the sound of the door closing again.

As for myself, I'm not sure that my issues can be solved in two minutes, but that doesn't stop Ax from trying. "How about we cut the scripted vows?"

"First of all, don't think we aren't going back to your sister at some point in the future."

With that out of the way, I consider his suggestion. It would make it easier to avoid saying things I'm not ready to say, but it's not like we can skip that part of the ceremony altogether. "We'd have to replace them with our own vows, and that's almost as bad."

"Right, but the vows are really between us, right? It's not for anyone else to understand, so what if it's not us standing up in front of everyone today? What if we're playing someone else?"

"Like roleplay?" I know right away this is the answer, even without the details worked out. This is familiar territory. We've said plenty of things to each other that we don't necessarily mean from behind the mask of another character. "Who would we be playing?"

He thinks for a few seconds. "That couple from your book—the one with the guy who wanted to give the girl a nightclub and said she was capable of more and all that. We could pretend to be them."

I nod, even though he can't see me. "We could say anything at all, and no one would know it's not real." Including, Ax.

"Right. No lies. No confusion. Just playacting."

Once again tempted to turn around and hug him, I squeeze both of his hands instead. "That's it. That's what we'll do. We'll roleplay."

Then later, when it's just the two of us, the mask comes down and you be you with him, Adly.

Immediately, I hear the door opening again. "I'll tell Giulia to have the priest scrap the vows," Holt says, because the motherfucker was listening at the door. "Come on, guys. I'm sweating, and it's not even my wedding."

"We good?" Ax says.

"We're good."

He unlaces his hands from mine. My entire body misses his heat the minute he steps away, but for the first time since this wedding was thrust upon us, I'm actually excited to meet him at the altar.

Behind me, I hear his feet cross to the patio door and then pause. "Adly, what happened with those two anyway? He gave her the nightclub...what does she do?"

A whole bunch of things, because that scene came in book two of a five-book series, but I try to sum it up as succinctly as I can under a time crunch. "She lives up to her potential."

Under my breath, I vow that I will too.

CHAPTER
TWENTY-THREE
ADLY

Pretending I'm someone else lets me disassociate, and the rest of the afternoon passes in a blur.

I come into myself now and then. It's like whiplash, snapping into the present all of a sudden, and finding myself in a moment that requires my full attentiveness before detaching once again.

The first time it happens, I'm all dressed and made up and ready to go, when Lina pulls me aside to give me a gift.

"The tiara is something borrowed. The dress is something new. The rings will be something old. You needed something blue, and I didn't have a lot of time, so I hope this isn't the most cheesy thing you've ever owned. I know it doesn't go with the dress, so I made it big enough to wear it on your ankle."

She hands over a handmade friendship bracelet strung with tiny pearls and pale blue beads.

"It's beautiful," I manage. The gesture is moving, but it's

the words spelled out with the letter beads that cause the lump in my throat. *Happily Ever After.*

Fortunately, I distance myself from the moment again before I think too hard about the possibilities of a true happily ever after for me, if happily ever after exists at all.

My perfect makeup job is once again threatened when Brystin gifts me a pair of oversized earrings that match the embroidery on my dress. "I saw them at Mirabelle's yesterday so I called her last night, and Lina picked them up when she picked up the dress."

Before I can find my voice to respond, Giulia adds the cherry to the emotional overload sundae when she passes over a jewelry box. "I've been holding onto it for the right time, and wouldn't you know it ties the tiara to the dress."

Of course I'm still wearing the tiara. Someone gives me a crown, I'm going to wear the fuck out of it until it has to be returned.

And she's right—the two-tone silver and rose gold necklace goes perfectly. It's elegant and understated in a good way, but very wedding appropriate with the two hearts linked together, as if they represent me and Ax.

The message with the necklace depicts the true meaning. *To my bonus daughter: I may not have given you the gift of life, but life has given me the gift of you. I am blessed and honored to have you in my world.*

"Don't cry or you'll mess up the incredible artistry I have worked on your face," Zully warns. "Since I'm about to become a household name and all, you really should try to make this look last until pictures, at least."

I disengage again then, losing another block of time to

the logistics of loading everything into the car and traveling to the church.

The next time I'm aware of myself is when we're lining up on the steps outside the church, preparing to walk down the aisle. My brothers look sharp in their suits, and Lina's ruffled, all-white tulle dress is an unexpected juxtaposition to my blush gown. Giulia's champagne mother–of-the-bride mermaid dress is the definition of sophisticated.

Even my father looks debonair in his tux with a silver-and-black vest and tie. The modern and fresh style age him down a dozen years, and I can almost imagine what a woman like Giulia sees in him.

It's awkward, though. Standing at his side when the whole wedding is happening under false pretenses, but I surprisingly don't have much guilt where he's concerned. He's the reason I had to do this in the first place, because he can't recognize the value of a woman in the corporate world. Because he still thinks of me as less capable than my brothers. Frankly, I think he only allowed me to run HR because I'm his daughter, and he doesn't think it's a vital role, not because he thinks I'm any good at it.

I'm doing my best to stay in character and avoid resentment, despite the constant clicks from the photographer trying to capture candid shots, when Dad turns to face me. "You chose a good man, Adly Jade. For whatever reason you chose him. I didn't know if there were any up to the task, but I think Ax Morgan was a very wise choice."

With no proof of the fact, I'm certain my father thinks I married for convenience. It's accurate, but also frustrating, since he married for love both times, a rarity compared to his brothers, and I'm irritated that he doesn't wish that for me, as weird of an irritation as that might be.

But shouldn't he be asking me how I feel? Shouldn't he be saying things like, *as long as you're happy*, or *if he breaks your heart I'll kill him*?

Instead, it's *I didn't think anyone could take your shit, but the fool you picked seems stupid enough to commit.*

At least, that's what I hear, and I automatically snap back. "Why? Because now you don't have to worry about who's going to take care of me? Looks like you're finally off the hook."

He frowns at me, probably not expecting such a cross response. "Don't be ridiculous. I've never worried about who's going to take care of you. You're more equipped to take care of yourself than either of your brothers."

"If I'm so much better equipped, shouldn't that apply to the office? Why am I not good enough for promotion?"

His lips purse together. "I never said you weren't good enough. I said you didn't belong there."

"Because I'm a woman?"

"Because you're my daughter, and I know what challenges the other roles at SNC will bring, especially to a woman. I don't want you to have a life that forces you to split your attention like your mother did."

I blow the tension from my lungs. "I'm not Mom," I tell him. "And treating a woman differently, even by putting them on a pedestal, is still a form of inequality. I deserve to make those choices for myself."

He seems about to argue, but he shuts his mouth and takes a beat before opening it again. "I guess that's a decision for you and your husband now. And as I said, I think you chose a good one. It's a compliment, Adly."

There's no use arguing. The man is set in his ways, and if he thinks it's a compliment, I can either be in knots about it all the time, cut him off entirely, or recognize his outdated values as his love language.

I'm not cutting off my family, and resenting him all the time does more harm to me than him. Besides, soon enough, he won't be my boss, and he won't hold so much power over me anymore.

So I say, "I love you too, Dad," and thread my arm through his since it's our turn to walk down the aisle.

The doors open for us, and I stand up tall and resume playing my character. It's the best trick, and I'm fully detached, once again unaware of my surroundings on a physical level. It's almost like I'm outside of myself observing, watching the activity take place without feeling connected to it.

Until I'm halfway down the aisle and make the mistake of glancing toward Ax. He's focused on me with an intensity that I've never seen. His expression is one of adoration and respect. He locks his gaze on mine with such ferocity, that my heart starts to kick harder in my chest and my skin feels lit up from the inside.

He anchors me in my body with that gaze.

I'm unable to look away. Unable to pretend myself out of being present, but also unable to be pulled away from his tether by anyone else. I know Hunter's standing beside Ax in theory, but I'm no longer aware of him. Giulia's likely already got a handkerchief dabbing at her eyes, and

Grandpa Irving's in the front row, probably beaming like he's a king.

I don't see any of that.

There's only us—me and Ax, and our game that feels more real than any game we've ever played, and yet for once, I'm not freaked out or overthinking. I'm just here with him.

I'm still playing a character, too.

At least, I think I am.

When it's time for the vows, and I face him, I center myself by thinking of my book, and the couple that we acted out that night at the bookstore. But their story of falling for the worst person possible morphs into my own experience, and I'm not sure who's talking when the words come out of my mouth.

"You surprised me, Ax. You weren't supposed to be 'the one.' You weren't supposed to be 'for me.' There were a hundred good reasons to stay away from you, not the least of which, your terrible taste in…well, everything but clothing. Anyone who knocks your style has no fashion sense."

Vaguely, I'm aware of the chuckle from the crowd, but I'm so tightly wrapped in our bubble that it feels far away and irrelevant like the laugh track on an old comedy.

They disappear into the distance as I let myself/my character get carried away. "I don't know what forever looks like. I can't think in terms that vague. A five-year plan is about as far into the future as I can conceive, but for the first time, when I see myself five years out, I'm not alone.

"That might not sound like a real romantic declaration, but the truth is, that's a huge upheaval to the life I planned for myself. Wrecking ball sort of upheaval, and so fucking unexpected." There's another faraway chuckle, this time mingled with some old lady gasps. "You surprised me, Ax Morgan. You turned me upside down and inside out, and the fact that I'm not mad at it, might be the biggest surprise of all. I hope that you decide to keep playing with me for a very long time."

Thank Giulia for sneaking a handkerchief into my pocket—and thank the designer of my dress for giving me pockets to sneak handkerchiefs into—because somehow I manage to produce tears.

Stupid, really, considering how short and unexciting my vows were. It should be a relief that they're done, and it is, but I'm almost more wound up when I realize it's Ax's turn to speak. For all the hours I fretted over what was appropriate to say to him, I forgot that he would recite something to me in turn.

He's a natural at improv, though. The pride on his face looks genuine. The emotion in his eyes seems real-ass real.

When he speaks, it's as if he's as disconnected from everyone else as I was, his words seemingly meant only for me.

"Funny how you're looking forward. When I think of us, I always start in the past. You've been a pain in the ass since you first showed up in my life. Always sassing and causing trouble before stripping off all your clothes so you could run around the yard. I'm not sure there's a lot of difference between your toddler days and last week, but uh…"

He waits to let the crowd react or to gather his thoughts or to swallow past the lump that seems to be lodged in his throat the next time he speaks.

"I never thought someone could match my level of sarcasm and still make me laugh. I never thought someone with so many damn walls could make me want to put in the effort to break through. You're still a pain in my ass. But you challenge me in ways I never knew I needed, Addles. I never cared about being more than I am, but you make me want to do more with my life, just so that I can share it with you. No one can tell you that you don't live up to your potential. You are the reason other people live up to theirs."

He takes my hands in his, and I wonder if he can tell how much I'm trembling. "I'm the luckiest human to know you, Adly Jade Sebastian Morgan. No matter what happens between us in the future, it will always be the greatest honor of my life to get to love you."

Love, he says. Bravely. Without hesitation.

I know he's acting.

But I wasn't brave enough to pretend love. Almost nothing he's said fits the story we were supposed to be acting out, either, not like he knew much about the plot in the first place. More confusing, he said several things that seemed to fit us specifically.

The greatest honor of my life to get to love you.

I'm a wreck through the rest of the ceremony.

I somehow remember Father John's advice at the rehearsal about exchanging rings. *Let him put it on to the knuckle, then you push it down the rest of the way yourself.* Apparently, putting a ring on someone else's hand can be awkward in front of everyone, and this tip helps, but it's also supposed to symbolize giving someone their life and your choice to accept it.

When I push his mother's wedding band to snuggle

against my pink sapphire—they actually fit surprisingly well together—I accept his life.

Then I put his father's wedding band on Ax's finger, push it to the knuckle, and when he takes it from me to move it the rest of the way down, I swear he's accepting my life in return.

And when Father John finally says, "You may now kiss the bride," Ax's lips meet mine, and the earth shatters beneath my feet, and I'm completely swept away.

It's like one of my favorite romantic storylines. Bigger even, and more trite. The universe seems to pause, holding its breath before erupting into a symphony of colors and sensations. Invisible birds sing. My heart feels too big for my chest. The new ring on my finger feels tattooed in place, and the *Happily Ever After* around my ankle doesn't feel so much like a lie.

FOR ALL THE activity leading up to the ceremony, it's nothing compared to the chaos of after.

There's more than an hour of photos taken. First in various arrangements with the family, and then everyone heads back to Adeline while the photographer positions me and Ax in every romantic pose possible.

After the vows and the uncertainty of whether there was honesty in them or not, I should be more confused than ever. Strangely, the whole thing just made me more committed to opening up to Ax. It's like the universe took the opportunity to give me a glimpse at a possibility and said, *Look at how this man could love you,* and it's with real, big, achingly good love.

Now I'm more scared that I might miss out on that real, big, achingly good love than I am convinced that it can't possibly exist. Knowing that I'll get a chance to tell Ax how I feel soon—when we're truly alone tonight, without family or friends or photographers—makes it easier to treat our photo session like another scene. We laugh and tease, and I get through it without feeling awkward or too intimate.

Then we're driven back to Adeline, where we're immediately ushered to the backyard. Everyone stands when we enter, and when my father introduces us as Mr. and Mrs. Morgan, our guests break out in applause, and my stomach flips.

Dad's supposed to hand the mic over to my cousin Scott, who got roped into being emcee, but he likes attention as much as any other male Sebastian. "I'm going to take this opportunity to exercise my privilege as acting CEO of Sebastian News Corp. I'm sure these kids are going to kill me for doing this in public, but I'm extraordinarily fortunate to have the power to give this gift to my oldest daughter and her new husband."

"Sweet he considers Lina his own, too," Ax whispers. His hand is laced in mine, and I'm not sure I ever want to let it go.

"He's going to follow it up with making this incredibly awkward somehow, in true Sebastian style. I apologize in advance."

Sure enough, Dad goes on to prove my point. "We aren't slated to announce this to the world until Tuesday, but I met with the board this morning, and they've agreed this is a splendid time to divulge that we've chosen someone to take the CEO position so that Arthur and I can finally retire— maybe this is a gift more for us than for Adly."

He waits for the crowd to laugh, and my stomach suddenly feels like it's lodged in my throat.

Is this really happening? Could he be offering me what I think he's offering?

"Ladies and Gentlemen, please congratulate our new CEO-elect of Sebastian News Corporation—Axel DiAngelo Morgan."

And for the second time in one day, the earth shatters.

CHAPTER
TWENTY-FOUR
AX

t's already been a day.

Not the best time to insert a joke to the level of magnitude of the one Samuel's trying to land, but as the applause breaks out, and I look around the room at reactions, I start to think this might not be a joke.

My father, for one. He's too smug for this to have been a surprise.

Hunter's father, Reynard, doesn't look surprised either. His jaw is set in a way that suggests he fought this decision tooth and nail, but the other board members are all clapping enthusiastically.

Except for Hunter, who I know for a fact wasn't at any emergency meeting this morning because he was with me and a bunch of the other guys at the cigar club. His expression is stone cold sober, but I've known him long enough to recognize the rapid lift and fall of his chest from trying to control his breathing.

Fuck. This better be a joke.

I turn to ask Adly but she's gone so pale that I'm already making plans how to get out of this if it's not a joke. "He's kidding, right?" I ask Giulia instead.

"I did try to get him to hold off on announcing, but he was so excited. Congratulations!" She hugs me then moves over to hug Adly.

In other words, not a fucking joke.

Alex takes Giulia's place in front of me. "Did you know about this?"

"Fuck no."

"Hunter's going to go ballistic."

I look over at Hunter again. When we make eye contact, I shrug, hoping he understands I had nothing to do with this.

He shakes his head, not necessarily like he's pissed at *me*, but definitely pissed.

Then with a flourish of his jacket, he takes off, crossing the lawn and heading toward the house. He didn't stay the night at Adeline, and wasn't planning to tonight either, having chosen a nearby hotel instead of enduring family hostilities. My bet is he's long gone before I have time to talk with him.

For the best. If I have everything straightened out by the time I see him, he'll be a much easier beast to soothe.

Meanwhile...Adly.

As soon as Giulia pulls away from her stepdaughter, I reach for Adly's hand, but she pulls away before I can clasp on. "I just need a minute in the restroom."

Her smile is sharp but it might as well be a knife for how it cuts into me.

Not only does it rip me to shreds, but the whole surreal fairytale vibe of the day is destroyed along with it. It's funny, because I hadn't bought into this wedding thing holding any meaning until I was living through it. I considered it a bunch of ceremony rigamarole bullshit. Entwine your life enough with the Sebastians, and you get a lot of that. I'm used to the farce of it all.

But then I was standing at the front of that church—not even pretending I was someone else, because that's what Adly needed to get through today, not me—and then the doors opened, and she walked in looking like a fairy queen, and all I could think was, *Fuck, I'm a goner.*

I was the realest I've ever been, standing in front of that altar with her.

She makes me want things I've never dreamed I wanted. The white house and the picket fence—metaphorically, because I'm a city guy through and through. The whole nine yards, and then some.

When we walked down that aisle together afterward, I vowed to myself that I would do everything in my power to make Adly mine for keeps.

Now that feels like days ago instead of mere hours, and I stare after her as she crosses the room, scared shitless that she's gone back to hiding in her near impenetrable fortress.

Another family member waiting to congratulate me pulls my attention away from Adly. I endure several handshakes and hugs before a hard clap lands on my back, and I turn to find Holt.

"Did you fuck this up?" he asks quietly. His tone is a contrast to his jovial expression, likely a show for any onlookers.

"I didn't do this," I insist. "Believe me."

I have the distinct impression he *doesn't* believe me. "You know, I thought it was odd when she said you weren't getting anything from this arrangement. Now this? Seems like a real convenient coincidence, doesn't it?"

Thankfully, Brystin steps in as the voice of reason. "Come on, Holt. You've said a million times that Ax could be a real contender for the position."

"No, he's right," I interject. "I think my new father-in-law saw an opportunity to use today to sway family politics to his side, but I swear on my mother's grave that I didn't ask to be part of this. I'll straighten it out."

He seems torn about how to respond. "Goddammit, Ax." He lets out a frustrated sigh. "I can't believe I'm saying this, but you actually do deserve the position a hell of a lot more than Hunter. Just…"

"Adly," I finish. "I know. I'll fix it."

"I'm not sure she'll even be that upset once she wraps her head around it." I have a feeling Holt's projecting rather than offering honest insight about his sister.

"Let me go check on her," Brystin says, patting my arm before she takes off toward the bathrooms.

Giulia makes an announcement that dinner will be served soon, a cue for everyone to start making their way to the tables. My father seems as though he's coming to find me, but if I'm going to snag Samuel for a conversation, it better be now, before the reception gets really underway.

I excuse myself from Holt and his badass big brother thing he's doing and jog over to Samuel, who is already on his way to the head table. "Hey. Can we talk for a second?"

"Meet you at our seats," he tells Giulia, then joins me,

walking a short distance from the garden setup so that we can talk in private. "We can go over logistics tomorrow. This doesn't have to distract from the evening."

As if I'm so excited about this announcement that I can't wait to dive into the details.

"No offense, Sam—"

"Dad," he corrects.

"Calling you a different name isn't going to change what I have to say." I'm terse, more terse than I should be with the man who is not only my father-in-law but also still my boss. "Look, this was a real swell gesture on your part, but absolutely unnecessary. I do not need to get on the nepotism train. I've done well enough on my own, thank you very much."

After a beat, I add, "Sir," because the respect-your-superiors code has been strongly groomed into me.

"A noble attitude. Not quite sure how it works in our family, unfortunately."

"I didn't marry Adly's family," I remind him. "I married her."

He chuckles, as though there's no difference in the two. "Anyway, I think you'll be happy to know that this isn't what you're claiming. Your name has been on the short list for quite a long time. It was only a couple of holdouts that did finally sway to your side because you've married in, but trust me when I say that if this was truly a nepotism situation, it would have been someone else in your place. You earned this on merit."

I wait through his whole speech, ready to attack, only to find by the end that the fight has died down a smidge. "On a short list? I didn't even put my name forward."

"That was your father's doing, I believe. It's been a year ago now, I can't remember exactly. I'm surprised he didn't tell you. Not so surprising that Hunter didn't let you know."

I ignore his dig at my best friend, though it doesn't go uncatalogued.

As for my father, of course he did. For all the times he's tried to get me to go after the CEO position, I should have guessed he was pitching me behind my back.

What really takes me aback from this conversation with Samuel, though, is that other people besides my father think that I deserve this job. Have thought that I've deserved it for some time. "The board honestly wants me to be CEO?"

Samuel's lip turns down, as though he's turned off by my insecurity, but fuck him, I'm human. "Do you think we'd put SNC in the hands of someone that we don't think is capable? This is our family legacy, Ax. Sure we want our name filling the top spots, but not at the cost of bad business."

"Right, right. I didn't mean any offense." I'm spinning so hard that it's difficult to hold on to the thread. "But what about Adly? I know your opinion on where a woman belongs, but how about the rest of the board members? Tell me she was on the short list too."

His eye twitches. "She has been discussed thoroughly. Not that that's public knowledge. I shouldn't even be sharing this with you now." And yet he expected my father and Hunter to break the rules. "Frankly, while no one believes the company is ready for a woman CEO, the biggest fault against her is her age. Holt was the youngest person ever offered the job, and you saw how that turned out. I think everyone would prefer you had another five years to your belt as well, but thirty-nine is better than thirty-three.

"And you have the resume. Viewing numbers have gone up since you became program director. You've widened the demography and expanded our audience. Your most recent ideas, in particular, have been strongly embraced by the board. There is no doubt in my mind that you are the right person for this job, but certainly take a few days to think about it."

Ah, shit.

I'm a sucker for Samuel Sebastian's praise. If I'd realized that earlier in my career, I might have worked harder to earn it. Unfortunately, it's only been the last few weeks that I discovered that I was even on his radar. It's strange how his appreciation can feel like taking a line of cocaine. My heart is hammering in my chest, my mouth feels dry, my skin hot, and I'm certain I could carry the world if he asked me to.

It's no wonder his kids have always seemed so desperate to earn it.

"I'll have a formal offer emailed to you with all the details," he tells me, in that tone that says it's time to wrap up. "Meanwhile, think about it. I'm sure you'll come around."

"Oh, he'll come around," my father says, inviting himself into our sidebar. "He has a wife to support now. He's not going to ruin her family name with his complacency."

If there were ever a time I wanted to punch a man...

But my father is beaming at me like he's proud to call me his son, and that's not the usual way he looks at me. His approval might be just as addictive as Samuel's.

Dad also isn't wrong in bringing up Adly. She's the only person I should be discussing this with. No one else matters if it ends up that I lose her.

WHEN ADLY FINALLY RETURNS FROM the bathroom, there's color in her face again. It's possible there's evidence of tear tracks on her cheeks, but she cried during the ceremony too, and I wasn't looking that hard before the CEO announcement.

This time when I reach for her hand, she lets me take it, but before I can offer to sneak away to talk, she says, "They're waiting for us to be seated to start serving."

Once again, our time is dictated by the wedding agenda. As I let her lead me to our table, I force myself to put worry aside and enjoy the night.

It's more difficult than it sounds.

All through our meal, I find myself studying her, trying to figure out what she's thinking or feeling. I tear apart each laugh, looking for signs that it was forced. I listen for subtext in every comment. When I rest my knee against hers under the table, I can't decide if she jerks away because she's angry, surprised, or just reaching for the bread bowl. When her leg returns to press against mine, I'm half convinced she thinks I'm the table leg.

After dinner, there's a million and a half toasts. She holds my hand on the table where everyone can see it, and maybe it's for show, but she squeezes it every now and again, and I start to feel hopeful. Like maybe everything isn't ruined, and there's a chance she'll understand, if only we could just have a conversation.

It's a goddamn year before we get the opportunity.

Unfortunately, it's not the talk I would have preferred to be having during our first dance, but as soon as I lead her out to the floor, the pianist still playing the arpeggio introduction of "The Luckiest," Adly brings it up. "So. CEO."

"Had no idea." I tug her into my arms. "Swear to motherfucking God, I'm as surprised as anyone."

"Mm hm." I'm not sure if she's agreeing or if she's trying to convince herself. "I didn't know you were going after it."

"I didn't, Adly. Never even interviewed. The only time I talked to your father about it, I was trying to get him to give the job to you." It's a shameless attempt to earn her good side, but I'm desperate here.

"You did that?" She swallows. "That's awfully... What about Hunter? You've always said you supported him in the role."

"I do. I did." I'm not explaining myself well. "I still do. And then, I don't know, I didn't realize how overlooked you were until I saw the crazy shit you were willing to do to get away from SNC."

"Crazy shit like marry you, you mean?"

"Yeah, crazy dumb shit."

"Seriously crazy dumb shit." She presses her lips together before opening them again to speak. "I don't want the job, Ax."

She sounds sincere, but there's sadness in her tone, so

I'm not sure. "You can tell me the truth, Addles. It's just us. You can be angry. I get it."

She shakes her head. "I really, truly don't want the job. It's too big. I want something I can have more of a role in shaping. SNC is not my dream." Her lip trembles. "I just wanted my father to want me for it."

I pull her closer, wrapping my arms tight around her and resting my chin against her head, my mouth at her ear. "Oh, baby, I'm sorry."

She snuggles her face into my neck and inhales, breathing me in. If anyone had ever told me that true happiness was a woman searching for my scent to calm her down, I would have fucking laughed my ass off.

Not any woman, though. This woman.

"Anything you want, Addles, and I'll do it. You want me to give your father a piece of my mind, I'll do. Right here, right now. In front of everyone. You want to never see him again, I'll take you as far as you need to go to make it possible. You want me to get him taken out, I'll hire a guy to do it. Not afraid of guns or anything. Just prefer to not have jail time."

Her laugh against my skin sends electricity straight to my balls.

She pulls her head back to look at me. "I want you to take the job."

I screw my face up at the idea. "Eh."

It's one thing to be grateful for the offer. It's another thing to take it. It's got bad idea written all over it. Even if Adly really didn't end up hating me for it, Hunter would, and no friendship is worth a job.

It's as if she knows exactly what I'm thinking. "If he's really a good friend, he'll be happy for you."

"Yeah, I'm not holding my breath for that." I run my thumb along the back of her corseted gown, and fleetingly wonder how hard it was to get it on. More importantly, how hard it will be to get it off.

"Then let me ask you this—do you want it?" she asks.

It takes me a second to remember that we weren't talking about getting naked.

Then another few seconds to really think about what she's asking. Do I want the job of CEO at SNC?

I want to say no.

I want there not to be any part of me that's curious.

I want to be whispering sweet things into her ears, peppering her with the compliments that she deserves, and charming her into imagining a future with me, not confessing that I could be willing to ruin my best friend's dream if I let myself consider it long enough.

I pull her close to me again. "I meant it when I said you make me want things I didn't know I wanted. I didn't ever know CEO was an option. Now that it is...?"

My voice trails off. I'm ready to say hard things out loud, but not that one.

She turns her face into me again, lets her lips brush against my neck. "Who knows? Maybe we could even work out an alliance between us. SNC and SHE as partners."

My stomach drops with the weight of an anvil.

Samuel said my most recent ideas were what swayed them to me. It's only when she mentions SHE that I remember the only idea I've ever really shared with anyone on the board besides Hunter was the one where SNC buys out the smaller network.

I'm actually buoyed by the possibility that I might have the power to stop that from happening if I take the CEO position, but I have to tell Adly. She needs to know, and she needs to hear it from me.

This time, it's me who pulls back to face her. "Hey, I need to tell you something."

But my fucking timing is terrible, because as soon as the words are out, the music ends. Any hope that I could steal another turn around the dance floor with my bride is killed when I see Samuel headed our way for his father/daughter dance.

"I need to talk to you, too," Adly says, squeezing me tight before letting me go. "Later. When it's just us."

I cling onto the promise of *just us* for the rest of the night.

CHAPTER
TWENTY-FIVE
ADLY

olt doesn't catch me alone until after the bouquet and garter are tossed. "You okay?"

I throw back the rest of my champagne and consider pretending not to know what he's talking about. There are so many things I could not be okay with at the moment, which is odd to think about because I actually feel pretty good.

It doesn't hurt that I've eaten my weight in wedding cake.

But it's Ax and the hungry way he's gazing at me from across the yard that has me feeling the most settled. Or rather, unsettled in a deliciously agonizing way.

I'm certain Holt doesn't want to hear that my libido has distracted me from Dad's "wedding gift," and I'm not ready to explain my other feelings where Ax is concerned.

The sting isn't about Ax, anyway. It's about our father, and his narrow-minded values.

"He means well," I say, knowing Holt will understand who the *he* is. "I'm sure he thinks this is the best way to show he loves me. While also scoring a win because he gets to pull the rug out from under Hunter, so narcissistic? Yes. But I'm not sure he knows any other way to be."

Holt tilts his head and scrunches up his features. "You don't have to be understanding about it, you know. It's okay to feel bad."

I do feel bad. It's just not a new feeling. It's the way my father has always made me feel, and I've matured enough to know not to expect anything different from him.

If he's never going to change, it has to be me that does.

"I'd rather feel smug." I dig out the strawberry from the bottom of my champagne flute and stick it in my mouth. "He can have the kind of leader he wants at his company. I can be the kind of leader I want to be at mine."

Brows furrowed with judgment, he swipes a napkin from a nearby table to dab at the strawberry juice running down my chin. "It's like you were raised in the wild."

With half-chewed berry sitting on top of it, I stick my tongue out at him.

"Scratch that," he says. "It's like you were raised by Steele."

I try to swallow and laugh at the same time and almost choke. My eyes water and someone claps my back as I cough. I peek over my shoulder to see Brystin.

"Do you need water?" she asks. "Holt, get her water."

I shake my head, the tickle in my throat dissipating. "I'm good." Not wanting to spend any more time talking about the CEO position at SNC, I offer a joke explanation for my coughing fit. "I just remembered that Grandpa caught the garter and lost it all over again."

Caught is perhaps not the best word. He wasn't even in the lineup. My husband must have a wicked throw, because his toss whizzed past the guys and landed in Grandpa's lap.

My husband.

My stomach flips at the phrase.

"Ax should consider a backup career in major league baseball." Holt seems to realize we're back on the topic I'd tried to steer away from and quickly redirects. "Sorry it wasn't me, baby," he says to Brystin, putting an arm around his fiancée's waist.

"I already have the ring. I'm good." She snuggles closer to him, but directs her attention to me. "Let me know when you want to do the send-off. We're ready when you are."

"You mean, our prison term is finally over?" I don't bother asking what the send-off entails. If it's like everything else this weekend, it's more than I would ever put together for myself, a little over the top, and also perfect. I've already been assured we aren't being sent on a honeymoon, thankfully. There's too much happening this week with our bid now submitted for SHE and Ax's promotion.

What's more interesting about her pronouncement is what comes next, when Ax and I are really alone for the first time all day.

I swivel my head in his direction and find him already staring. His gaze is intense. Like he's undressing me with his eyes.

The heat in my face spreads down over my collarbone.

I turn back to Brystin, and find Zully has joined us.

"Yeah, I think they're ready, Brys." She winks at me like she's in the know.

The woman is too good at reading a situation. Scary good.

"In that case," Brystin says, "I should let you know that all of your things and Ax's things have been moved to the guest house. Grandpa cleared out so the two of you can have some 'privacy.'"

Holt covers his laugh with a fist. "Sorry, sis. There's a murphy bed in the second room, at least."

I bite my lip about the sleeping conditions. Apparently, my brother hasn't figured out that's not an issue for me and Ax, and I'm not about to be the one to tell him.

Zully doesn't have the same restraint. "You do realize they're fucking, right?"

"Ha ha. Hilarious." Then Holt must notice that I'm doing everything in my power not to look at him. "Wait. AJ, is she serious? No. No. Ax is He Who Can't Be Named?" He leans toward the others to explain. "She was doing some kinky sexting shit with someone she had saved in her contacts as that."

Oh my God, I want to die.

And is there a reason he can't get the stupid contact name right?

"I'm not even going to ask how you know who your sister was kinky sexting with," Zully says. "But Brystin, tell me all the details when you ask him later."

"I do not have Ax saved in my contacts as He Who *Shall Not* Be Named." But I'm feeling saucy and secure, like this thing with Ax is going to last, so I wait a beat and add,

"Anymore." Brystin and Holt gasp in unison. "He's listed as Axhole now."

"Axhole. I like it," Zully says.

"Me too." Though I think it might be time to change it to something more fitting. Like *My Axhole*.

Right now, with my embarrassment out of the way, I'm stuck on something else Brystin said. "Grandpa cleared out the guest house? Where's he sleeping?" The man notoriously requires a lot of personal space, and now that I look around, I don't see him anywhere.

"He's flying back to the city tonight," Brystin says. "Elias was wheeling him inside a few minutes ago."

After excusing myself with a string of curse words, I gather my dress in my hands and run up to the house. I catch them in the foyer, preparing to leave.

"We almost had a clean getaway," Grandpa tells Elias when he sees me. He's a fan of slipping away without any to-do.

"After putting me through all this attention, you don't get to pull an Irish goodbye."

"Think you'd know by now that the person with the checkbook gets to do any damn thing they like." Despite his orneriness, he stands and pulls me into a hug. "If I were five years younger, I would have demanded a dance with you."

"You wouldn't have had to demand," I say, my mouth at his ear.

He draws back. "Not so sure about that. It's like pulling teeth to get you to show your heart."

It's astounding how much better he understands me than my own father.

Guilt unfurls inside of me like a flag, letting itself be known. "Hey, Grandpa, I shouldn't have—"

He cuts me off with a "Zsht." Then taps me on the nose with a single finger. "I don't give a damn about the money, Adly. I care about leaving you happy. I have the trusts set to pay out when they do in hopes that you'll have a chance to realize they aren't the same thing before you're burdened with all that cash."

It's the message he's given his grandchildren over and over since we were little. Firmly believing it was money that fucked up his kids, he strove to create a different philosophy of life for us. Not an easy task when his sons are kings of capitalism, but he has tried.

"Then I should have come to you in the first place," I tell him. If I'd told him that leaving SNC was what would make me happy, he might have given it to me without the rigamarole.

"Then you wouldn't be with Ax right now, would you?" He reaches out to pat my cheek. "I know he makes you happy, Adly Jade. Do you?"

And there's the question I'd yearned for from my father. Fitting that it comes instead from the man who's taught me more about unconditional love than anyone else.

Until Ax, at least. If what I feel for him is what I think it is.

I have to swallow before I answer. "I do, Grandpa."

"Took you long enough." He hugs me again before sitting back in his wheelchair. "Get me out of here, Elias. I was trying to skip the sendoff. Too many tears for my liking."

I swipe said tears from my cheek as he wheels out the front door, just in time for Giulia to exclaim behind me, "There you are. Good. Are you ready to go?"

Turning around, I discover Ax is with her. He comes up next to me and silently slips his hand in mine. Like that's how they belong. Together. Linked.

"Ready," we say in unison.

"Perfect! I sent everyone else around the outside of the house. They should already be in the drive." She cracks the door and peeks her head out. Satisfied with what she finds, she swings it open for us and steps aside.

Our family and friends are lined up on both sides of the stoop and down the drive, all of them waving lit sparklers that glimmer in the dusk.

Sparklers!

Hand in hand, Ax and I run past them. I'm not sure exactly why we're doing a sendoff from here when the backyard is closer. The tradition of it, I suppose. I decide we'll just cut off at the path leading to the guest house. It's about a quarter of a mile from the main driveway, and my feet are killing me, but I can manage the walk knowing relief is at the end.

Of course, Grandpa Irving or Giulia or someone had a better idea, because when I finally look ahead instead of at the faces on either side of us, I'm so surprised that I come to a full stop. "Oh my God, a Cinderella carriage?"

"It's amazing," Ax says.

It's completely ridiculous, is what it is.

Little white twinkle lights sparkle out from the greenery and begonias wrapped around the curved bars that create the pumpkin shape. A velvet bench waits inside along with a bottle of champagne in a bucket of ice and two flutes. In the front, two big white horses stomp nervously behind a driver in full tuxedo and hat.

In other words, it's perfect.

The driver steps down from his perch to help me up the steps. There's rapid camera flashing as a photographer attempts to capture the moment, but I don't stop to pose. There have been enough pictures for the day.

Ax slides in next to me, and as the door of the carriage closes, I hear my father announce, "There goes Mr. and Mrs. Morgan!"

Cheers erupt, and the horses take off at a trot.

Without asking the driver to verify, I'm guessing he'll take us down the driveway to the main road and then up the private drive to the guest house. It's a pleasant ride for such a beautiful night, but now that I'm (sort-of) alone with Ax, my hands are sweaty and my heart is thumping.

"Champagne?" Ax uncorks the bottle, and I hold up a glass to catch the bubbles. Cristal drips down my hand, and I squeal.

Then Ax leans forward and licks the sweet alcohol from my knuckles, chasing away both my voice and brain function.

My breath goes too when he looks up at me with hooded eyes. "You know what else tastes good with dessert wine?"

There's too much innuendo in his tone to not know exactly what he's suggesting.

Ax follows my wide eyes as they dart to the back of the driver's head.

When his gaze returns to mine, there's a challenge there. "This carriage is probably a big hit for weddings, anniversaries, prom night." His voice is low and seductive as he kneels on the platform in front of me. "If that driver hasn't seen action before now, then he's not paying attention."

I take a sip of my champagne to stifle a giggle. "My prom date was not that smooth."

"Fuck Tad Murdoch. He can't stand to get his hands dirty, let alone his face." Ax unbuckles one of my shoes and removes it, then moves to the other and does the same.

I silently award him ten points for releasing my toes from their misery.

Then he trails his fingers under the hem of my dress, up the back of my calves, his eyes locked on mine.

Goosebumps spread down my arms, and familiar anticipation/panic turns my stomach into mush. It's the same feeling I have every time I'm getting busy with Ax. The thrill of what he'll do to me—how he'll make me feel, how he'll make me come—interlaced with the fear that I won't survive letting him this close.

It's that fear that drives me into character time and time again. Becoming someone else keeps the real me safe and hidden.

As much as I don't want to run from Ax anymore, impulse and habit has me reaching for a scenario before I can stop myself. "That's why I gave Tad the slip and came out with the chauffeur's son instead. Just be warned—if my daddy finds out that you've touched his precious daughter, he's going to have your hide."

I regret it immediately, wishing I'd been brave enough to be naked and vulnerable with him.

It's just foreplay. There will be other chances.

Still, I worry what Ax is thinking. It's not like either of us said that things are different now, but the charge between us feels so altered to me that it's hard to believe he doesn't feel it too. In which case, he might think I'm trying to reverse course, hiding behind the same old games we've been playing.

I watch him carefully, trying to read him. Hoping he can read me.

He lowers his eyes to his task, letting his fingers brush past the backs of my knees, then the outside of my thighs. When he meets my stare again, desire's written all over his features. "He'll have to peel you off my face first, because I plan to be suctioned on tight."

My clit throbs with the promise, and even if Ax doesn't understand where I'm hoping we'll go tonight, an orgasm or too before things get serious isn't the worst idea.

Besides, roleplay in front of a stranger is kind of hot. Pouring my heart out in front of one, not so much.

So roleplay it is.

When Ax wraps his fingers in my panties, I lift my hips without hesitation so he can pull them down past my knees and then off my feet.

Ah, this is why he took off my shoes.

Ten points for thinking ahead, then.

He stuffs my panties inside his vest and pushes my knees wide apart before disappearing under my dress. Seconds later, his tongue laps across my clit, and I moan.

Only to be rewarded with a pinch on my inner thigh that I interpret as a reminder to be quiet.

I bite my lower lip, trying to stifle the pleasure coursing through me, while the horses' hooves clip-clop steadily across the pavement, a rhythmic soundtrack to our clandestine encounter.

Draped across the velvet cushions, cocooned in twinkle lights, I feel the heat of Ax's breath on my skin, his tongue tracing delicate patterns on my swollen clit. Shivers ripple across my body as he expertly explores my folds, his tender caresses punctuated by sharp bites and teasing flicks of his tongue.

Each low groan and gasp escapes me like a puff of steam into the chilly air, and it seems like the longer we indulge, the more I yearn for that blissful, insatiable release that only Ax can provide. My breath hitches, and my champagne flute slips from my fingers to the platform and spills.

Whoops.

Hands now free, I bring my fists to my mouth to silence myself, digging my nails into my palms to maintain control.

Meanwhile, Ax's fingers delve inside my pussy, thrusting with a rhythm that mirrors the horses' gait. My hips rock against him, seeking friction, seeking release.

It's not enough, though.

It's not what I want.

His fingers mimic the width of his cock, but they aren't nearly long enough to fill me the way I need to be filled.

"Please," I whisper. "More, please."

I'm not sure what I'm asking for. I'm not expecting Ax to pull out his cock and fuck me with the driver right there in front of us. All I know is that I need.

Fortunately, Ax understands.

Replacing his tongue with a finger on my clit, he emerges from under my dress. "My fingers aren't good enough for the boss's daughter?" The rumble of his voice electrifies my skin. "Not refined enough for the likes of you?"

He pushes my dress up to my thighs, careful to keep my naughty parts from view in case the driver happens to look back. Then Ax props my bare feet onto the bench, spreading me wide. "If the girl's made of money, maybe she needs to be fucked with money."

He reaches for the Cristal and takes a long swig.

Then with a devilish twinkle in his eyes, he runs his tongue up the neck of the bottle.

It's obvious what he's thinking, and fire ignites in my veins. What would that shape feel like inside me?

"Rich enough for you?" He doesn't wait for my answer before he props the tip at my pussy and starts to press in. "Thick enough?"

I bite my cheek to silence a moan.

The sensation is new and intriguing. I much prefer the glide of his smooth cock, but the uneven ridges of the bottle's opening hit my insides in interesting ways, causing me to wriggle and writhe.

With each inch that penetrates me, I'm more aroused. Ax's thumb starts to work its magic on my clit, teasing me with a tantalizing combination of pleasure and sensory overload. My hips arch towards the bottle, meeting Ax's firm hand with a rhythm that echoes the horses' cadence.

When his mouth returns to my clit, I'm a goner.

I throw my head back and open my mouth to let out a silent cry. The twinkle lights become one with the night sky, swirling together to form a dazzling cosmic tapestry. The horse-drawn carriage is just another part of this outrageous erotic fantasy, and I clutch onto the velvet cushion beneath me in an attempt to keep my bearings.

It's no use, though. Ax's tongue laps at my clit with playful eagerness like a thirsty cat lapping at a bowl of milk. Each flick and swirl of his tongue sends trembles down my spine, building the pleasure within me as he deepens the thrusts of the bottle.

My body arches in response, begging for more as he expertly teases me with his skilled movements. It's overwhelming, yet I can't get enough, and I surrender to the bliss coursing through me as my climax builds and builds, becoming more intense with each passing moment. I can feel the constriction in my chest, my heart pounding like a wild animal, begging to burst free.

Suddenly, I can't hold it in any longer. All my muscles tense, and an orgasm ripples through me. My fingers dig deeper into the cushion for support. My eyes start to water. My mouth opens to let out a silent "Oh." As the force of my climax eases, a dazed euphoria settles over me, and though my limbs are heavy and relaxed, I'm floating away like a hot air balloon, soaring to the heavens.

Except, before I can fly away too far, Ax is there, pressing soft kisses along my thighs, reminding me I'm here. Reminding me I'm tethered.

Reminding me that he would be my home, if I let him.

I can't think of anything else I want more.

When I've come down from my high, I drop my feet to either side of Ax, grab his face with both of my hands, and kiss him hard. Like he's my oxygen.

He tastes like me and champagne and the mint sprig he was chewing on earlier.

He tastes like a future I didn't realize I longed for.

He tastes like safety.

He tastes like mine.

CHAPTER
TWENTY-SIX
AX

We don't stop kissing until the driver pulls up to the guest house. Adly's lips are red and swollen, and her eyes are glassy with lust when she pulls out of my arms.

She's never looked more beautiful.

"Go on inside," I tell her after we're both down from the carriage.

She looks back at me with as much curiosity as concern but seems mollified when I nod my head toward the driver.

"I'll get changed." It's a sensual promise until she thinks about it. "If I can manage to get this dress off myself."

"I'll be right behind you, if you can't."

Maybe not *right* behind her. It takes less than a minute to tip the driver so that he'll forget anything he may have seen or heard during our ride, but I stay long after the horses have clopped off down the road so I can get my head on straight.

I'm not used to being confused by a woman. Probably because I've never been in this deep with one before. I've never been interested enough in anyone to deal with the hassles of commitments and obligations and loss of freedom.

Adly never counted.

Sure, she was a hot teenager who grew up to be an even hotter woman, and I'm not going to try to fool myself into thinking I didn't want her for an extremely long time, but I never believed she was anything but off limits.

It's not ambition that I have a problem with—it's rejection. Why put myself out there when I was perfectly satisfied with the status quo?

But then that night in (what was then) Holt's office, Adly opened the door a crack, and I peeked in and liked it so much that I kept my foot in the way so she couldn't slam me out again. That's how I lived for a long time, happy with whatever she threw me, fully aware that she was only giving scraps.

I married her that first time in the courthouse feeling lucky as fuck to be the guy who could help her out. Because she doesn't let just anyone help her. She doesn't trust anyone enough to accept favors, but she accepted mine, and that was some sweet motherfucking victory.

I think I could have lived forever like that.

I would have.

Then she went and started messing with my head. Started opening that door wider and wider. Let me linger on her threshold. Made me want more of her.

Made me want all of her.

The confusing part was when she started acting like she

might want more of me, too. That's when I started getting ambitious. That's when I began to think there could be something forever about us. That's when I let myself really fall.

I married her today feeling lucky as fuck to get to love her, but what I didn't say in those impromptu vows is that I don't want to love her in pieces anymore. I want to love her whole.

But I know we don't always get what we want, and I don't want to be the asshole who overstays his invitation, so I keep looking for signs and signals to tell me what she's after.

Is it forever?

She alluded to that in the church, but that could have been an act.

Then when we were dancing, and she was snuggled in my arms, she talked about *just us*, and fuck, that really did feel real.

So when I was on my knees, I thought she'd let me adore her cunt with my lips and tongue and no masks. No scenes. No game. The *real* just us.

But she slipped into a role again, and maybe I'm not surprised, but I sure as hell am confused. Who is it that she wants to walk in after her tonight?

If I were brave, I wouldn't give her a choice. It's all of me or nothing at all.

I'm chickenshit, though. Still willing to settle for pieces. I'm not ready to risk any of her for nothing at all.

And so I put on another mask before pushing open the door and stepping inside after her.

It's my first time in Adeline's guest house. It's as over-the-top opulent as the main house with its architectural details and rich velvet curtains and Brazilian cherry wood floors.

It's also been one hundred percent staged for romance with dozens of flowers and flameless candles and soft piano music emitting through the sound system speakers. Someone went all out to make this feel like a real wedding night.

Giulia's doing, hopefully.

Or Brystin's. I can't handle the thought of Adly's grandfather or father, or even Holt, spending time and attention on what essentially amounts to our honeymoon suite, so I decide not to think about it anymore.

Honestly, I'm not thinking much about anything at all, because seconds after I walk in, Adly emerges from the bedroom without a lick of clothing on.

And damn.

I don't think I've ever seen her completely naked. I've seen every part of her body bare at some time or another, just not all at once. Apparently, I've been missing out, because as beautiful as I've always known her to be, the woman standing before me is on a whole other level.

The candlelight casts a warm hue over her skin. Her chestnut hair cascades loosely on her shoulders and down her back. Her perfectly round and perky breasts, with their hardened peaks, stand out proudly against her toned body. The strip of hair on her pelvis directs my gaze lower to the mesmerizing hole between her legs that I crave, but every inch of her is a masterpiece. Her broad shoulders exude strength while still looking fragile like fine porcelain. Her slim waist begs for my hands to explore. Her legs are strong and lean, showcasing both power and elegance.

I can't stop staring. Can't stop wanting.

She's the one who speaks first. "I managed to get the dress off by myself." Her smile is coy, and I almost drop the mask in hope that she wants tonight to be real too.

But how long before *she* turns it into a scene?

I'd rather be one step ahead of her, anticipating her needs, knowing her wants.

Warding off rejection.

I force my lips downward into a frown. "Yeah, I can see that." My tone is purposefully biting.

She's instantly on alert. "What's wrong? Did something happen?" She takes a step toward me, her arms in front of her chest, as though she's attempting to be less naked.

I hold my jaw taut while I undo my jacket and pretend my cock isn't rock hard and pressing against the prison of my boxer briefs. "Maybe you should tell me, my dear wife. Did something happen?"

Her forehead crinkles in confused worry. "If I did something, Ax...if you heard something..."

There's something intoxicating about her concern. She could easily decide to hell with me and leave me moping on the living room sofa to crash by herself after a long day.

The fact that she doesn't makes me feel too guilty to keep her guessing.

"Yeah, I heard something." I throw my jacket on an end table and start working on my tie. "Our carriage driver, in fact, appreciated my tip so much that he thought I might like to know about the rumor going around about my wife getting fucked by our priest."

It takes a full two seconds before she gets it.

Then it clicks, and she understands that I'm playing the enraged husband of the woman who went into the confessional last night and left debauched.

Her hand flies to her mouth to hide her smile, but it's evident in her eyes. Her shoulders sag in relief, and her chest shakes as she suppresses a laugh.

She stares at me for a minute, as though considering.

When she drops her hand again, she's in character, panicked and pleading. "It's not what you think. You have to let me explain."

"Only thing I need to hear you say is that it's not true."

"Baby…"

"That's not an answer. Are you or are you not still a virgin?"

She hugs her arms around herself and shakes her head.

"That wasn't yours to give away. That was *mine*." I throw my tie down with a feigned huff.

Or maybe not exactly feigned, because I'm a little resentful it was such an easy choice for her to play tonight, when I want nothing more than to hold her and kiss her and love her.

But if this is all I get, then I'll pretend with her.

I'll just put my grudge into the scene. "Come here," I command.

She doesn't move. "It was for you, baby. All for you. I wanted to know how to please you."

"Do I seem like I'm pleased? Now I won't say it again—come here."

Cautiously, she moves toward me. "He said I wasn't ready for you. He said I was too small, that I could never take your cock, and it would ruin the experience. He needed to break me in. For you, baby."

My dick likes her begging so much that it twitches in my pants.

But I'm not just turned on—I feel *owed*. My character's needs bleed into my own, and I'm not sure if I feel owed because my pretend wife pretend gave her body to a pretend someone else or because my real wife won't give everything to me.

Complicated, I know.

Either way, there's an edge of legit anger when I grab her by the hair and tug her to me. "You gave him *my* cunt?" When she only nods, I snap at her. "I need it in words. Tell me you gave him my cunt."

My free hand slides through her pussy lips, roughly rubbing at her clit before my fingers dip lower to thrust inside her.

"I gave him your cunt," she says, her voice so breathy I might believe she were frightened if her eyes weren't dilated and her pussy so wet.

"Louder." My fingers saw in and out of her while my thumb presses against her swollen bundle of nerves. "Tell me again what you did."

"I gave him your cunt."

"And this mouth?" I lift my pussy soaked fingers to shove between her lips. "Did you give him *my* mouth?"

We didn't kiss last night in our roleplay, and she didn't suck my cock, but she answers the way I expect. The way I hope. "I gave him your mouth."

"I'll have to fuck him out of you, you know. Everywhere

he touched. Did you give him this?" I reach around to spank her ass cheek. "Did you give him *my* ass?"

She presses her lips together tightly and shakes her head.

I'm not sure if she's saying she didn't or that she doesn't want to admit the truth, but I decide to go with the latter. "You gave him everything? Every part of you that is supposed to be mine? I'm your husband. You belong to *me*." She gasps when I spank her again.

And again.

My red handprint on her skin is the brand that I want it to be, but it will fade. The ring will come off her finger in a year. I don't know how to claim her for real. How to keep her, and I'm no longer in character when I ask her, "What do you have left to give? What do you have left that's only for me, Adly? What do I get? Tell me what's mine."

She goes still.

Then in almost a whisper, she says, "My heart."

If only she knew that's all I want from her.

All of a sudden, I don't think I can play this particular scene. Not when it's turned to this. It cuts too deep.

The pain has to be clear on my face, and I wonder if she thinks it's just another part of the game. I open my mouth to make sure she knows, to tell her I can't do this anymore. I can't *just* play anymore. I won't.

But before I can find the words, her hands land gently on either side of my face. "Ax, I'm not playing right now. This is me. I'm being me. I'm trying to tell you..." She gives an awkward shrug of her shoulders as her thumbs caress my cheeks. "I'm trying to give you my heart."

Her words hang in the air, and I stare at her for a long

moment, my eyes searching for the truth in hers. "Your heart." My whisper is barely above a murmur. "You want to give me your heart?"

She nods, somber and earnest and a little terrified, her expression open and honest in a way I've never seen before. "Well, *your* heart, I mean. It's already yours, Ax. I'm already yours."

There's a small voice inside, urging me to beware, telling me this could be just a new scene, a new way for her to dance around serious commitment.

But I tell that voice to fuck off, because the woman standing in front of me is peering up at me like I'm some kind of lifeline, and while I'm smart enough to be cautious, for the first time in what feels like a very long while, I allow myself to grasp on to hope. "Don't fuck with me right now, Adly. There is some shit you can't say and not fucking mean."

"Yeah. I know." She moves in even closer, so there's only a breath's distance between us. "I fucking mean it. Do you...?" She searches my eyes looking for answers I'm more than willing to give. "Do you want—?"

I don't let her finish. "I fucking want, Addles."

It's the first time I've been this sure about anything. She is the only constant thought in my mind. She's the only future I ever dream about. She's the first thing I want to see in the morning, every morning, for the rest of my life, and she's the only woman that I have wanted that with.

The only woman I will ever want that with.

Without another word, I reach up and cup her face in my hands. Her skin is soft and warm against my palms, sending a shiver down my spine. My thumbs glide over her cheeks, mirroring her tender touch. Eyes locked on hers, I lean in slowly, and kiss her.

She kisses me back.

Slowly, at first.

Then with more demand, more urgency, as if we can't get enough of each other. As if there's only *this* in the world. Only *us*.

"I fucking love you, Ax," she says when I let her up for air.

"God, you better fucking mean it because I love you so much, baby. So fucking much."

"Me too. I should have told you sooner."

"Me too, baby." My tongue slips inside her mouth for another long kiss. "Should have told you so many times."

Silently, I vow to tell her so many times from now on.

"So...you forgive me for the priest?" Her giggle vibrates against my lips.

Jesus, she's perfect.

"I reserve the right to revisit that at a later time. Right now, we're good." This time as I kiss her, I sweep her up in my arms and carry her to the bedroom.

There are more flameless candles and the bedspread is covered with rose petals, but beyond that, she's all that I see as I drop her lightly onto the bed.

Immediately, she rises to her knees, and starts unbuttoning my shirt while I work on my cuffs. With her help, I peel off layers of clothing. Our lips meet in between before wandering to explore. She leaves a trail of kisses and tiny electric shocks on my jaw and neck and torso. I nip at the skin by her ear, by her collarbone, under her breasts. Her body is a map of all the places I want to visit again and again, places I've marked with my tongue and teeth several times before and yet never really claimed until now.

Finally, we're naked before each other, honest and bare, with no place to hide. "I'm going to make love to you now," I tell her.

"Ew, gross," she teases as I push her to her back and crawl over her.

"So gross." With my eyes fastened to hers, I reach down to play with her clit. She spreads her legs to make room for me, and I settle in, my cock notched at her pussy. "I can grab a condom."

I didn't use one last night at the church. Both of us were too into the scene to realize, I suppose. Not very responsible, but I know she's on birth control, at least. It's not like I've been with anyone else since my last bill of clean health. Tonight, I'm proposing the lack of prophylactics be a choice instead of a carried-away-in-the-moment accident.

She runs her hands through my hair. "I don't want anything between us anymore, Ax. Just you."

It's the best thing she could say to me.

"You let me in, baby, and I'm never going to leave." If she doesn't realize I'm talking about more than sex then I don't know what conversation we've been having instead.

"Promise?"

The gravity of the moment hits me, and my throat tightens. "I've never meant anything more."

"Okay," she says, like she's truly letting herself believe it. "Okay. Don't hurt me, okay?"

Never.

"*Salute,*" I say instead because our negotiations are true contracts, and this is a promise I intend to keep.

"*Salute,*" she whispers.

Gently, I push inside her, eliciting a soft whimper from her lips. She feels like hot velvet wrapped tight around me, and I groan. "I've never loved anyone else like this, Addles. You've got me by the balls in every sense of the phrase."

"Only by the balls?"

She has full possession of the rest of me too. Those fucking Sebastians own everything, and for once, I'm not mad about it.

"You've got me," I rephrase. "You've got me."

Kissing me, she wraps her legs around my waist and pulls me deeper, hips undulating in time with our connection. Together, we ride the waves of pleasure, and when our pulses synchronize, I forget what it felt like when the only heart that beat in my chest was mine.

"Let's talk about your sister."

I throw my head back against the tub and groan. "Why do you want to ruin such a nice night?"

She's straddled on top of me, but while she seems to be content with soaping my chest with a loofah for far longer than it needs soaping—not complaining—my cock would rather she scooted back a bit and took a ride.

He's a greedy fucking asshole. I've already come twice tonight. He should be satisfied.

Adly's come too many times to count, because I'm a god in the bedroom, which I only now realize puts me at a disadvantage since she's not yearning for another round like I am.

I run my hands over her hips and pretend I'm not waiting for an opportunity to position her where I want her.

Or that's what I was doing until she brought up Bianca. Good thing, I suppose, to find my little sister is a boner killer.

Adly seems completely oblivious of my plight. "You can't drop a bomb like that and not expect me to want to fix it."

"Uh...I can because I did, and there's nothing to fix."

She leans forward, distracting me with her tits until she kisses the sensitive spot by my ear. "I want to share everything with you, Ax. Please, talk to me."

It's like she has a secret manual that tells her exactly the right words to say to me. Wish I had one for her.

Sighing, I lift my finger to tease her nipple, a smug smile forming on my lips when it pebbles under my touch. I didn't plan on telling her about Bianca today. It just came out, probably because I've wanted to share everything with her for longer than I care to admit. So many times I almost told her about my sister, and I've never told anyone about her, except for Hunter...until today.

Since it doesn't seem like she's going to let my cock back in her pussy until we've had this conversation, I guess it's in my best interest to humor her a bit. "Well, the status quo doesn't seem to be hurting anyone."

"You mean, avoiding the poor girl?" Adly seems horrified. "She's barely an adult, Ax. Remember being that age? Confused and afraid of rejection."

"Fuck, that was me four hours ago."

"Oh, baby." This time when she leans forward, she

kisses me, but as soon as my hands get busy groping her ass, she places her palms on my chest and pushes away. "Why did her father keep her away from you in the first place?"

I attempt to clear the fog of lust from my mind and shrug. "Doesn't approve of people with money, for one. Never liked the way my father treated my mother, for another. I guess he thinks the apple doesn't fall far from the tree and figures that I'd be a bad influence on her."

She studies me with compassionate eyes. "It doesn't mean he's right."

"Doesn't matter if he's right. Siblings don't have any right to contest that sort of thing."

"Except now she's old enough to make up her own mind, and she obviously wants to give you a chance."

"A chance to what? Show her that I'm exactly what her father thinks I am? An asshole with no morals or ambition or home of my own?"

Adly purses her lips together. "That's *your* father talking." I can practically hear her silent *tsk*.

It's cute, but she's misguided. "*He's* not wrong."

She leans back and scrunches her face up into an expression that could be considered unattractive if she wasn't the most beautiful woman in the world. "Does he know a different Ax Morgan than I do?" she asks.

Obviously, she's in delulu land. Maybe that's the downside of too many orgasms.

Or the upside, because the way she looks at me is real, real nice. Like she actually sees someone different than the guy I see when I look in the mirror, because there's admiration and respect and approval.

I don't think anyone's looked at me like that since my mother died, and that was eighteen years ago now.

It does something to my insides. Heals something that's been broken for a long time, and instead of trying to prove to her that she's off her rocker, I'm suddenly more interested in letting her prove that she's sane.

I lift a soapy hand to knead the muscle at the side of her neck, concentrating my gaze there, too chickenshit to look at her face. "What Ax Morgan do you know?"

Without glancing up, I know she's grinning. "The one who was willing to inconvenience his entire life to help me, even when I wouldn't tell him what I needed the help for."

It wasn't an inconvenience to get to be her hero.

I'm not ready to let her understand how whipped she's had me for the last year and a half, if not longer. Especially when I'm not sure I'll be able to rescue her dream, even if I do take the promotion. There's only so much power a CEO has when he's working under a board. If I don't deliver what they're after, they'll sack me and go to the next guy who will.

Hunter's image flashes in my mind. Thinking about the stony expression he gave me as he left the reception makes my stomach churn.

It's a reminder that there are still things left to tell Adly.

I decide to start small. "Confession—Hunter told me about SHE before you did."

"Hunter knows? Wait...what?" She seems to be trying to fit puzzle pieces together in her head.

"Alex told him, apparently."

I can see when it clicks. "Goddammit, Alex." She blows out a huff of air, but doesn't seem all that surprised.

"Hunter's the reason the price got raised."

"Goddammit, Hunter." She grins though, like she's not interested in being mad.

I chuckle, sitting up a little as I do. Unintentionally, the movement brings her lower on my pelvis. So close to where I want her. "Can you just…"

She doesn't resist when I nudge her hips upward. Without needing any adjustment, I'm lined up at her pussy, and when she lowers again, she sinks down on my cock with a gasp, sheathing me like she was tailor-made.

I groan. "Yeah. That's better."

Even more so when she uses those yoga-toned thighs of hers to lift herself up and down. And, fuck, when she clenches that cunt of hers around me…

My eyelids droop with pleasure, and a hilarious thought occurs to me. "You know if Hunter hadn't gotten the price raised, we wouldn't be where we are right now. In a way, we owe this," I gesture between us, "to Hunter."

Her movement stutters. "No. Nope. Uh uh. No way. I'm not giving him any credit for this." Her voice pitches up at the end of her sentence, my cock apparently hitting a particularly sensitive spot.

I'm overly pleased with myself about it, since she's really the one doing the work. The Lord's work, in my opinion, and damn if she isn't a goddamn apostle the way she enthusiastically picks up the tempo.

Obviously, I don't want to think about Hunter anymore. I do feel guilty, though, because the guy has had his fair share of hard, and I feel an obligation to stand up for him since I think there's a lot she doesn't know.

Maybe just not right now. "Look, your brother isn't

always the bad guy. But it does feel weird singing his praises while you're bouncing on my cock."

When she laughs, my cock vibrates inside her. "Then don't sing his praises. Sing your own instead."

"Eh. You sing them."

I really don't expect her to be singing anything except my name, but she somehow takes the suggestion as a challenge. "You're an honest man, Ax. Hard to find that in our world, but you are. And decent."

She pauses to bite her bottom lip when my thumb lands on her clit. "A guy who knows how to make a woman feel cherished. A man with a wicked tongue and a mouth that should be outlawed."

I lean forward to use that mouth she's praise/bashing to bring her nipple into my mouth, eliciting a shaky cry on her inhale.

Still, she continues to tout my talents. "You're a boss in the bedroom. And a badass in the boardroom." Her sentences become shorter, choppier as I tease her with my fingers and my lips. "Naturally able to charm. And command. A man who belongs at the helm. Visionary. Smart. Innovative."

It's a head trip to hear so many nice things about myself from the woman I respect most in the universe. A real ego booster when she's fucking herself on my cock at the same time, wearing herself out in the process. I'm more than happy to take over the task, but I'm too self-centered or too concerned about her feelings not to ask the question that pops into my mind, despite the ill timing. "Hey, do you really want me to take that job?"

She stills, my cock lodged firmly inside her as she slides

her fingers into the hair at the base of my neck. "There isn't a single man on earth who is better suited for it, Ax. If it's what you want, you have my full support."

I've never imagined the planets aligning for me like this. The job, the woman—it's like the dream ending that I never believed existed has landed in my lap—literally, at the moment.

While I don't have any sense yet of what I can do for Adly in return, I silently vow to do whatever it takes to give her the perfect fairytale ending that *she* never believed existed.

I kiss her, then—a dirty, sloppy, tongue-down-her-throat-like-it's-my-cock kind of kiss. With my hands braced on her hips, I hold her still and fuck her like only the badass hero of the story does.

BREAKFAST IS BROUGHT to us in the morning, and after not getting much sleep the night before, we don't venture to the main house until early afternoon. It's mid-summer in Connecticut, and the weather is perfect for the half-mile walk. I wouldn't have minded if it had been snowing or the temperature were in triple digits, though, because Adly's by my side.

Damn, I'm so whipped.

There's so much still undiscussed between us—like, if we're staying married or if I get to move into her room or if she wants to have babies, all that jazz—and I already know I'm going to roll over and say yes to anything she asks.

Good thing she doesn't tend to ask for a lot, except I'm

discovering I really like giving. She's going to have to learn to put up with it.

When we arrive at the main house, several family members are outside, finishing up lunch. There are a lot less people than there were the day before, most of them likely having left already. Alex, Riah, and Zully aren't in sight. Steele and Simone don't seem to be around either.

It's Brystin who makes eye contact first, so we walk over to her table. "There's the—"

"If you're about to say lovebirds, happy couple, or anything in that vein," Adly interjects, "then I just want to remind you that I will return every ounce of humiliation to you when it's your turn to get married."

"...butter," she says, an obvious last-minute substitution to what she really meant to say.

"You don't know how much I appreciate that," Holt tells his fiancée. "I do not need to be reminded about..." He shudders, apparently reminding himself of whatever he doesn't want to be reminded of.

He turns his attention to me and points. "You are a sick man. Dare I even ask what you have Adly saved as in your phone?"

I'm not sure what he's getting at, though I have my suspicions, so I answer honestly. "Mrs. Morgan."

Adly's head swivels toward me. "Really?" She sounds unexpectedly pleased.

"Yeah, really." I'd changed it the day she'd changed me to *Axhole* in hers. Before that, she was listed as *Sassypants* because I didn't want Hunter to ever accidentally see her name on my phone, and the name fits her saucy mouth.

Some time I'll have to ask her what I was listed as before.

Right now, I'm more curious about Holt. "What's his problem?" I don't bother to be discreet with the question poised to Adly. More fun to talk about him behind his back in front of his face.

She exaggerates a roll of the eyes. "He's just figured out his baby sister has sex, and it's messing with his mind."

"Ah." I squeeze Adly to me, very familiar like. "Guess we shouldn't tell him that the first time for us was on his desk."

Her cheeks pink, but she rolls with it. "He needs to stop hiding the good liquor in his office."

"He needs to stop choosing Hunter's birthday as his security code." I swing a glance toward Holt. "Too obvious, man."

When his mother's birthday and death day didn't work, I tried Holt's rival on a whim. Like I said, too fucking obvious.

Brystin laughs, and Adly squeals, "You did not!"

The conversation continues, but I hear my name called behind me, and excuse myself to head over to the table where a couple of Adly's uncles are sitting.

Henry Sebastian stands to greet me with a handshake. "I want you to know I was always an Axel Morgan fan," he says. "You've had the best credentials for a while now."

"He didn't have the name," August says, like he's reminding his older brother of a past discussion. Or discussions, possibly.

"Thank you, sir. I'm honored."

"Deserved, deserved," Henry says. "Honestly, probably a better situation than letting Hunter have the spot."

Guilt eats at my esophagus and when Henry releases my hand, I rub at my chest with my fist. I want this job, but I'm not ready to say yes without speaking to Hunter first. His friendship means something to me, and I want to honor that.

"Hunter had some good ideas, though," August says.

Henry shakes his head, unimpressed. "They were probably Ax's ideas." He puts a hand on my shoulder. "You know, the minute you became a Sebastian, you clinched the deal with a few of the board members, but what really won everyone over was your plan for SHE."

The next twenty seconds plays out like one of those nightmares where I know something terrible is about to happen, but I've lost my voice or I'm not wearing pants or I'm stuck in a vat of super glue, and even though I can see the disaster before it happens, there's nothing I can do to stop it from unfolding.

I try, though. "We really don't have to talk about it right now."

But Henry's voice is louder, and he bulldozes over me. "I'm sure you know the network is for sale. For what it will add to SNC, purchasing it at that price is even a bargain."

I've had this kind of nightmare before.

Which is why I don't need to turn around to know that Adly's heard every word.

CHAPTER
TWENTY-SEVEN
ADLY

've heard that phrase about the ground dropping out from underneath a person a million times in my life, but this is the first time I truly understand it.

One minute, I'm securely standing on the solid earth of Holt's terrace, laughing because of something stupid he said, turning to share it with my husband...only to hear him being congratulated by my uncle for a brilliant master-mind of manipulation that I foolishly fell heart, head, and soul for.

The ground has definitely dropped.

There's a whoosh in my ears like the ocean, and I can feel my pulse in my throat, as if a big blob of heartbreak has taken residence in my torso, displacing all my organs. A haughty voice sing-songs in the back of my mind. *I knew it, I knew it. I knew it.*

I'm trying not to jump to conclusions, however. Ax deserves a chance to explain, and much as I want to grill him right here and now, I've spent my whole life in the limelight and know when a matter needs privacy.

Ax must not have learned the same decorum. "Adly, it's not how it looks."

Without saying a word, I spin on my heel and head inside the house through the door that leads to the breakfast nook, only to find that it's occupied by Lina and Reid.

Ignoring their greetings, I move toward the living room.

As expected, Ax follows. "Let's talk about this, Addles. I can explain."

I don't process his words, don't let them sink past the wall that went up the minute I heard the word SHE pass over Henry's lips.

For what it will add to SNC, purchasing it at that price is even a bargain.

The living room is too open. There are no doors to shut.

I pass through the space, aiming toward the library before remembering that the room has two stories and multiple entrances. Too easy for someone to eavesdrop.

With Ax still following, I turn down the hall leading to Holt's bedroom. He's not currently occupying it, after all, and for a multitude of reasons, it feels like a safe place to communicate.

Or lose my shit.

It's a mystery at the moment which reaction will win out.

Finally, I march over Holt's threshold.

Without being told, Ax shuts the double doors behind him, securing us in. "Adly, I know how it sounds. And I should have talked to you about this before. I just didn't—"

Taking a breath, forcing my shoulders high, I cut him off

when I turn to face him. "Answer just two questions for me." It's hard to look directly at him without remembering his mouth on me last night, bruising my lips, making me come.

"Oh. Okay. Okay. Whatever you need." He's flustered, probably preferring to dump excuses, but I don't need them.

I need answers.

I plant my gaze on a spot on his forehead. "Did you or did you not know I was attempting to purchase SHE before you told the board that you thought SNC should purchase it?"

He takes a step toward me. When I back up, he doesn't try again. "I didn't talk to the board at all. It was an offhand conversation with your father. I meant it when I said I didn't know I was being interviewed."

I've learned the longer an answer is, the more room there is for lies. "It's a yes or no question, Ax. Yes or no will suffice."

"It won't suffice because there's no context." His voice is level but his words are tight.

I don't let his frustration deter me. "Yes or no. Did you know before you gave the idea to SNC?"

He jaw twitches as he thinks. "Yes, I knew." He immediately tries to expound. "But–"

"Thank you," I say, cutting him off, surprised that I can talk around the lump in my throat and the knife in my back. "Second question. Did you or did you not have the CEO position on your radar when you offered to marry me?"

This time, the question seems like a relief to him. "I

didn't, Adly. I didn't. I swear to God. It never crossed my mind. Not even fleetingly."

"Yeah. Sure looks like it never crossed your mind."

"Looks are bullshit. You of all people know that. I never had any intention of pursuing a promotion. That job was supposed to be Hunter's."

My eyes prick. "So you threw my dream on the chopping block for your buddy."

Guilt skims across his features before he recovers. "No. No! I was actually mad at him when your father asked me about my ideas." He shakes his head, as if realizing the detail is unimportant, and tries again. "Look, I knew. Okay? I knew that Hunter was planning to snatch up SNC, but like a dickhole, when your father and I were talking, I wanted the fucking credit, so—"

"*Was* it your idea? Did you *deserve* the credit?"

His expression sinks. "Hunter would have come up with it himself eventually."

"So it *was* your idea." I'm not sure why I want to hear the answer when it's clear as day on his face, but I do. Want to hear it from his own traitorous mouth.

He gives me another evasion instead. "I didn't mention purchasing SHE specifically."

It's a guilty response. The kind that sidesteps the truth without actually telling a lie.

I'm the one who takes a step toward him, this time. "You said, 'Hey, you could buy a smaller network that's up for sale with a younger demographic that could easily be absorbed into SNC,' and even though you never mentioned a specific network, you thought there was a chance in hell that he would come up with a network that wasn't SHE?"

It's not like there are plenty of other small networks to choose from. If there were, I wouldn't have had to try to grab up this one now.

He knows it too. "I guess I didn't think that far."

"Didn't think past your own self, you mean."

"I was spitballing, Adly. This was at the beginning. Before..." He trails off like it's not worth saying.

I probably don't want to hear it, but I can't help myself. "Before...what? Before we were married?"

He looks at his shoes. "No."

Part of me still wants to parse out what his backstabbing came before, but I can't get past the detail that, whatever he was going to say, it was *after* we were married.

After we'd negotiated and made an agreement. After we were outed, because Ax didn't have the opportunity to "spitball" with my father after city hall and before the next round of negotiations.

Maybe it doesn't matter when it happened, but fucking me over after we'd signed the marriage certificate feels particularly malicious.

I knew he'd hurt me. I fucking knew.

"I'm such a fool." I can't look at him. Can't even look at that spot on his forehead. I turn so I'm not facing him and the patio doors smack my line of vision. We'd stood out there just yesterday, back-to-back, and he knew just what to say to make me feel less guilty about the lies we were about to tell each other.

I'd thought it was sweet.

Now I realize that it was probably all part of an elaborate manipulation game.

And I fucking fell for it.

I twirl back to face him. "Every time I asked you why you were helping me out, you stuck to your 'no reason' story, and it took some convincing, but I believed you in the end, Ax. You fucking snowed me."

"I didn't marry you to get a fucking job out of it, Adly." It's the first time he's sounded sharp.

It makes it easier to bite back. "No, you married me to get *the* fucking job. The one everyone's after. I shouldn't be surprised that you'd play dirty to get it. Everyone else has."

Everyone except me. Probably why I was never on the consideration list.

If I had any heart left to be broken, this last realization would shatter the rest to pieces because I'm suddenly convinced that my gender wasn't really the issue—it was the fact that I wasn't cutthroat.

Normally, I'd be proud of that. Right now, I just feel stupid and inadequate. "Congratulations, you make a better Sebastian than I do. Welcome to the name. Guess you deserve it."

"Jesus, fuck." Ax swipes his hand over his face and paces away, then returns just as quickly. "You want to know why I married you, Adly? I married you because I wanted *you*. I wanted to be near you. I wanted you to have a reason to let me the fuck in. I didn't have a plan. I shot from the hip because there was no way in hell I was letting someone else steal that chance to get close to you. There wasn't anything nefarious about it, Adly. I just wanted to love you."

It hits me like an arrow between the ribs, piercing the spot where my heart was only this morning. It hurts most because I wish I could be the kind of person who believed him.

But I'm just not. "Nothing says love like selling out a girl's escape plan. It was the only thing that mattered, and you've ripped it out from under me."

"Or... Or, Adly, hear me out." He holds his hand out in front of him, cautious and pleading. "If I take the CEO position, I can try to convince the board to leave SHE alone."

If that's supposed to make everything better, he's sadly missed the mark. "How ironic, isn't it? You offering to use your promotion to try and save me. I wouldn't need saving if it weren't for your promotion."

Then, because I'm hurt and mad and in the mood to lash out, I add, "You wouldn't *have* the job if it weren't for me."

"Really?" His lid spasms. "Is that how you feel?"

I feel his wound as clearly as if I'd turned the sword on myself. My breath shudders as I inhale, and I want to take it back almost as much as I want him to hurt.

"It's not about how I feel. It's about the truth." I have to bring my hand to play with my lips so that I don't use it to reach out for him instead.

"Mm. Funny, you seemed to feel differently last night."

Reminders of last night make my insides ache. For the briefest moment, I'd been his, and he'd been mine, and I meant it when I said he deserved the CEO position.

It doesn't change the fact that my family would have only ever given it to a Sebastian.

Or the husband of one.

I cross my arms over my chest and jut out my chin in response.

He nods, pain clear in his narrowed eyes. "Regardless, I

didn't use you to go after the job, Adly. I didn't want the job. I wanted you."

I'm not sure if he meant the past tense, but it's all I hear.

I'm not brave enough to ask for clarification, and deep inside I know it doesn't matter. If he purposefully fucked me over, I can't forgive that. It's not forgivable.

Unless he didn't.

Unless it really is a misunderstanding.

The miscommunication trope in books is my least favorite. Instead of talking it out and clearing the air, the couple breaks up, and as a reader, I want to throw my book across the room and vow that I'll never be so shortsighted in real life.

Am I being shortsighted?

Or am I finally being wise?

As if Ax can sense the warring of my thoughts, he starts to reach for me, only to pull back when I tense up.

He clasps his hands in front of him, a way to keep them put, perhaps. "I fucked up, Addles. I assumed there was no way to keep SNC from taking SHE, and that was dumb. And I should have told you. I should have given you a heads-up, but I swear, on my mother's ring that you're wearing, that I never wanted to sabotage you, and I will do everything within my power to fix this."

I bat the tears from my eyelashes, my lip trembling. "And I'm just supposed to believe you?"

"You're going to have to trust someone for once." It's matter-of-fact. There's no plea in his tone. No attempt at persuasion. Just a plain old statement of how things are.

I wish he wasn't right.

"I do trust someone," I tell him. "The only person I've

ever been able to trust—me. And my experience says that all this beautiful stuff you're saying about wanting to be near me and doing anything to make it right? Those kinds of declarations are only real in books. Nowhere else. It's fantasy, just like everything between us.

"I think you just got carried away with the role you were playing." It's cruel. To me as much as him, and the tears are flowing freely by the time I finish my speech.

Ax visibly crumbles. "Don't say that, baby."

"Sorry, but I think we both need a dose of honesty."

The truth is, I'm the one who got carried away. I swore off these kinds of relationships so I would never get caught up like this. So I would never have to position my heart against my head. So I would never have to question if I'm being swayed by facts or fiction.

It's all Grandpa's fault. This stupid fairytale wedding shit that made me think…made me *hope*…

I shake the romantic notions from my head. "I'll give it a few days before explaining to my family. After everything they've done this weekend for us…"

I have to take a break to swallow, and when I pause, he slips in, desperate and urging. "Tell them what, Adly? After everything, you're just going to throw this away?"

I'm not sure how I manage to keep my spine straight. "Just keeping my end of the bargain. We agreed I'd be the one to break us up, after all. So this is me…" The sob catches in my throat, and I can't finish my sentence. Can't look at him. Can't listen to anything else he has to say.

It's time to leave the fantasy and go back to reality, and that means I can't be here anymore.

"Don't follow me." Wiping my eyes with the back of my

hand, I circle wide around him so I don't accidentally touch him, and charge out of the room.

I find Holt where I left him in the backyard.

As soon as he sees the state I'm in, he excuses himself from his conversation and pulls me around a row of tall bushes so we can talk privately.

Like only the most awesome brother, he skips asking what's wrong. "What do you need?"

"A car ride home."

Then, because business is what comes first, what's *supposed* to always come first, I tell him the rest. "And I need you to drive with me."

I'll cry more about Ax later, when I'm alone. When I have time.

Right now, we have to make a plan.

CHAPTER
TWENTY-EIGHT
ADLY

do not cry about Ax later, when I'm alone.

I cry about him as soon as the limo pulls away from Adeline.

Blubber is a better word for it. With my feet curled up underneath me, sitting across from Holt and Brystin, I go through an entire box of tissues as I catch them up to speed.

In general, I'm not a crier. When I do, it's a few trickled tears that can easily be passed off as watery eyes. Dad enforced a "Just say ow" method of coping with pain, which probably did a lot of psychological damage, while ensuring all three of us could withstand any obstacle with our heads held high.

My head is not held high. My eyes are faucets. My heart cannot be mollified with a single "ow."

It takes a while to explain everything, especially with how many breaks are required to just plain sob, but when I'm done, I wipe my eyes, hiccup, and look to Holt and

Brystin to tell me something comforting. Anything to stop the churning of my stomach and the incessant urge to cry.

Instead, they meet my story with several beats of stony silence.

Finally, after exchanging a glance with Holt, Brystin makes the first effort. "So Ax said he wanted to marry you just so he could be near you?"

Said like that, all soft and unassuming, it sounds like a reasonable thing to say.

"It is why people tend to get married." Holt laces his hand in Brystin's. "It's why I want to marry you."

She blinks up at him. "Me too. It's kind of sweet, really."

I'm tempted to throw one of my balled up, snot-filled tissues at her, but manage to contain myself. "It's not sweet. It's an excuse."

Holt, at least, seems to understand. "Because you think he married you just so he could get the CEO job? Admittedly, that was my first reaction, too."

"Yes!" Now we're getting somewhere. "Seems pretty damn obvious to me."

Holt makes an expression that looks like shrugging but with his face. "I don't know. He swore on his mother's ring that he didn't go after the promotion. No man says shit like that lightly."

Ax swore on his mother's ring to me too. Maybe he just knows people fall for that line.

"To me, the only obvious thing is that the guy is nuts for you," Brystin says.

Holt agrees. "He couldn't take his eyes off her all weekend."

"Those vows were…" She pats her palm over her heart. "Mm."

"I was taking notes." He sounds like he's expecting bonus points for it.

"I was thinking about trading out my fiancé." The grin she gives him is teasing.

He narrows his eyes. "Please be kidding."

"So kidding." She lifts her face so he can press a kiss on her nose.

Fucking great.

My whole world is falling apart, and I go and get myself locked in a car with a pair of lovebirds.

Though, each point they make yanks at a different string in my battered heart. I felt it too, when Ax looked at me. Like he would burn the world down for me. Like he meant every word he spoke in his vows.

"He was *acting*," I tell them, mostly to remind myself.

"I didn't know Ax was an actor," Brystin says. "He's good."

Holt nods. "He deserves an Oscar."

"Oh my God, is this the Axel Morgan fan club?" My head is starting to pound, as much from all the tears as from frustration. "He's not an actor-actor. It was a ruse. Part of the strategy. He exploited our situation."

I point that last part to Holt, hoping that he'll feel as wronged as I do if he remembers that it's not just me getting fucked over here.

Despite that, it's Brystin that comments. "That's high-level conniving you're talking about. Ax always struck me as kind of a himbo."

"Yeah, right?" Holt agrees.

"All beauty, no brains." She giggles.

Holt laughs with her. "Hunter's underling."

As annoyed as I was when they were fawning over Ax, I'm outright enraged at the suggestion that he's just a pretty face. "Now listen here—Ax is probably the smartest person employed by SNC. Ever. The most strategic, for sure. Smarter than Hunter by far. Ax knows the company inside and out. His ideas are cutting edge. He is *not* a himbo."

There's another exchange of looks between the two, as though I've proven something that they already knew.

"You know," Holt says as he stretches his arm out on the seat back behind Brystin, "Ax is on top of his shit. Has more of a finger on the pulse than probably anyone else there. When I was CEO, the board frequently talked about him as a possible backup for me, if I failed to do the job properly. His name was right up there with Hunter's."

Brystin frowns. "They talked about you failing right in front of you? I'm so glad you're out of that toxic situation."

"It's probably more toxic for an actual Sebastian than for someone without the blood ties. Ax as CEO actually makes a lot of sense. I thought you would feel the same way."

I *do* feel the same way.

Or I *did*.

But..."He told SNC to buy SHE."

This time Holt actually shrugs. "I would have told them the same thing. It's a good idea."

I don't know what isn't getting through to him. "He sold us out, Holt!"

"Yeah, and Alex sold us out first because he told Hunter we wanted to buy SHE." He lets that sit for a second, confirming my suspicion last night that this was the secret

Holt and Alex was keeping from me. "Do you think Alex is out to sabotage us too?"

"No, you assHolt." I throw my tissue at him. I'm not in the mood to be patronized and don't have the patience to offer him the same restraint I showed with Brystin.

Which is for nothing because, when the snot-rag bounces off his thigh to the floor, she's the one who picks it up and throws it in the trash compartment.

Then she leans forward to gather the rest of them from the seat next to me. "Alex told Hunter about SHE?" she asks, as she tosses the tissues away.

"He thought it was brotherly to give him a heads-up," Holt says.

She sighs. "Oh, sweet child."

I stare at them with my lips parted, feeling like I'm in the Twilight Zone.

Holt was raised in the same household I was. How does he not understand the rule of business first? "You guys are missing the point."

"What point?" Brystin takes Holt's hand in hers, as if she's responding for them jointly. "Tell us. We're listening."

"Our company." My teeth are gritted. "Are you going to just let it slip through our fingers? Don't you care?"

"Of course I care." Holt's tone is firm but not mean. "I've put all my eggs in this basket. More importantly, I believe in it. I believe we—all three of us—can do something special with it under your management, Ad."

My eyelashes feel newly wet again, and I blink them several times. "SNC has all the money and power. How are we supposed to compete with them over a bid?"

"Same way any small company competes against the big

guys. We give it our best shot and hope that the personal attention we deliver wins over the money and power of SNC." It sounds like something Holt has told himself many times before. As if this isn't the first time he's faced the idea of going head-to-head with our father and the rest of our family.

I guess I'd been so focused on the money part of the escape plan that I didn't stop to think about the various ways things could play out.

Now that I am, it feels like I'm looking at a long, steep slope. "It's impossible. Sebastians always win."

"Good thing we're Sebastians, too."

The lump in my throat doubles in size, and my lip trembles. "I'm not anymore. I'm a Morgan."

"You'll always be a Sebastian." He makes it sound like it's a good thing.

And of course it is.

"But I want to be a Morgan." The tears start again, and I'm beside myself with this want. Because as much as I want to leave SNC and get away from my father's narrow-mindedness, I'd give it all up to have Ax.

To really have him. To *believe* I have him. To believe I'll always have him.

Through my sobs, I hear Brystin's quiet voice. "I think that's the actual point, Holt."

"Ah, AJ. Come here." Holt retrieves his arm from the back of the seat and gestures for me to join them on their bench.

Without hesitation, I cross to settle into the crook of his arm, and bury my head in his shoulder as he wraps me in a hug.

I don't know what I would do in this world without my brother. He's the whole reason I got brave enough to leave SNC in the first place. I have no idea what he did to make this ride today happen so quickly, what was said to the remaining guests about our departure, or where or how my stuff is getting home, but all I had to do was say that I needed him, and now he's here for me. For no reason except that he loves me.

How many times has Ax been there for me in the same way? All because...he loves me? Is that why? How am I supposed to trust that?

As if Holt knows the questions I'm warring with in my head, and when I'm no longer crying so hard that I can't speak, he asks one out loud. "Do you think Ax was genuinely using you for his own gain? Like more than any other person that we know has?"

"I don't have any proof," I say into his shoulder.

"What does your gut say?" Brystin asks.

I pull back from Holt, taking the wad of tissues that Brystin offers to wipe my nose and dab at the wet spot I've left on his black button-down while I consider.

There's no rule that says the CEO spot could only be filled by a Sebastian. If Ax had really wanted the CEO position, wouldn't he have tried to go for it before? Why would he have spent so much time coaching Hunter if he was planning to try to steal the job out from under him?

Would Ax really have needed to marry me at all?

I think about his vows, how he said I made him want more. Made him finally believe he could go after things—like this job?

It's possible that I'm not the reason he got the CEO offer, but I might be the reason he felt like he could deserve it.

Then I accused him of the opposite. To his face. Crushing his spirit, no doubt, in equal if not bigger ways than he crushed mine.

When I think about hurting him, I want to go back to my side of the limo, curl into the fetal position, and stay there forever, but I force myself to stop wallowing and truly answer the question. "My gut feels all over the place where Ax is concerned. Like I'm at the high rollers' table. My heart races and my hands get sweaty, and I feel like I'm going to throw up."

She tilts her head to study me, her face screwed up in confusion. "Haven't you ever been in love before?"

Holt tries to hide a laugh and fails. "It wasn't really encouraged in our family," he explains to her. Then turns to me. "First time for me too, sis." He lifts a hand like he's expecting a fist bump.

I leave my hand at my side. "Fuck you, I've been..." I stop myself before I tell a lie. I've always felt like I've fallen in love a million times because of all the books I've read.

Maybe it's not exactly the same as the real thing. The real thing that I was sure didn't exist a few days ago. "If this is what love feels like, why the fuck would anyone want to feel more of it?"

Brystin gives me a small sympathetic smile. "It's only that way in the beginning. When you're still rolling the dice, putting it all on the table. That part's hard. But when you win, girl...?"

Holt finishes for her. "The prize is fucking everything."

BY THE TIME we reach the city we still have no plan for how to go forward with our bid for SHE, mostly because I can't stop moping about Ax for long enough to think about it.

So much for business first mentality.

When Holt suggests it's a conversation best saved for when we're fresh and Alex is on the phone, I decide that sounds like an excellent idea.

But the thought of going back to an empty apartment makes my chest hurt. I can't even let myself hope Ax will show up eventually, because if he doesn't, I don't know what I'll do.

And while he's called and texted a few times since I've left Adeline, I can't bring myself to read what he's said because I'm chickenshit.

I can practically hear Ax bawking in my head.

On a whim, I ask Holt to have the driver drop them off first so I can make a stop before going home. Obviously, I can't run away from the situation forever, but a quick escape might not be the worst thing, and while alcohol is always a fun option, I prefer my escapism in the form of books.

According to the clock on my phone and the sign on the door, Under the Cover has just closed when we pull up. There's a light that's been left on in the back of the store, but I can't see anyone milling about, so I use the key that Ax gave me and slip quietly inside.

It's the first time I've been here since he brought me. Unsure where the main light switch is, I use the light on my phone to guide me to the contemporary romance section in search of something funny and low-angst. Small town, maybe, with lots of feel good scenes and no drama.

I'm so intent on my task, that I don't notice I'm not alone until the person is nearly on top of me. "Excuse me, can I help you?" the woman asks.

I swear I jump out of my skin.

When I can breathe again, I apologize to the woman. She's about my age with tight curly hair and spunky glasses. The owner, I assume. "I'm so sorry. I'm Adly Morgan. Ax made arrangements for me to be here. I think."

It occurs to me that I don't know how Ax would have introduced me, and wonder if I should have said Sebastian. Funny how quickly I've become attached to a name that I hadn't ever intended to use.

When the woman looks at me strangely, it also occurs to me that maybe I *don't* have permission to be here. Did Ax break in after all?

"Made arrangements for you to be here is one way to say it," the woman says. Then she extends her hand. "Hi. I'm Carley. Great to finally meet you. I'm just finishing up closing. Don't mind me. Leave me a list of everything you take, and I'll be sure to update the inventory."

"Uh. Okay." It's weird, though. Her telling me not to mind her, and come to think of it, I don't think she's billed me yet for the last round. "Well, thank you. Are you the owner? I should tell you, I absolutely love this store. It's my favorite place on earth."

Besides Ax's arms.

The pang that comes with the thought is quickly forgotten when Carley gives me another strange look. "I'm the manager. The current owner is some guy in Florida. Until the sale closes next week, anyway."

"The store is being sold?" Fabulous. Yet another thing I love that I'm about to lose. "Please tell me the new owner is keeping things as is?"

Carly shrugs and gives me the first real smile since approaching me. "Depends. Are you considering making changes?"

"*Me*?"

"I'm sorry. I might be ruining a big surprise, but it was my impression that Mr. Morgan was buying the store for you. You are his wife, aren't you?"

I open my mouth but the ability to speak has gone.

Ax is buying the store...for me?

But why would he...?

A scenario forms in my mind—it's second nature at this point. One where Ax knew that SNC was going after SHE, and believing there was no way to stop it from happening, he decided to buy this store so that I'd have something to fall back on.

It's a fantasy of an idea. I have absolutely no proof, but my gut says it's exactly what happened.

Even if the details are muddled...he bought me a bookstore.

He bought me a bookstore.

He loves me. He has to. People don't pull out their checkbooks to buy happy endings for women that they're planning to fuck over. He loves me, and I'm still a fucking fool because I let believe myself believe the worst instead of the truth.

I force myself to find words. "I'm his wife."

"Phew. I was scared for a minute that he had someone else on the side. Anyway, maybe act surprised when he tells you?" Her dimples twinkle when she smiles.

"Yeah. I'll do that."

Suddenly, I don't have any interest in escaping. The only romance I want is my own. I pull out my phone, and still ignoring the texts he sent, I select *Axhole* from my contacts and press CALL.

He answers after one ring. "Addles?"

The sound of his voice feels like a blanket warm from the dryer. I want to curl up in it for a long, long time.

But first I have to take the risk, roll the dice, let him in. Trust. "Ax? Will you help me figure out how to get SHE?"

He doesn't hesitate to answer. "Yeah, baby. Of course. You don't even have to ask. Want me to meet you somewhere? Tell me where. I'm yours."

"Um..." I hadn't thought further than the question. "Where are you? I'll meet you there."

His breath is audible over the phone. "I'm at home."

Home. As if it's a place instead of him.

"Okay. I'm coming." I hang up, say a quick goodbye and thank you to Carley.

Then, thinking only of the prize, I head home.

CHAPTER
TWENTY-NINE
AX

Time moves like it's stuck in molasses after Adly's phone call.

Honestly, it's better than the hours before, when I didn't know if she'd ever talk to me again, let alone allow me in the apartment. Even though I left Adeline on Adly's heels, I was truly expecting the lock would be changed when I arrived home.

Highly unlikely considering that there hadn't been time, but the Sebastians are like magicians. Money makes the impossible happen.

I was relieved when the key turned for me, only to be thrown back into turmoil when I walked in to find the apartment empty. I sent another, "let's talk" text that she left unread, and paced the length of the hallway from her bedroom to the kitchen over and over, like a man who'd forgotten what he was looking for and where he put it for the better part of an hour.

I legit felt out of my mind.

When she finally called, her voice was an instant remedy. Doesn't matter that the conversation was short and that nothing was resolved. I still have a shot to fix this, and I'm holding onto that like it's the holy grail.

I *can* fix this. I will make this right.

My ears strain, listening for the door as I find mindless tasks to keep me occupied. I flip through every news article on my FlipBoard—twice. I unpack my suitcase. I unpack hers as best as I can. I set out all the gifts I was sent home with on the dining room table except for the painting that I place on the cabinet in the foyer.

Then, when almost an hour has passed, I hear the lock turning and run to meet her at the front door, bracing myself for a chilly greeting. I haven't forgotten that we have rules about boundaries in the apartment, but after the last couple of days, they feel outdated and moot.

Point being, I have no idea what to expect when she crosses the threshold, and I force myself to behave with restraint.

But it's all for nothing because as soon as she sees me, she runs into my arms and throws hers around my torso, burying her face in my neck. "I'm sorry," she says, breathing me in like I'm her favorite scent.

I planned out monologues of explanations on the drive to New York, only to realize that those are the only two words that need to be said. "No, I'm sorry."

"I panicked and overreacted."

"I'm the one who panicked when I made that suggestion to your father about buying SHE." I pull her in tighter. "And then I should have told you."

"It was a smart idea. I shouldn't have said you only got the CEO position because of me."

"I *did* only get the CEO position because of you, but I don't want it if it means I don't get you."

She pulls back just enough to look at me. Her eyes are puffy from crying, and her lips still swollen from kissing last night and this morning, and she's the most beautiful woman I've ever seen, even before she says, "If you turn that job down, I will never roleplay with you again."

"Does that mean there's roleplay in our future if I do take the job?" Fuck the roleplay. The real question I'm asking is shrouded in the longer sentence—*do we have a future?*

I realize it's probably the wrong time for this kind of sentimentality. SHE is on the line, and we have a small window of time to fight for it. "Never mind. Focus on that later. Let's talk out a plan."

I start to turn out of our embrace, but she tugs me back. "Ax, you're the *only* future I'm sure of right now."

Fuck, I'm such a sap because my insides suddenly feel like mush, and all I want to do is pick her up and carry her to the nearest bedroom so I can show her what kind of future I imagine for us. Specifically with my mouth and hands and cock.

But I man up before I get carried away. "That's unacceptable. Let's figure out how to solidify the rest."

There's a flash of vulnerability in her eyes right before her gaze lands on the new art piece. Then her brows knit in question. "Is that the painting you bid on at the Ida Sebastian Academy auction?"

Holt was right when he suggested it for her foyer. I just

failed to place the winning bid. "It's a wedding gift. From Scott and Tess."

Her expression brightens. "We have wedding gifts?"

God, she's adorable.

It takes a few minutes to pull her away from investigating the pile of wrapped packages, picking each one up to shake and feel the weight before cataloging the possibilities of the contents in her mind, but eventually, we make it to the couch to discuss business.

Facing each other, I prop my elbow on the back of the sofa and rest my head in my palm. Adly curls her feet under her, a glass of wine in one hand, the fingers of her other hand playing up and down my thigh.

If I weren't so focused, that latter hand would be a distraction.

"I could underbid you," I suggest, after telling her I got the official email offer this afternoon. I'm invited to a board meeting on Thursday to accept or turn it down. I figure that will be my opportunity to negotiate plans for SHE.

Purposefully underbidding, though, is a messy solution. If I got caught, I'd be fired at the least, jailed and fined at the worst.

"Even without the legal ramifications, our bid is too close to value for you to underbid. We submitted it yesterday, and Bob told Holt that he needs a couple of weeks to decide. He would have jumped on ours if he didn't think he could get a better offer somewhere else."

I already know they don't have any more money to up their bid. "Have you considered finding another investor?"

"At this short notice?" She takes a deep breath in and exhales. "Then there would be a matter of negotiating power. Who else is going to come on to the project and let me run everything?"

I think about the millions I have saved away after years at SNC. It's not billionaire money, but it could make a difference. "Me."

She smiles, changing the pattern of her fingers on my thigh to circles. "Conflict of interest. You can't be CEO of SNC if you have stock in SHE."

"There are ways around it." Hunter would know how. "Or I don't take the CEO position, and then it's not an issue. Ow!" I bat her hand away when she pinches me. "We have to discuss all the options. Not just the ones you like."

"So what then? Hunter becomes CEO, and you know he'll come after us with an ultra-competitive bid. Even if we won SHE by some miracle, he'd find ways to bring us down afterward."

"That was always going to be the situation with Hunter at the helm, whether he tried to buy out SHE or not."

"But now we don't have to worry about that." Banned from my thigh, she brings her fingers to my arm to trace my tattoo. "You are the right person for that job, Ax. And also, the best shot I have is with you there. You really want to help fix this, then stop trying to convince yourself that the answer is to turn it down."

Her tone isn't as stern as the words. Almost as if she's reminding herself of the fact as much as me.

"Okay, then let me convince the board to change the strategy." I spent a lot of the drive back to the city thinking of other options, and there are a couple of ideas that could be viable.

"What strategy? That's the best plan. There isn't a better

one." She sounds more tired than defeated. "I might need to consider that it's not in the cards for me. Besides, I would be a stellar bookstore owner."

It could be coincidence, but it's too pointed. "You know about the bookstore. I'm sorry."

"Why are you sorry? It's the extreme grand gesture. I'm probably pregnant because that's how hot it is. It's so big I can't begin to say thank you."

She's kidding, but the idea of babies with Adly is a real turn-on.

But not because I gave her a bookstore. "I felt bad knowing SHE was a longshot, and I wanted a backup escape for you. I realize that, like always, I wasn't aiming high enough for you. You deserve your own network. Let Carley run the bookstore."

"Wouldn't it be amazing if we all just got what we wanted because we deserved it?"

It's not the way the world usually works, but I'm determined to make it happen for her. My dream is her, and I'll do anything for her to get her dream, even if that dream isn't me. "You have to trust me. I'm going to come up with a better plan."

She frowns, and I know I've hit a nerve. Trust is a big thing for her, and I know she's trying, but it's frustrating for me too. I'm here. I've been here. I keep being here. What more does she need to believe I'm in this? Haven't I proven myself yet?

It's not an argument I want to get into right now, though. "We'll talk it out first," I tell her. "You don't have to trust me blindly."

"No, I want to trust you... I, um..."

She stares down at the couch, seeming to be searching for the right words. Words that aren't necessary. "I get it, Adly. You don't–"

She cuts me off. "Let me get this out, okay? I need to say this." She shifts, her hand leaving mine as she takes a swallow from her wine before reaching over to set it on the coffee table.

Her change in demeanor sends my pulse into rapid-fire, and I'm afraid suddenly that there's a bomb she's been carrying, and when she presents it, this comfortable moment between us will blow up, along with the promise of a future together.

Maybe that's just PTSD talking. The downside of wanting more, I've realized after this afternoon's drama, is that I care when I don't get it. I hurt. I hurt a lot.

But if I want her to trust me, I have to trust her too.

"I'm listening." It's all I can do to keep the tremor from my voice.

She sits back again, her forehead wrinkled in thought. "I'm sure you know my mother didn't really die from a brain aneurysm."

The turn in conversation throws me. The last thing I expected to be talking about tonight was her family's cover-up of Sonya Sebastian's suicide. It's a secret held so tightly that I haven't even ever seen conspiracy theories about it on Reddit. Maybe because it happened so long ago.

"Yeah. Yeah, I do." It was a constant source of trauma for Hunter, of course. He was only eight when she died, and while the Sebastians did everything to make sure the world didn't know the truth, they made sure that Hunter "knew" it was his fault.

Real fucked up, if you ask me.

The whole situation, really. Sonya had an affair with Hunter's father, only to be kicked to the curb after she birthed their son. In true Sebastian fashion, Reynard used his money and status to make sure Sonya lost all custody.

When Samuel married Sonya, I think he thought he was being a hero. Through him, she could see Hunter now and again. Had more contact than she would have otherwise, but I think it just made it harder for her to get over her broken heart. She had Holt, Steele, and Adly, and still pined for the son she'd lost. Her suicide note only mentioned Hunter.

Adly's never talked to me about it, but I imagine it was equally traumatizing for her.

"No one told me," she says now. "Holt was seven when it happened, and he must have eavesdropped enough to figure it out. I'm not sure when Steele found out. He doesn't like to talk about it, but I think he was young. No one told me until I was eighteen."

I flinch. Even I knew long before that.

"Holt's the one who finally sat me down, and afterward —when I was still mad at him for telling me, before I accepted that I'd rather know the truth than live with the lies—I asked him why he told me. He said, 'Because no one else is going to tell you the truth.'"

She pauses, and guessing her point, I'm desperate to argue it.

But it feels like she has more to say, so I force myself to keep still, keep listening. Force myself not to react until she asks for a reaction.

"That's only one of the times I learned the Trust No One

lesson. I learned it every day watching my father say one thing to his brothers and another to his father and another to us. I learned it when the men talked business and strategized creative ways to bend the truth. I learned it from the boys who asked me out on dates just so they could get access to the Sebastian world—backstage invites to concerts, a ride on our Macy's Parade float, recommendations for universities. The list goes on.

"Might have been easier to deal with if they'd just be honest upfront about their intentions, but no one ever was. No one ever is. That's what Holt reinforced for me that day. No one tells the truth. No one can be trusted."

I can't hold back anymore. "Fucking Holt. That's a fucking bleak and depressing out—"

She raises her hand and pinches my lips together with her fingers. "Hold on, hold on. I'm not done. Be patient."

It's hard, because I really I want to get Holt on the fucking phone to ream him out for painting such a dismal portrait of humanity.

I mean *some* humans are pure shit. But not all.

Not most, in my experience.

But I never had to deal with people wanting me for my money or my power like she has, and I gather it makes for a far different life than I had, so I concede a nod for her to go on.

"Holt wasn't wrong. *I* was wrong." She releases my lips and moves her fingers to play with the evening stubble on my jaw. "See, I thought he meant not to trust anyone ever. But I think now he couldn't have meant that, because what about him? I can trust him. Because he loves me, and I think that's the key. Trust the people who love me like Holt loves me.

"And I know you love me. So...I'm going to trust you." She shakes her head, as if scratching out her last sentence. "I already do trust you."

My chest feels tight, like my heart is trying to fight through my ribs to get closer to her, and my arms ache to pull her into my lap so I can kiss the bitterness from her confession.

I need her to know that I hear what she's saying, first, what she's trying to explain, and I cup her face, stroking her cheek with my thumb. "Addlecat, you can trust me because I love you, and I vow to prove every day from now on that you can trust me, because I love you. But I am never, ever going to love you like your brother does."

She lifts her hands to cover her face. "That's not what I..." She drops her hands so she can swat me with them. "You know what I mean."

Of course I do. I understand her better than I did before, too, and I'm fuckall grateful that she felt comfortable enough to explain.

It's also been a long day, and my brain, at least, is fried. We aren't getting further on this tonight.

So instead of getting serious, I tease her. "Do I? Maybe we should clarify." I grab her by the hips and drag her over to me, draping her legs over my lap.

Then I run my hands up her thighs, letting the edge of my thumbs skate the lines of her panties. "Does Holt love you like this?"

"Oh my God." She dissolves into giggles.

Next, I bend to nip at her tit through her shirt. "Does he love you like this?"

"You're an ass."

Hand inside her shorts, under her panties, my thumb finds her clit. "What about this? Is this how your brother loves you?"

Her eyes close briefly as she moans.

Then she leans forward and grabs my fully erect cock through my pants. "Stop talking about my brother unless you want me to think he's responsible for what's happening here."

"Fuck that shit." I slip my hand out of her shorts, and offer them to her lips. "Lick off your sweetness for me."

She does, and I thought I was already rock hard, but now I'm fucking stone, and it's my turn to groan.

Nudging her legs open with mine, I settle between them. "Now, where were we?"

Our mouths meet in a slow kiss. Her breasts press against my chest and I feel the heat radiating from her body. "I believe we were discussing how much your brother loves you," I murmur against her lips.

"That was not what we were discussing," she says, reaching down to stroke my cock over my clothes.

I chuckle and kiss down her neck, nipping at her skin as I go. My hands return to her hips, about to push her shorts and panties down, but I'm still laughing about her brother in my head, and suddenly, Hunter enters my mind.

I pause, debating if I really want to interrupt the sexy stuff to bring him up.

Loyalty wins out, and I sit back. "I know this might be

hard to hear, but I learned a similar lesson about trust from your brother."

She tries to reconcile a time when Holt would have taught me anything, and realizes that's not who I'm talking about. "My other brother."

She sighs. "I hope we aren't always going to talk about my brother when I'm about to get cock." But she places a hand on my shoulder, encouraging me to go on.

"Preferably not. But Hunter did teach me what it means to have someone's back. He's been there. He's proven himself. To me, anyway." I realize she didn't have the same relationship with him, but she has to understand that he means something to me. He always will.

I'll choose her if she needs that, but I'd rather choose them both.

She seems to get it. "Have you talked to him yet?"

Since he walked out of the reception, she means.

I shake my head. "You were my priority."

There's a softness in her eyes as she massages the tight muscle at my neck. "Will he understand?"

Her tone is compassionate, and I can tell she cares about my relationship with him, even if she doesn't have any hope for her own relationship with him.

It's all I needed. "I guess we'll find out."

Then, stretching myself over her again, I lower my hand to tease her wet pussy. "Now stop talking about your brothers so I can give you cock without it being weird."

I spend the rest of the night building trust, showing Adly how much I love her.

We don't mention her brothers again.

CHAPTER
THIRTY
AX

Being back at work on Monday is surreal as fuck.

I'm supposed to be finalizing the rollout of next year's program lineup like I'm not considering pulling the plug on a few of the shows when I take the CEO position.

When I'm not distracted by all the changes I want to make to SNC, I'm thinking about alternatives to acquiring SHE. My computer has so many notes docs open that I have to triple check which one I'm in every time I jot something down. I'm still behind from last week's Fourth of July holiday too, so it's go, go, go from the minute I walk in the office until I force myself to quit for the night.

Adly's in the same boat. She's expected to catch up on her HR shit like she's not about to put in her two weeks' notice. Like she isn't simultaneously making her own CEO plans.

The only reason either of us make it out of the building before midnight is each other. Not because we're looking out for each other's health or anything. There's just only so long either of us seem to be able to go without touching. Without kissing and fucking and getting lost in each other.

We get very little sleep before the whole chaotic schedule starts again.

We also do very little talking. Serious talking, anyway. Without either of us saying it directly, it's as though we've put the logistics of our relationship on pause until the business bullshit is sorted out.

After all this is said and done, do the rings stay on? Am I back to sleeping in the room down the hall instead of her bed? Do we start dating? A weird concept when we've already stood in a church and exchanged vows, but also just as weird to think we might actually be married now, for real, without ever having discussed kids or religious preferences or retirement goals.

I can't think about it right now. Not until after my meeting with the board, and not because Adly isn't the priority. Just the opposite. The work shit is noise that keeps pulling focus. Figuring it out is the only way we get space to concentrate on us.

Tuesday, I barely make it until noon before slipping down to her office for a round of Delivery Man Has A Large Package, for old times' sake.

As soon as the official workday is finished, she heads downtown to meet with Holt. I have another obligation before I can join them, but I call in via Zoom along with Alex while I'm in the car.

"I talked to Bob Peterson today," Holt says. "I'd hoped I could get him to accept our bid right now before SNC made a play. I don't know if he's gotten wind of a potential second offer or if he's just holding out because he's a greedy fuck—whichever it is, he's not accepting any offers until Friday."

"Your meeting with the board is Thursday?" Alex asks.

I assume he's asking me. "Yep. Every time I talk to Samuel, he acts like my acceptance of the position is already a done deal. I'm sure that's the viewpoint of most everyone. If I had to venture a guess, I'd say that the real agenda for the meeting is formalizing a bid strategy."

Conveniently just in time to submit before Bob's deadline.

Adly lets out a grunt of disgust. "Someone's leaked to Bob. The timing is too coincidental."

Her anxiety triggers some caveman mode, and I have to make sure not to offer assurances that I can't deliver, just to make her feel better. "The financial predictions I put together suggest it's actually not as good of a buy for SNC as it first sounded. I found some other options that don't carry as much risk." Well, *one* option. But it's damn promising. "It's such a big difference in the bottom line that they'll have to consider it."

"Awesome." Adly couldn't be more sarcastic if she tried. "Now if only everyone on the board were a reasonable human being."

Making deals with rich fucks is always about the money. Always. Greed wins, hands down.

Except when it's about power.

I know full well some of those men are more interested in getting Holt under their thumb than they are about making a profit. I'm holding out hope that at least a few of them aren't completely petty.

If not, I might have another trick in my back pocket. Tomorrow's meeting will determine that.

Right now, my car is pulling up to the curb for tonight's business.

I leave the Zoom call, texting Adly a separate goodbye so that we don't have to be all gushy in front of the others, then I pocket my phone and get out of the car in front of Hunter's building.

I can't remember ever feeling this nervous to talk to Hunter. We've been friends too long for this to be the first time I've fucked him over. He's fucked me over too. We've figured out a way of dealing with those snags in our friendship.

But this time the stakes couldn't be higher. For me. For him. In different ways.

I don't know what to expect, and that not-knowing has put a pit in my stomach and turned my mouth into a desert as I ride the elevator up to his floor.

At his door, I pause before trying my key. He changed the locks when he felt like Alex had betrayed him, and Alex is his blood.

Though, I'm not sure blood weighs the same to the Sebastians as it does to others.

When my key turns, I'm relieved, but still unsure as fuck how he'll greet me.

I decide it's best to give him a head's up that I'm here,

and knock sharply on the open door before calling out, "Housekeeping!"

He calls back without hesitation. "In the den."

I find him at the game table with a glass of scotch and a deck of cards. Besides the loosened tie and missing shoes, he looks like he's just come from the office.

Since he doesn't actually have an office, I try not to think about where he was today that required business attire. So much of his life the last few years has been preparing for SNC. I'm not sure what else would occupy him, and despite the fact that we've shared most everything over the years, it doesn't feel like I'm in a place to ask.

When he sees me, he mutes the television, but he nods at the screen. "She's phenomenal." I follow his gaze and realize he's watching Brystin's news show on SHE. "SNC took a hit when she left. It will be a real coup to have her back in the fold."

I pause before replying, trying to suss out his angle. Obviously, he's not pussyfooting around the elephant in the room, but where does he see the two of us in relation to SNC now? His straightforward tone gives nothing away.

The fact that I no longer support acquiring SHE complicates my answer.

I settle on something vague. "I think that's certainly how the board feels."

"You told them to feel that way."

The undercurrent of animosity in his voice sends me to the bar cart to pour my own glass of scotch.

I told him at the rehearsal dinner that I'd shared the idea with Samuel, but I'm sure he's talked to the other board members about the reason behind their decision to offer me the CEO position. They aren't supposed to talk about what happens at meetings with anyone else, especially Hunter since he was in the running for the position—hence why he's been excused from all CEO-related discussions, even though he's normally on the board himself. My father's one of the members who keeps his lips tight, but he's one of the few who aren't a Sebastian. They aren't known to follow rules.

Hunter's father would have told him it was the SHE proposal.

I take a sip of my drink, relishing the burn, and wonder if Hunter resents me for giving the idea to Samuel after all.

When the alcohol settles, I turn to face him. "I bet SHE was always on their radar. Holt ending up there has to be an embarrassment to Samuel. I'm sure he was looking for someone else to come up with the acquisition idea because he knew he'd be accused of ulterior motives."

It's the first time I've considered this, but it sounds right.

Hunter's brows lift as he ponders. "That's probably accurate," he says, and now I'm sure I'm right.

The realization makes me feel like a pawn on someone else's chessboard, and for half a second, I start to doubt that I deserve the job I've been offered.

Again.

It's a fleeting thought. The last couple of days thinking about how I'd run the place has given me confidence. There are politics involved in choosing me, yes, but I can do the job. Better than Hunter can, probably. At least just as well.

He lifts his drink. "Manipulative little fuckers, aren't they?"

I don't usually like to encourage Hunter's self-loathing

by ragging on the Sebastians as a whole, but I can't disagree with this particular statement so I raise my glass. "That they are."

A beat passes in silence.

It's my place to say something, no doubt. I purposefully didn't try to plan this conversation, though, deciding it was better to respond to Hunter in the moment instead of making assumptions about what he might say.

Now I'm regretting that decision.

I'm usually good at thinking on my feet, but the words aren't coming. Probably because I know they'll be hard to say.

Hoping they'll come easier without so much literal distance between us, I cross the room and take a seat across from him.

As if it's automatic, Hunter starts dealing the deck of cards. Four cards face down to me, four face up between us, four face down for himself—Casino. A game we've played so many times over the years, we could play it in our sleep.

I pick up my cards and make a play.

On his turn, he sweeps. "How long have you wanted it?"

Immediately, I know he isn't talking about the game.

Not the card game, anyway. Jockeying for the CEO position at SNC could very much be considered a game in itself.

No one has asked me this particular question yet. Holt and Adly were more interested in whether or not I'd pursued the job. Hunter is the first to sense the deeper implications of the situation we're in.

For that, he deserves a frank answer. "I don't know. Maybe the whole time." I scoop up a couple of spades on my turn. "Maybe I was always wishing it was me instead of you." Maybe I didn't want to be just another person who envied him, and so I buried the wish.

Or maybe it felt too out of reach. "I never thought that it was a possibility, though. Not without the name," I tell him, which is the God's honest truth. "But then I married Adly, and doors seemed to open."

He lets out a gruff laugh. "Those doors were open to you even before you married Adly."

He takes the ten of diamonds, the highest scoring card in the game, but it's a minor loss when weighed against the value of his statement because it means he believes I always had a shot at CEO.

His faith in me means something.

Or I could take another point of view and be pissed that he never encouraged me to go after the job earlier. Was it because he really believed I didn't want it, or because he wanted it too badly himself to care about my feelings?

I have no proof. When Adly had no proof, she jumped to the worst scenario.

But I already know that Hunter cares about me. We have blood brother scars on our palms. We've been through too much. I'd be a jackass not to let our past have merit.

So I consider his statement thoughtfully. "I guess I could never see myself walking through those doors without following you in."

I really was content to be the shadow. It was easier. It was good enough.

It's not good enough anymore.

On my turn, I stare at the cards in front of me. There's

more than one move I can make, but I don't make any. "What if I take it?"

Holding my breath, I lift my eyes from the game to study his face.

He freezes and looks up at me from his own hand, but he doesn't look surprised. "It will put a real strain on our friendship."

It's a warning.

But a strain isn't the same as an ending, and hope flickers briefly in my chest.

Of course, that's only the first bomb.

Might as well let the next one drop. "I'm about to add another strain—I'm in love with your sister."

This time he does seem taken aback. "Oh. That's rich." His laugh is humorless. "Fucking amazing."

He sets down his cards and crosses the room to the cigar box on the bar cart, but when he opens it, it appears to be a joint that he retrieves. He lights it in silence and takes a long puff.

I know it must feel like I've chosen the other side. His father has pitted Hunter against his half-siblings his entire life, brainwashing his son into believing that there's justification to the rivalry.

I think he knows somewhere down deep that most of it has been built out of petty jealousy and nothing with any real validity. He's too smart not to see it logically.

But emotionally? He's been groomed. He's been indoctrinated. That's some hard shit to shed.

I get that, and because he is my buddy and because it didn't cost me anything to align myself with him, I did.

The last thing either of us could have expected was for me to fall in love with one of the enemies.

It has to have thrown him as much as it first threw me.

He's mid puff when he recognizes my conundrum. "Oh shit." He pounds his fist on his chest as he coughs. "You're strung up by your balls, aren't you? Married to the woman you're supposed to be selling out. Ouch."

To his credit, he appears only mildly smug about it.

I let out a long stream of air, releasing some ridiculous fantasy I'd had that things could go differently—okay, I suppose I did think a little about what I'd say after all. There are very few serious problems I've encountered over my life that he hasn't helped iron out, and a part of me had imagined I might be able to tap Hunter for ideas with Adly's problem. We're fucking unstoppable when we put our heads together.

I see now that it was as insensitive as it was preposterous.

He's managed to carry this conversation with stoicism, but I can read the guy. The hollow beneath his eyes, the slightly higher pitch of his voice, the stiff way he holds his cards, the sharp line of his jaw—he's hurting.

Of course, he fucking hurts.

He could have tried to mask it behind rage and blame— it would have been understandable—but I guess he respects me too much to do that. Respects our past.

I respect it too.

After the things we've been through together, it's hard not to have a bond based in truthfulness.

So, respectfully, I don't ask for his help.

Truthfully, I tell him, "I'm, uh, working through some different scenarios."

He tilts his head as if considering some of his own. "You'll figure it out."

There's malice to his tone, but it's also possible Hunter always had more faith in me than I did. Right along with my father. The difference being that Hunter didn't make me feel like it was my failing.

Across the room, Hunter runs his hand through his hair. "This fucking sucks, Axelrod." His voice is raw from more than just smoke.

The distance between us is wide again, but I force myself to ignore the urge to close it. He's the one who created it.

I set my cards down, and run my hands up and down my thighs. "I need you to know—I didn't try to fuck you over."

He turns away from me to face the cart. "Well. I didn't try to fuck you over, either. It just happens sometimes."

He no longer tries to disguise his bitterness. It has teeth. It's a wounded animal, so driven by instincts, it would chew through its own paw if it were the only chance to survive.

I stare at the floor, searching for the right words.

Before I can attempt any that come to mind, there's a crash. Startled, I stand when I see that he's swept half the bottles off the cart to the floor. Liquor pools at his feet amidst pieces of glass and the few containers strong enough to withstand the outburst.

It's a rare display of emotion. Hunter's skilled at playing

numb, and I'm both honored and gutted to witness his true feelings.

Still with his back to me, he holds on to the ends of the cart like it's the only thing keeping him on his feet, the joint dangling between two fingers of his grip. "You were my brother because you were never a Sebastian."

Something lodges at the back of my throat. The recognition that I've crossed a line that can never be uncrossed plunges like a self-inflicted knife into my stomach. "I know." My voice croaks. "I know."

It's fucked up that I've had a better experience with his family than he has. His father is cruel and abusive. His mother, dead, and Hunter made to believe it's his fault. He was manipulated into making Holt his rival by his father and his uncle. Alex resented him to the point of destroying their relationship. Even Adly has let herself believe the rhetoric where Hunter is concerned.

Besides Grandpa Irving, the Sebastians have never shown Hunter anything akin to love.

Me taking the CEO job is just a symptom of the bigger betrayal—becoming one of them.

Am I crazy to believe that this can be overcome?

"I'm still me," I tell him. "I won't become them."

"That's not a promise you can keep." He turns to face me, disregarding the mess he's made. "I would never have wished this burden on you. I would have protected you from them."

If he'd been given the job, he means.

He was raised to believe it was his responsibility to fulfill his father's supposed destiny, that if he carried the weight of this obligation, the rest of his siblings would be spared. It's self-aggrandizing and martyrdom all wrapped up in one package, and I can't blame him for buying into it after witnessing how far Reynard went to instill the belief.

But fuck, it would be a whole lot easier if he just set that shit down.

"Now you don't have to," I say, knowing one phrase can't erase a lifetime of indoctrination. "Now it's my turn to protect you. You're free now, Hunter. You can figure out what you want to do with your life—what you really want to do. Not what you think you're supposed to do."

He wags his head in a *la de da de da, don't you know every-thing* gesture. "It was the only thing I wanted."

It's possible that's true.

"Then double down on your campaigning so you can come in and clean up after me when I'm fired." God, I hope that's not what happens, but I'm not naïve about surviving in Sebastian-infested waters.

Still, Hunter takes it for the placating statement that it is, rolling his eyes. "At least you didn't try to convince me we could really be brothers now that you've married my..." He hates to refer to Adly as his sister, but in front of me, it's an outright lie to call her his cousin. He settles on..."*her.*"

"Never." We were already brothers. We will *always* be brothers.

In *my* heart, anyway.

Hunter may choose to see things differently. "Now that you are a Sebastian, you should know—I tend to keep them at arm's length."

I pretend it doesn't sting. "Maybe that won't always be necessary."

"That would be a real turn of events, wouldn't it?" He

lifts the joint to his lips, and maybe I'm supposed to believe the spite in his eyes is for me, but it could be for the Sebastian empire and the toxic family dynamics that led to this predicament in the first place.

I choose to believe the latter.

On his next exhale, he waves the smoke away from his face and nods toward the card table. "I'd ask you to stay and finish the game, but I think it's best if you leave now."

The dismissal is another sting.

Not because I didn't see it coming or because I don't believe it's warranted. I just don't know when I'll be allowed back in this apartment. When I'll lift my glass again with him. When he'll deal me in for a game of Casino.

It's me desperate for a hint of our future that has me asking, "Should I keep my key?"

He considers as he puts his joint out in the ashtray on his desk. "How else will you dispose of the questionable shit on my hard drive if I die? The paparazzi shouldn't be allowed to have that much fun."

A particular evening several years ago with three stupid-hot girls and the camera on comes rushing to my mind. "Probably best for my own ass that shit gets destroyed."

"Meanwhile, you'll have to trust it in my hands." It might not be intended as menacing.

He crosses to me, finally, his hand stretched out toward mine, and I know before I take it what this is about. "This means I'm owed a Get Even."

Strangely, this statement makes me feel better. It's a threat, but there's history with it. It's another game like Negotiations, which also began with me and Hunter, but

Get Even was born more out of a need for a coping mechanism.

I can still remember the first time we played, that summer during our teens that we spent at that fucking place we never talk about. Camp, we called it. Evil reform school, more like. Hunter had accidentally gotten me in trouble, and after I'd taken the cruel and unusual punishment, he'd felt like shit about it.

More though, we'd needed something to have control over. Something with rules written by us. A justice system that made sense in a situation that was far from just. *"It's cool,"* I'd told him. *"Now I'm owed a Get Even."*

Who remembers what I did to him? The revenge wasn't the point. Being even was.

It became a staple to our friendship, pulled out whenever one of us felt slighted. When he got Valedictorian over me in high school, for example. When I graduated summa cum laude in college, and he only graduated magna cum laude. When he fucked my Latin tutor. When I fucked his first girlfriend. There was lots of Getting Even over women.

That was usually the revenge, too—fucking the other's latest girl.

It feels like a fairly benign threat considering Hunter is never going to try to fuck Adly.

It also feels hopeful. Like he cares enough about our friendship to try to balance the scales. I let my hand close around his, and we shake. "That seems fair."

It's possible I just gave him permission to sabotage me in my new job, but if that's what it takes for us to be right, then that's what it takes.

If it doesn't happen at all, if things are never right again between us, that will have to be all right too. Adly will never replace my friendship with Hunter, but I think I could live my life without anyone, as long as I have her. She's the only future that matters anymore.

One day maybe Hunter will have someone that makes him feel the same.

That's the prayer I offer under my breath as I step out of his apartment.

Then I close the door behind me and walk toward what lies ahead.

CHAPTER
THIRTY-ONE
ADLY

t's time," Ax says, sweeping into my office on Thursday afternoon.

I don't admit that I've been watching the clock like it's my job for the past hour. It didn't matter that I knew he was stopping in on his way upstairs to his meeting with the board—I couldn't get myself to focus for shit. And it's not even my meeting.

He's probably feeling that tangled up in nerves himself, if not more so.

Without bothering to finish the email I'm currently struggling to write, I'm out of my desk chair and crossing to him.

The past few days have been weird and exactly right, both at the same time. Without talking about it, we're starting to figure out a work/home routine. The boundaries I once thought were so crucial are completely gone at the apartment, but elsewhere, I'm still tentative about approaching him without being in character.

Now, I use the excuse of straightening his tie as reason to touch him. He switched up his normal suit rotation this morning at my request to wear his navy Canali two-piece. It's sharp without being pretentious, and he wears it like a mother-fucking badass.

While I finish tucking his tie into his jacket and smoothing out his lapels, he fidgets with his cuffs. His nervousness is palpable. "You still have a few minutes. Do you want to run through what you're going to say?"

I've only seen sections of his presentation, partly because of time, but partly because this won't be a traditional meeting. They're scheduled to be in the Lounge rather than a conference room. The setting is much more relaxed, with long curved upholstered benches and armchairs and a bar. It's meant for schmoozing and posturing, usually used for wooing important figures, but the board tends to meet there a lot as well.

The fact they've decided to meet there today signals they feel Ax's acceptance is just a formality. We're both not sure that he'll be given the chance to pitch any ideas at all, but he's determined to try.

"Uh..." Ax shudders with what seems like anxiety. "I think I'm good. Do you need me to run through anything?"

"Not if you don't." Of course I'm dying to know everything he plans to say and what points he'll emphasize and how he'll pivot if challenged, but I'm doing my best to relax and trust him. Alex, Holt, and I have put together the best bid possible, but we have no influence over SNC. This is Ax's chance to give us a shot at SHE.

He takes a deep breath and for the first time since he's walked in here, he seems to finally focus on me. His hands settle on my hips, and his gaze flickers from my eyes to my mouth. "You could give me a kiss goodbye. I'm off to war, and the enemy is well armed. You might never see me again."

A smile plays on my lips. "Don't talk like that, soldier. I won't have it. I won't kiss you goodbye, because we'll see each other soon, but I will kiss you good luck."

My mouth parts and surrenders to his tongue, and I throw my arms around his neck as the kiss deepens. I can't believe I wasted so much time never touching my lips to his. What was I afraid of? That I'd hand over my heart as quickly as I handed over my panties?

Now that I've done just that, it's hard to imagine why I ever thought it was such a bad idea.

Before the kissing, though—even before the sex—Ax has been part of my work life for so long that it's strange to think of working somewhere without him. If everything goes as planned, I'll be doing just that, across town in another building.

I still want that.

But the realization that things will change puts a sharp pang of melancholy in my chest. No more quickies in the middle of the day. No more having to move my entire schedule around because Ax has created another HR scandal. No more throwing daggers at him with my eyes across a conference table.

If I can't buy SHE and have to stay here a little longer, it wouldn't be the worst thing, I suppose.

"No matter what happens," I tell him, wiping my gloss from his lips, "it will be okay."

"Yeah?" It doesn't sound like he's skeptical. More like he's just confirming I really feel that way.

I test a couple of the worst-case scenarios in my mind to see if I really do. In every one, I'm good as long as Ax is with me.

But seeing that we haven't once broached the topic of our real future since negotiating our fake one, it feels like it might be too much to put that on him right now.

Instead, I just say, "Yeah. I really think so."

"I think so too."

There's no alcohol—no toast and, "*Salute*"—but it feels like a promise all the same.

Ax takes another deep breath and stares down at me like he would prefer more kissing, which is my sign to get him on his way. "Go. Before I end up rumpling your suit."

He raises a brow as if he's considering whether or not he has time for that.

He doesn't.

"Go!" Laughing, I shoo him out the door, lingering on the threshold as I watch him head toward the elevator. "You got this!" I call after him. "Text me immediately!"

Without slowing his stride, he whirls around to give me a thumbs up, then turns out of sight.

I spin to face my empty office, jittery with nervousness. Is there any point in trying to work? It's four in the afternoon. Too early to break out the alcohol?

I'm still pondering when there's a rap on my open door.

When I turn to see who it is, Holt's standing there. "It's time."

He's as anxious about today as anyone, obviously, but he hadn't mentioned anything about stopping by, so it's a surprise to see him.

Especially since he isn't supposed to be able to get in the elevators that lead to the exec offices. "How did you get up here?"

He shrugs it off like it's a ridiculous question. "Security knows me."

"Oh." More like Security *likes* him. He had his flaws, but morale did peak under his short tenure as CEO. Now that I think about it, there are probably a lot of staff members who would bend the rules to do him a favor.

"So are you going to spend the next hour or so wearing a hole in the carpet or are you coming with me to watch?"

"Watch?" The Lounge is behind solid oak doors with no windows to the interior, so he can't be talking about Ax's meeting. Is there something else happening that I forgot about?

A smug smile spreads on Holt's face. "You don't know about the Electrical Room." He doesn't wait for me to confirm. "Come on. We're going to miss it."

Five minutes later, we're outside the Lounge in front of a door labeled Electrical Room.

"Has this always been here?" I swear I've never noticed it before.

"It's meant to be inconspicuous," Holt says, entering a code into the panel. He grins when the screen blinks green. "Dad didn't change it after he came back."

"Your passwords still work? Are you fucking kidding me?" There are a few doors in the building that I just assumed I'd lost access to after Holt left. The private rooftop, the Lounge, the executive sauna on the top floor. Now I find out I could have been using them this whole time?

The lost opportunities flutter from my mind as I follow him into the narrow room and discover two rows of theater style chairs facing the wall that backs up to the Lounge.

Oh, and it's not a wall—it's a window. The giant mirror behind the bar in the Lounge room is a fucking two-way.

"Oh my God." There is a secret surveillance room at SNC that I never knew about, and I'm tripping out.

Then I remember the last time I was inside the Lounge myself, and how Ax and I stayed later than everyone else and… "Oh. My. God!"

Holt's focused on some sort of remote that he found on a side table, but he seems to understand the source of my horror. "If no one knew you were in there, no one would have any reason to watch or listen in. Besides, only a handful of people have the code, let alone know this room exists."

Right, right. That makes sense.

Except the part where he said "listen in" because, while we can see into the Lounge, we can't hear anything.

Mind-blowing all the same. Though I'm not sure that it's less maddening to watch what's going on if I can't hear anything.

While Holt continues to futz with the remote from a seat behind me, I cross to the window-wall and put my hand up to the glass over Ax's figure. He's standing at the bar in the back with my father, nodding so much that he must feel like a bobblehead.

Just like Dad to monopolize the conversation.

Apparently, I suck at lip-reading because I can't make out a single word, and so I give up and decide to take a quick roll call of the people in the room. All four of my uncles are here. Plus Ax's father and the three other board members who aren't family, as well as Cole, one of my cousins that has been invited to join.

The only person missing is Hunter.

Well, and Holt would be in there, too, if things had gone down differently.

I wonder briefly if he has any regrets, but that thought gets lost when the door opens and another familiar face walks in.

"Hunter's here," I warn, in case Holt finds this whole spying thing less palatable with our half-brother in attendance.

Before he can reply, sounds of chatting and general commotion suddenly enter the room through speakers installed high on the walls. "And the Lord said, let there be sound."

"Pretty sure that's not what he said." *But oh my God, we can hear what's happening in the Lounge.* I mean, at the moment it's just a bunch of chatter with no discernable strings of conversation, but still. "Shit, Holt! This is so…." So many adjectives come to mind that I can't settle on one right away.

"Illegal?"

Illegal. Amazing. Creepy. Useful. Surprising and *predictable.* "…Sebastian," I say.

He pats the chair next to him on the front row. "Come, my fellow Sebastian, and take a seat. Looks like they're about to get started."

I give him shit as I cross to curl up beside him. "It's Morgan now. Could you get it right?"

"Too good for eavesdropping now, are you?"

"Never." The thought of spying on my husband without him knowing, though, does make me feel a spot of guilt. "I told Ax I trusted him. Maybe I shouldn't be here."

I don't make any move to leave.

"Your call." Holt rests his foot on the opposite knee. "But you didn't follow me up here because you didn't trust Ax, did you?"

"No. I followed you up here because you were the pied piper of secrecy, and I am a rat with a large appetite of curiosity."

He reaches over to the mini-fridge next to him—because of course there's a mini-fridge—pulls out a craft beer and tosses it to me. "And now you're drinking. You shouldn't be going anywhere, under the influence."

"And if I get one more WWI, they're going to take away my hall privileges."

"Walking While Intoxicated?" When I nod, he does too. "You'll have to be carried around everywhere, and that's terribly inconvenient."

I'm about to disagree—because inconvenient for whom? —when someone in the Lounge taps a glass with a spoon, like they do when they're trying to get everyone's attention. "Gentlemen, I'm sure no introductions are required," Dad says. "Let's welcome the man of the moment—Axel Morgan, our new Chief Executive Officer."

There's spattered applause as well as more clinking of glasses and stomping of feet.

Hunter, sitting alone at the bar, only sips on his drink.

He's the closest person to us, the details of his expressions easy to make out when he turns to face the mirror, which is fairly often. Probably every time he has a reaction he doesn't want the others to see.

It's weird and wrong to have this much of a close-up on him, but I already figured I was going to hell for the books I read, so what's another offense to add to my naughty list?

"Now Axel hasn't formally accepted our offer yet," Dad continues when the cheering has died down. "Would you like to take this moment to say a few words?"

This time there are shouts and calls for him to speak.

"Here we go," Holt says, popping a Raisinet in his mouth.

I gape at him. "Where did you get chocolate, and why aren't you sharing?"

He hands over the box. "Had it in my pocket. Shh. I want to hear this."

Like I don't?

But I pour a handful of somewhat melted chocolate-covered raisins in my hand and return the box in silence, eager not to miss a word.

"Thank you, everyone," Ax says when the room settles again. He goes on to express his gratitude for being selected and for recognizing his expertise and commitment to the company and then issues some compliments to board members.

Basically, ass kissing without being too obvious.

Soon he launches into words I've heard him practice. "Before I can formally accept this position, however, I want to revisit the plan to acquire another network."

"You don't think we should expand?" Henry asks, clearly wary.

Ax points at him. "I think we *should*. As long as we purchase the right company. And I don't believe it's SHE."

He proceeds, all ears and eyes trained on him as he explains why SCOOP, a fledgling news outfit in California, is a better target.

After a long list of advantages the company offers, he sums it up. "The lower price helps us maintain cash flow, their audience is younger, but it more cleanly crosses over to ours, and it will give us an opportunity to create the stronghold we've always wanted on the west coast."

Ax's father stirs his martini with a stick of olives. "Our demographics *are* weak once you get west of Colorado."

The comment spurs a few more around the room, statements that—in general—seem to support interest in pursuing SCOOP instead of SHE.

Ax showed us his research earlier this week. It wasn't hard to see the advantages of the proposed acquisition, and in less than fifteen minutes, both Holt and I were convinced that it is by far a better choice for SNC. We weren't as confident in Ax's ability to convince the family.

Hearing what's being said now, I wonder if we didn't give the board enough credit.

I throw a hopeful look to Holt now. "Can it be this easy?"

He doesn't answer, nodding for me to pay attention to the scene in front of us. I look around the room, trying to see what he's telling me to see without success.

And then I do see it—the exchanged glances between

Dad and Arthur. Henry's tap of the nose when he nods at Kevin. Cole's refusal to look anywhere but at his shoes.

"They've already made up their minds," I say, my stomach plummeting. "It doesn't matter what Ax says."

Sure enough, after a less than thorough debate about the pros and cons of switching gears, Dad slaps his hand on Ax's back. "These points are well thought out, Son. But we've seen the financial prospectives for SHE, and we truly believe it's the way to go. There's no need to try to sell us on anything else. Your first idea was gold."

With that, the room breaks into several conversations, everyone content to move on to more casual subjects.

When Ax tries to regain their attention, his voice is lost in the crowd. He shakes his head, clearly frustrated.

It's a frustration that I know all too well. How many times have I been silenced or ignored because I was a woman, or too young, or too naïve? I hate having to watch Ax be brushed off in the same way.

Silently, I vow to give everyone a voice when I run my own company.

Which is seeming more and more unlikely as the minutes pass.

But then someone knocks on a table, silencing the room. "Morgan's still talking," Hunter says, nodding toward Ax. "I think we should hear what he has to say."

Ax looks back toward the mirror—toward *us*—momentarily causing my heart to spasm until I realize he's just catching Hunter's eye, and I suspect that something passes between them that I don't have the insight to decipher.

A thought hits me, one I would never have considered

before Ax started trying to sway my mind about Hunter. "Is he...on *our* side?"

Holt doesn't seem so optimistic. "He probably just wants to give Ax every opportunity to hang himself."

"Yeah." Maybe.

Or maybe our brother's more complicated than either of us understand.

But now Ax has the room again, and I push away any other thoughts to listen to him.

"Here's the thing." Ax makes direct eye contact with several men before he goes on. "The optics are bad. SHE is a network focused on women's programming, specifically women between the ages of eighteen and thirty-four. Their audience has already been critical of the network's male owner, despite the fact that Bob Peterson is very hands-off, and other important voices have agreed that there need to be more women at the top in the news industry. There will be a lot of negative attention if the company is sold to a male-dominated organization.

"Looking around the room here, I think we can agree that's what we are."

There are a few laughs, a few pats on the back. A few strokes of dicks.

I open my mouth and stick two fingers in, pretending to vomit.

"Ditto," Holt says, but it doesn't seem very convincing when he pops another Raisinet in his mouth.

Ax gets the focus back easily, this time. "It makes us look like bullies, guys. It guarantees a loss of the very audience we're trying to obtain, which means all that money would be spent for nothing. We'll also have to spend more on PR to overcome the bad press, and we'll need to expect up to fifty percent turnover during the transfer process. I can't imagine any of the most popular newscasters and hosts staying."

The idea of losing money is never acceptable to the SNC board, but the grumbles and comments seem to indicate they're just as upset about the idea of not acquiring all the talent at SHE.

"What's that? Brystin might not come crawling back to us?" Holt asks in faux shock.

I dramatically throw my hand to my heart. "But why wouldn't she want to work in our toxic, male-dominated environment? We're antiquated, but still the best at everything!"

We're so busy laughing, that I don't notice the Electrical Room door opening until a gruff voice says, "You two!"

I jump to my feet, stunned to find the man behind the voice in the doorway is none other than Grandpa Irving.

CHAPTER
THIRTY-TWO
ADLY

'm pretty sure my life flashes before my eyes.

If Grandpa's here, I have to be in trouble.

There's also an inexplicable smell of...buttered popcorn?

Maybe coming from the Lounge, though I haven't seen anyone start the machine up, and anyway, it's the least of my concerns.

Seemingly unruffled by our guest, Holt waves to the man peeking over Grandpa's shoulder. "Hey, Elias."

"Hey," Grandpa's assistant answers.

Panicked and caught, I search for an excuse for being here, something to say to counteract the trouble that I'm most probably in. "No wheelchair today, Grandpa?"

I've said before I'm not good at thinking on my feet.

He shuffles in, using the wall for support as he climbs to the top row of chairs. "Sometimes a man needs the full power of his height." He sits down directly behind me. "Figured I'd find you two here. What did I miss?"

I'm still reeling about our new arrivals, and don't even try to answer.

Holt, on the other hand, launches into a recap, only to be interrupted a few words in. "You make a better door than a window, girl," Grandpa snaps.

Chastened, I fall back into my seat so he can see over me into the room.

"Much better. Elias?" This time Grandpa snaps with his fingers as well as his voice, and Elias, who has followed Grandpa up to the top row of chairs, hands over a bag of popcorn.

Not the microwave kind, either, but from an actual movie theater.

"What is going on here?" I mutter to Holt, too low for Grandpa's hearing aids to pick it up clearly.

Which is probably why Grandpa assumes I've said something else. "If you wanted your own damn popcorn, you could have gotten it yourself."

Despite his words, he hands the bag out for us to grab some for ourselves.

I take some, obviously, because Raisinets are infinitely better when mixed with popcorn.

Holt's mouth is still full when Grandpa nudges him with a thump to the head—a *soft* thump, but enough to send Holt into a fit of coughing. "You were catching me up, remember?"

Holt holds up a finger until he's taken a sip of his beer and is able to speak again. "So right now they're discussing the negative optics attached to SNC going after—"

He's midway through his first sentence when Dad starts talking in the Lounge, and once again Grandpa thumps Holt's head, this time to silence him. "Shh. We're missing it."

I'm too invested in what's happening in the Lounge to give any more thought to the strangeness that is Grandpa sharing his popcorn while we spy on a room that I never knew existed before today, despite having practically grown up in this building.

Munching quietly, I turn all my attention to Dad.

"...ultimately a problem for SHE, not for SNC. Differences in corporate philosophy always arise when one company absorbs another company. We don't change the way we've done business for thirty years to capitulate to the ideas of a fledgling company."

"Oh my God, he is so old!" I mean Dad's way of thinking, but remembering who's behind me, I throw a, "No offense, Grandpa," to the back row.

Holt adds, "Uh...Blockbuster, anyone?"

Cole seems to be thinking along the same lines when he speaks in response to Dad. "So we just let ourselves be eradicated from history and not acknowledge changing attitudes and behavior?"

Ax points at Cole. "That right there! We can't forget when Blockbuster didn't take a little company called Netflix seriously."

He pauses to let the room have a chuckle about one of the largest media mistakes in history.

Holt sits up like he'd just come up with a million dollar answer. "Did I not just—?"

He's silenced by another thump from Grandpa. "Zippit, boy!"

When the room settles, Ax goes on. "The problem is that you want to advance. But you can't just bow down to every new method that comes along, without knowing if that method is going to pan out."

SHE is going to pan out. I know it will.

I don't bother saying it out loud because I don't want to be thumped on the head, but also, is that what Ax thinks? Does he not have faith?

Wiping my now-empty, popcorn-greasy hand on the bottom of my skirt, I sit forward, as if that will help me hear better.

"So here's my suggestion," Ax says, and I swear I hold my breath. "Put your eggs in both baskets. The Sebastian name is what holds all the credence, does it not? You already have Holt working at SHE. Brystin will be a Sebastian soon. If Adly takes over as CEO and gives critics what they're asking for—a woman at the helm—then just like that, you have a second Sebastian stronghold. Let *them* buy the company. Let *them* take the risk."

Ax has the Lounge captivated.

A giggle bubbles inside me as I see where Ax is going.

"Oh…this is good," Holt whispers. Apparently, he doesn't want to get thumped anymore either.

I nod, afraid that speaking at all will break the spell Ax has the room under, despite not even being in the same room.

Uncle Arthur pooh-poohs. "Adly and Holt can't afford that price tag."

"She has her trust fund now," Hunter says. He doesn't

bother turning his head toward them, so I can see the twitch of a smile on his lips.

Because he thinks he's throwing me to the wolves, or because he's actually trying to help? Impossible to know.

Reynard perks up at that, his eyes calculating. For good or bad or neutral, I think I just witnessed him figuring out why Ax and I got married.

"Well, maybe that's enough," August says.

Ax waves his hand, dismissing the conversation about money. "That's their problem. Not ours. They can find investors. They can raise the funds. The point is that we don't take on any of the risk, but the Sebastian name still gets the benefits."

"Adly as CEO?" Henry shakes his head. "How old is she, again? You just got married. She should be working on birthing your babies, not running companies."

My chest feels warm with rage. Behind me, I swear I hear Grandpa growl.

"Isn't she already pregnant?" Arthur asks.

"I think that was just a rumor, Arty," August says.

Ax ignores the stray comments to address Henry directly. "Sir, if and when my wife ever decides she wants to have babies, I guarantee she'll take three weeks off and be back in the office with the kid strapped to her back."

I preen, despite myself.

Also, I might get a little choked up. Nothing a swig of beer doesn't wash away.

There are quite a few men in the Lounge that don't take it for a compliment, and while I can't make out the exact comments, the tone of their grumbling and the expressions on their faces make it clear how they feel.

It's a terrible feeling—being smug about who I am while also knowing that the traits I'm most proud of are the ones that disappoint some of my family most. It makes me question my identity sometimes. Shakes my confidence.

The look on Ax's face says he's feeling all that for me in my place. "I know this isn't your way," he says. "This is the new way. This is the new basket. You don't want anything to do with it? Let it happen over there."

He grows serious, not that he wasn't before. "But these new ways *are* happening. Because of the philosophies of this organization, there are opportunities that are unavailable here, leaving the younger generation of Sebastians unprepared."

"*Philosophies* is code for misogyny," Holt declares, and this time I'm the one who kicks him to be quiet.

Ax moves from the bench he'd been perched on to face the men, giving us a primo view of his backside that is only trumped by the words coming out of his mouth. "Letting Adly go somewhere else where she can thrive and grow and command without the barriers that exist here, is a win for her and a win for the family name. Not to mention that I'm sure every one of you would like your own to have the chance at happiness, wherever they may find it."

"Not at the expense of business," Henry says.

"Never at the expense of business," I grumble.

"No expense to the business at all," Ax reminds him, "since they would be their own entity."

There are definitely board members who are interested in this proposition. I catch snatches of individual conversations that include phrases like "real strategic thinking" and "creative solution to our women problem."

But not everyone's shares on the board are equal.

Cole and Hunter have bigger shares than the non-family members. My uncles all have equal but bigger shares than Cole and Hunter, except for Arthur, whose share is as big as my father's since the two of them ran SNC for most of their careers.

Then there's Grandpa, who still holds the majority shares, but he's officially been a silent board member for the last twenty-five-plus years. It's in writing that he can't vote, so it's not like he can walk in and overrule any time he wants to. His shares don't count where the board is concerned.

It will change whenever he departs this life and the shares are passed down, though, and everyone is very aware that his will can still easily be changed.

But that's the future.

At present, the votes that matter are Dad's and the uncles', and as I watch the expressions on their faces as they consult, the buds of hope that had blossomed only a few minutes ago inside my chest start to wither and die.

I'm already braced for the worst when my father stands to address the room. "There is merit to the way you think, Ax. This vision of yours has legs. It could very well go the way you've suggested, bolstering the family name across the board."

I exchange a look of shock with Holt. He takes my hand, and we squeeze each other until our knuckles are white.

But then Daddy goes on. "The experience in this room, however, says that people will think the worst, rather than the best. Having members of our family associated with a network that we don't own makes us look divided and broken and weak. The only way to ensure our power remains intact is to keep the family united."

"Translation—imprisoned," Holt mumbles next to me, stealing the words from my mouth.

Is it really any wonder that I have such a hard time trusting people when the family attitude is that everyone is the worst?

Then Dad makes the statement that's meant to put the entire discussion to rest. "Acquiring SHE is a nonnegotiable if you are to have the CEO position in this company, Ax."

I should have seen it coming, but I audibly gasp.

"Then I'm afraid, sir," Ax says, in a much more polite tone than I would be able to muster, "that this role isn't meant for me."

In a small, secret room, with a stupid kernel of popcorn stuck in my teeth and while my hand is being crushed by my brother, my heart breaks.

It's bad enough when my family is fucking over my dreams. It's a whole other thing when they're fucking over the man I love's dreams.

What's even the point of this sacrifice? So neither Ax nor I get what we want? That doesn't make things better.

"I'm sorry," Holt says quietly.

Grandpa's hand settles comfortingly on my shoulder.

Then Ax turns around to face the mirror, and this time he doesn't look at Hunter—he looks directly at me.

As if he can tell I'm crushed and teary-eyed, he smiles.

As if he knows I'm here, and he's reminding me it's all going to be okay.

A tear runs down my cheek, just as Grandpa stands up behind me. "That's my cue."

Cue?

Elias helps Grandpa out of his seat and down the step toward the door.

I turn to Holt. "Grandpa's here because of Ax?"

He shrugs, and then points to the screen...er, window.

I look up just as Dad approaches Ax. There's a lot of noise in the room at present, but I strain my ears and can make out the conversation.

"It's too bad that you have to let your emotions get in the way of an opportunity like this," Dad says, shaking my husband's hand.

With a grin on his face, Ax replies, "It's too bad that you don't have emotions."

Holt laughs.

I'm too...too a lot of things, really. Pissed? Disappointed? Motivated? Lit up?

"Holt," I say, letting myself consider crossing a line that I have always thought too far. "Have you ever thought about the family secrets?"

"What about them?"

"Making them less secret?" I spin my head toward him to gage his reaction.

His brows are raised in surprise, but before he can respond, Ax once again addresses the room. "Well, gentlemen. If we're done here, I'm going to..."

He nods toward the door, which is out of view from where I'm sitting. His expression changes, though, indicating that there's something interesting in that direction.

Or someone interesting.

Ax turns back to the room. "I really wish I didn't have to do this, but you've left me no choice."

He walks out of view, toward Grandpa's booming voice. "Boys, it's time we have a talk about your inheritance."

There is almost nothing I'd rather witness than my uncles being put in their place by my grandfather, but right now, all I care about is my husband.

I bolt from my chair and run out of the room, just in time to meet Ax coming out of the room next to me.

When his eyes hit mine, he's surprised. Then elated.

And then I'm not paying attention to his expression because I'm too busy running into his arms. "I heard every word," I say, gripping him tighter than I ever have.

"The secret room?" he asks.

I pull back to look at him. "You know about...?" Of course he does. That's why he signaled Grandpa.

With a sigh of emotion, I cup Ax's face with my palm "You were incredible. All of your points were smart and nuanced and just amazing."

"I think it's pretty safe to say that they won't be going after SHE."

Ax's confidence stirs my optimism. Threatening his sons' inheritance is a power move that Grandpa rarely pulls out, after all.

On the other hand, I'm not sure how far the move carries, and I don't want to get my hopes up that everything will be wrapped up in a perfect bow.

Especially when Ax sacrificed so much. "But your job! Will you—"

He cuts me off with a finger to my lips. "We said we'd be okay, no matter what happened. Remember?"

I'm about to argue. When I'd made that statement, it had only been my job on the line.

But then I remember what I heard today, what my father said. What he was willing to sacrifice for the sake of "the family name."

Does family even mean anything when its members care more about money and power and status than about each other? Is that the kind of entity that I feel compelled to protect?

Point is, I have options.

"Yeah," I tell Ax. "We'll be okay."

I'm not sure the same can be said about the rest of the Sebastians.

Only time will tell.

CHAPTER
THIRTY-THREE
ADLY

Ax and I don't stick around to witness the aftermath of Grandpa's talk with his "boys." It's a chance for me to practice trusting that things will work out, and while it's not the easiest thing I've ever done, I'm giving it a try.

Ax is a good distraction, it turns out.

When I get out of bed the next morning, I'm exhausted, but not because I spent the night tossing and turning and worrying.

Well, tossing and turning, maybe, but definitely not in a bad way.

After that, it's like dominoes falling how everything comes in line—from the pancakes that we don't burn, to the all-green-lights drive to work (a real plus when getting naughty in the back seat), to the line-free wait for the employee elevator, to arriving to still-hot coffee from Sassy who actually showed up for work on time.

At exactly seven after ten in the morning, Holt texts.

> Grandpa came through!

A few minutes later he calls with the details. "Bob Peterson reached out to let me know he's accepted our bid. There are no competitors. You are officially about to become the CEO of your very own business, sis!"

After about six months of legal runaround where a hundred other obstacles could potentially pop up, anyway, but his point is that SNC is not going to be a problem for us.

I actually cry.

"The threat to their inheritance actually changed their mind?"

He seems to understand me even through my blubbering. "The tipoff that the FTC has promised to file antitrust lawsuits if SNC tries to acquire SHE might have scared them off as well."

"Grandpa really does know how to hit them where it hurts."

"That wasn't Grandpa." The smugness in his tone gives him away.

"Wow, Holt! I didn't know you had it in you." That's a lie, obviously. Of course he had it in him. He's a Sebastian, after all.

As excited and terrified and over the moon as I am about SHE, there are still bows that need to be tied. Tentatively, I ask the question I'm pretty sure I already know the answer to. "...and Ax?"

I can hear the puff of air Holt blows out before replying. "I'm sorry, AJ. Seems that a few of them are feeling spiteful.

No one likes to get their ass handed to them by their nona-genarian father."

I refuse to let it burst my bubble. I hoped it would work out differently, but I didn't expect that it would. As Ax pointed out yesterday—it's a bad idea to put all your eggs in one basket.

As soon as I hang up the phone, I get to work. First I print the resignation letter that has been waiting on my hard drive for more than two months.

After that, I open a brand new Word document and make a list.

A long list.

A much longer list than I anticipated making, in the end.

Then I put both of the documents in a manila folder and head upstairs to my father's office. It's another domino falling into place when his assistant informs me that, "Samuel is free and able to see you now."

Excellent.

"Adly, my dear." He's behind his desk, but he stands to greet me.

We haven't spoken since before the board meeting yesterday, and while he doesn't know that I saw the whole thing, he's got to believe that Ax filled me in, and I can tell from his tone that he's planning damage control.

I imagine the excuses for Ax's revoked promotion on the tip of his tongue:

I got ahead of myself when I made the announcement.

The decision hadn't been finalized.

These things happen in business. It's complicated. Let the men handle it, darling.

Crossing to face him from the other side of his desk, I cut him off at the pass. "Daddy, would you say that all you want is for me to be happy?"

He frowns at me like it's the most absurd thing I could ask. "Absolutely, honey. It's all any parent wants for their child."

I gag internally.

The funny thing is that I think he really means it. He doesn't see the disconnect between his actions and my happiness because he can't believe that I could know what I want and need better than he could.

Unfortunately, I don't think he's the only man with this outlook.

Instead of calling him out on it as I'd love to do—partly because I'm well aware it won't get me anywhere—I open my folder and pull out the first document. "Then I'm sure you'll be elated to know how exceedingly happy it makes me to give this to you."

And then I hand over my signed resignation letter.

It's a six-week notice because I'm not an asshole. Besides, the finalized purchase for SHE will take much longer than that, and I'd rather leave things clean behind me so I can truly look forward without baggage.

Probably not something my father understands or appreciates, but I take pride in my work ethic, with or without his approval.

"What's this?" His forehead furrows as he skims through what I've written.

It only states I'm resigning and not why, which I'm more than willing to share with him.

"I'm buying SHE. With Alex and Holt. Our bid was accepted this morning. Yes, I know Ax mentioned it to you. He was really doing you all a favor, giving you the opportunity to see the upside of having the Sebastian name at a competing network, though this has been in the works for a while."

"Adly, now—" He has the stern, "puffed" look he always gets when he's mad.

I'm a thirty-three-year-old married woman who doesn't need to be lectured by her father or her boss, so I shut that down real fast. "I'm sure you have lots of thoughts and feelings about it, Daddy, despite how very much you want me to be happy. I'll have Sassy send over a list of therapists that are in-network if you need someone to talk to about it."

His mouth opens and shuts like he's too taken aback for words, and this isn't even the good part.

While he stammers, I open my manila folder and take out the other document. "You'll want to sit down for this one. It's quite long, and this is the only chance I'm giving you to discuss it with me, so buckle up. We're in for a ride."

He does sit.

As do I.

Only fifteen minutes later, we come to an agreement. Much sooner than I'd anticipated. Another domino falling in place.

When I stand to leave, he remains seated behind his desk, a scowl etched so deeply on his features, I'm not sure it will ever go away. "Your mother would be ashamed of you."

I don't know why he thinks bringing up a woman I've

never known will have any effect on me. "My mother's dead," I say plainly. "See item four on the list you just read."

His eyes slit. "Well, she's rolling in her grave."

"And so is yours." I reconsider. "Or maybe they're both so beyond us and our petty family politics that they've tuned us both out. Let's pray that's the case. Otherwise, I have to believe they didn't make it to heaven."

Because let's face it, watching the Sebastians struggle through life has got to be hell.

Though, I do imagine it's entertaining as well.

"And Daddy, you're leaving soon for your tee time, aren't you?" He's golfed on most Friday afternoons for the last ten years, if not longer.

He grumbles something incoherent. Cursing me out under his breath, most likely. "I may be late, considering the phone calls your request requires."

At least he's calling it a request instead of blackmail.

More importantly, his office will be free later this afternoon.

"Better get on it, then." I address him over my shoulder as I cross to leave. "Call me when it's done, please. And happy golfing!"

I actually do hope he enjoys his game. He's still my father, and unlike him, I like seeing the people I love get to do the things they love.

That's exactly what I'm thinking about when I text Ax after Dad calls me with the all clear.

> Give me twenty minutes then meet me in the place it all began.

Outside Dad's office once again, I pray I wasn't overconfident. The lights are off and his assistant has gone for the day, but there is still a security code to enter.

Being the notorious snoop that I am, I've tried to break in before. Obviously. I've tried all the dates that I thought might be important to Dad—the day he married Mom, the day she died, the day he married Giulia, his mother's birthday, his mother's death day, his kids' birthdates—nothing worked.

Then Holt pointed out yesterday that Dad was too lazy to change the security on the Electrical Room when he returned as the acting CEO, and that had me curious. Could it really be possible he never changed the code on his office either?

Holding my breath, I enter in Hunter's birthday, and voila. The door opens.

Sometimes it's so much easier than it should be.

I didn't have the same confidence that there would still be hidden liquor from when Holt occupied the space, so the new bottle of 30-year double cask Macallan in my hands came from home. I'd purchased it a while ago for a special occasion, having become fond of it after that December night with Ax.

When he appears in the doorway, I'm seated in Dad's chair, my feet propped on the desk, scotch in hand. "Looking for this?"

Without missing a beat, he answers similarly to how I'd replied back then. "Not after it's had your dirty mouth all over it."

"You didn't seem to have a problem with my mouth

when it was wrapped around your cock this morning." I've already gone off script.

The smile on his filthy smug lips says he doesn't mind.

He closes the door behind him and prowls toward me. "You know, your father will have your job if he catches you in his office."

I gasp dramatically. "Oh, dear. It's too bad I already handed in my resignation letter, isn't it?"

"You got it?! SHE? The bid went through?" His entire face glows. Like when my cousin Reid looks at Lina. It's super gross, and I'm one thousand percent a sucker for it when it's Ax looking at me that way.

"No competing bids," I say, as proudly as if I had made it happen by myself.

"That's incredible, baby. I'm so happy for you." He stands next to me, expectantly, and when I don't jump into his arms as he likely expects, he spins the chair toward him, forcing my feet off the desk.

Then he leans over, caging me in when he braces a hand on either arm of the chair.

His eyes are dark and hooded as he peers at me, and my skin tingles with anticipation. "You should kick me out of this seat," I tell him.

"So that I can rail you over the desk? Don't worry, I'm already choreographing how that will happen in my head."

Nudging him backward, I stand. "That does sound nice, but no." With a little choreography of my own, the bottle of scotch is on the desk, I'm facing Ax, the chair is behind him, and with a little push, he falls into it. "Because it's *your* seat."

He's smart, so he knows that I'm trying to tell him that the CEO job is his after all.

I'm smart, too, so I'm prepared when he cocks his head at me and sighs. "Addles…"

Straddling him, I climb onto his lap and cut him off with a short kiss. "Don't. I know what you're going to say. And just don't."

"Then go ahead and tell me."

"You're going to say that you don't want the job anymore. You can't be the leader of a company that chooses to operate out of fear. And that you especially can't work for a board comprised of traditionalists and misogynists. And you really can't work for people who are so willing to put knives in the backs of their family."

"Hm. I guess you do know what I was going to say." He appears genuinely surprised.

As if I don't know him by now.

"It's noble." I smooth his lapel with my hand as I talk. "And I don't doubt that you feel that way, which really does make me melt, but I also know that more than one thing can be true at the same time, and that you really want to do this job. You know you will kill at it. You will turn this company on its head, and it will take time, but you will bring about change.

"And I need you to do that, Ax. Because this network is part of my family legacy, and I need you to make this a better place so that one day, our daughter can sit in this seat without having to punch through ceilings." For the second time in one day, my eyes are misty.

It's Ax's fault, because his eyes are misty too. "If she wants to, you mean. She should have the option."

"Yeah. She should have all the options. She could decide to run the bookstore instead."

"Or something else entirely different."

"That would be cool too."

He wipes a tear from my cheek, frames my face with his hands, and presses a long kiss to my lips.

When he pulls away to study me, I know I've convinced him. "How did you get the board to change their minds?"

It's my turn to be surprised. "How do you know it was me and not Grandpa?"

"Because the old man called me this morning to say he did what he could, but he wasn't a magician."

I don't know if that's exactly true. He seems pretty damn magic to me.

"I put two and two together," Ax continues, "And figured it meant Grandpa could only save one—SHE or my job—not both. I'm glad he picked the one he did."

"Me too. Because then I got to be the one who saved the job."

"Adly Jade... Please tell me it didn't cost you too much." It's clear he's not talking about money.

"Nothing at all," I say, brightly. "It was you who inspired me, actually. I mean, you did pretty much black-mail me into marrying you."

"You *blackmailed* your family?"

"I know, right?" I had expected to feel icky about it, but I don't. "I'm not sure why I didn't do it sooner. Thought I was better than the rest of them or something."

He pulls my hips closer as he lifts his mouth to press a kiss on my temple. "You *are* better than the rest of them."

"Well, *of course* I'm better than them. But it turns out it doesn't matter if I'm better if I don't speak their language. So I put it in terms they'd understand."

That last part I might have learned from Grandpa.

"You are fucking incredible." Ax gazes at me like I just invented a new form of currency. "What did you hold over them? There are so many things to choose from, and that's just the things I know."

"All of them. I waffled between a couple at first, unsure which would have the most impact, and when I couldn't narrow it down, I made a list of every family secret I knew, that I was willing to share, and asked Dad what he thought the board might be willing to give me to keep them quiet.

"He hadn't even finished reading the list before he caved. Got you an extra mill added to your salary too."

"Damn, woman." It's clear he's impressed.

Admittedly, I feel pretty damn smug myself.

The truth is, though, that Ax really is my inspiration. "Look, you really outdid yourself when you grand-gestured me a bookstore. I was determined to prove my love as well."

He brushes a strand of hair from my face then cups my chin. "You proved it the minute you let me in."

I purposefully roll my eyes. "Boring. This gesture reads better."

Then, partly because my legs are starting to fall asleep, I push out of his lap and circle around the desk to take him in.

It's weird seeing another man behind my father's desk. It's not Ax's style at all, and I imagine he will replace it with something more modern and stylish—as well as the chair and the carpet and...the whole interior, really—but even without those details in place, with the New York skyline behind him, he looks like he was born to be in command.

"How does it feel, Mr. CEO?" I bite my lip so that I don't start crying again. I'm just so proud and happy, and also I can't help thinking about my own desk—the one I'll be sitting behind one day soon, across town, in a much different building.

It's not just the beginning of a new chapter for us. It's a whole new freaking book.

Fitting, too, that where it all began is where it begins again.

Ax seems similarly moved. "It's, uh...it's..." He shakes his head, as if just as determined not to be emotional, and spins around slowly, taking in his view. "Anyway."

When he turns back to face me, there's a different look in his eyes. The one that makes my skin hot and my pussy squirm.

"Mrs. Morgan." It's that bossy voice of his that turns my insides into mush. "I hope you didn't come in here to beg for an extension on the payroll budgets."

I'd be lying if I said I hadn't thought we might end up playing.

Like a switch, I'm tuned in and turned on. "Please, sir. I've been so busy. There was a holiday and a wedding and a deviant sex god who kept distracting me."

"Tell me more about this deviant sex god." It's a rare slip of character that has me fighting a smile before he's back in his role. "I mean, excuses, excuses, excuses."

I brace my hands on his desk, leaning forward so he can get a better view of my tits. "You don't understand, sir. I need this job. There has to be something I can do to make it right."

Ax flicks his tongue along the bottom lip of that wicked mouth of his. "I'm sure we could make a bargain of some sort."

Then he reaches for his belt buckle.

It's long after everyone else has left the building before *my boss* and I come to an arrangement.

Needless to say, we're both quite satisfied.

EPILOGUE
ADLY

Eighteen hours later

At home, that weekend, we talk about us.

Rather, we negotiate.

We're in the bedroom with a bunch of flameless candles lit—Ax's idea because he knows I'd never admit that I like real-life romance. Not for the first time, we're drinking Macallan straight from the bottle rather than using shot glasses.

It is the first time we've done this naked.

"Kids?" Ax asks. He's on his stomach, his head propped in one hand while the other draws lazy spirals on my thigh.

I'm sitting against the headboard with my legs stretched out, admiring the view of his ass. "Mm...what was that?" I replay the words—word—he just said, in my head. *Kids.* "Yes, please. You?"

"Hell, yeah. I'll knock you up tonight, if you want."

I actually believe he's trying to curtail his enthusiasm. He really wants kids.

He'd make a hell of a dad, too. There's a pang in the area of my uterus, just thinking about it.

"How about give me a couple of years?" I'm absolutely picturing myself at work with a baby strapped to my back, but not when I'm first starting out.

I do believe that I can do anything. Just not all at the same time.

"Of course. We have time."

Well. There is such a thing as a biological clock, and mine is ticking, but that isn't the only way to be a parent.

"I wouldn't mind adopting, either," I say, to make sure we're on the same page about that. "There are so many kids that need homes, and there are plenty of other Sebastians to pass down that DNA."

On the other hand, my life would be complete if the baby in my arms smiled up at me with Ax's mouth.

He scrunches up his face as he considers. "We still get to keep fucking, though, right?"

"Duh."

He shifts to painting long strokes down my leg with his palm. "I want family with you, Adly. It doesn't have to be the traditional definition."

Yep. I'm wet.

"I think we're in agreement then." I lift up the bottle. "*Salute*," we say.

I drink and hold it out to Ax.

He climbs up the bed to sit next to me before taking it.
Bye-bye, nice view.

After he chugs his swallow, he kisses me. That's the addition to the game, we've decided. Agree, *salute*, kiss.

Frankly, with those lips of his, we should have been doing it this way all along.

When the kiss is over, Ax bends one of his legs and stretches the other out beside me. "We staying here?"

Momentary panic rushes through me. I love my apartment. I've put so much into my apartment. It's the first thing that was ever truly mine, and I can't imagine letting it go or living somewhere else.

But then I take a breath and remind myself that all new beginnings are born out of endings. Even the best books have to be put on the shelf so that another can be read.

I glance around the room, forcing myself to look for the ways I've grown out of the place. "It would be nice to have more closet space."

"There's no room for a baby here."

"And SHE is all the way downtown." Which is a reason to move sooner rather than later, as far as I'm concerned. Though, this apartment is only a short drive to SNC, so Ax would have to compromise. "Something in Chelsea?"

"That's about the distance I was traveling when I was living with Hunter." He lifts the bottle, his brow questioning.

I nod.

"*Salute.*" He takes a swig. "I'll call a real estate agent on Monday."

This time the kiss is longer, and I'm starting to think we might be nearing the end of this negotiation session.

We've accomplished a lot already. We've also made decisions about religious affiliations (Catholic church for Palm Sunday, Easter, and Christmas, and we agreed to do the marriage prep that Grandpa got us out of) and political positions (we have different ideas on the party system, but both agree to always vote), and we had a lengthy discussion on investment strategy that nearly ended in a fight.

Until I straddled Ax's face and gave him something else to do with his mouth besides piss me off.

Strangely, we were *both* more amenable after I'd had two orgasms.

Now that we've discussed all the usual points of contention in relationships—something we never got the chance to do before this since we never dated—I'm feeling pretty good about our chances at a future together.

Just one more thing he needs to know. "Extended family is still important to me, Ax." Warts and all, I can't just disavow my father and his brothers. They're too much a part of me.

Fortunately, Ax understands. "As it should be. They're important to me, too."

"I'll want to go to all their stupid events."

"I'll be right by your side."

"And I'll be by your side when you reach out to your sister." I grin at him like I've caught him in my trap.

He doesn't miss a beat. "So then you'll try to work things out with Hunter?"

Fuck, maybe I was caught in *his* trap. "Oh, you're good."

I have the advantage, though, since Ax believes it will be a while before things are okay between them again.

"Sure," I promise. "I'll try."

"Salute."

He sets the bottle down on the nightstand and pulls me over his lap for this kiss. Straddling him, I can feel his cock as it thickens underneath me, so I'm surprised when he breaks away for more conversation.

"We're really doing this, then, aren't we?" He brushes a stray piece of hair from my lips. "Making a go of this husband and wife thing?"

After everything we've just discussed, a silly bit of doubt niggles at me. "If you would rather—"

He cuts me off. "There is *nothing* I'd rather. I'm locked in for the duration, Addlecat. You can't see it, but there's an invisible tattoo that says *forever*, right here." He points to the skin above his heart.

"That's pretty fucking romantic, actually." *Doubt officially unwarranted.* Not to be outdone, I point to the skin above my heart. "Mine says...HEA."

"What does that mean?"

Obviously, I haven't schooled him well enough. "It means happily ever after."

Abruptly, he pushes me to my back and stretches out over me. "Is that how we live, Addles? Happily ever after?"

I nod emphatically, too moved to talk, and then too busy doing other things to want to talk.

I mean, I can't see into the future or anything, but I'm choosing to believe we will.

Wait. That can't be it! There are so many things you still

want to know about Ax and Adly, but most of those questions involve a certain Sebastian, don't they?

You'll have to grab the final installment in the Brutal Billionaires series---Brutal Bastard---to find out what happens with Hunter and his plans to Get Even.

Spoiler: the alphahole we all love to hate might just meet the woman who will bring him to his knees.

Meanwhile, sign up for my new release newsletter at this link to get a bonus epilogue that gives readers a quick glimpse at Adly and Ax's future, plus access to all my bonus scenes.

AUTHOR'S NOTE

Under the Cover is a real live bookstore!

It's just not located in Brooklyn. It's in Kansas City, Missouri, but almost every other detail is the same, including the reading nook and the Stevie Nicks mural and the upbeat, quirky manager named Carly (Morton) who is featured in the book is really the owner (smut peddler).

I highly recommend readers stop by if you're ever in town. The store has been covered nationally, as have several other romance themed stores around the country recently, not only because romance rocks (duh) but also because this is an age and time when women are carving out their own spaces in the world, particularly where sex is concerned. These stores are designed for us and by us (people in our community), and like Adly, I truly find these spots to be my happy place.

Cheers to romance bookstores (salute!), and keep your eyes and ears open, because who knows? One day I might have a bookstore of my own.

xo Laurelin

WANT MORE SEBASTIANS?

Meet the Sebastians in a world of power, sex, secrets, and brutal billionaires

Man in Charge - Scott Sebastian office romance, boss/employee romance, alpha billionaire, arrogant playboy heir, public spice

Man for Me - Brett Sebastian billionaire romance, friends to lovers, office romance, he fell first, short read/novella

Brutal Billionaire - Holt Sebastian billionaire romance, imagined love triangle, boss/employee, forbidden, morally grey, alphahole, "good girl"

Dirty Filthy Billionaire - Steele Sebastian billionaire romance, kinky, class differences, "you owe me", short read/novella

Brutal Secret - Reid Sebastian billionaire romance, forbidden, age-gap, curvy girl, forced proximity, first time, awkward heroine, obsessed hero, new adult, no third act breakup

Brutal Arrangement - Alex Sebastian billionaire romance, forbidden, brother's girl, obsessed hero, good girl to bad girl, morally grey, pop star, alphahole, imagined love triangle

Brutal Bargain - Adly Sebastian marriage of convenience, forbidden romance, enemies to lovers, he falls first, brother's best friend, fake relationship, forced proximity, family saga, billionaire Romance

Brutal Bastard - Hunter Sebastian coming soon

Check out the Sebastian family tree at www.laurelinpaige.com/sebastian-family-tree

ALSO BY LAURELIN PAIGE

WONDERING WHAT TO READ NEXT? I CAN HELP!

Visit www.laurelinpaige.com for content warnings and a more detailed reading order.

Brutal Billionaires

Brutal Billionaire - a standalone (Holt Sebastian)

Dirty Filthy Billionaire - a novella (Steele Sebastian)

Brutal Secret - a standalone (Reid Sebastian)

Brutal Arrangement - a standalone (Alex Sebastian)

Brutal Bargain - a standalone (Ax Morgan)

Brutal Bastard - a standalone (Hunter Sebastian)

The Dirty Universe

Dirty Duet (Donovan Kincaid)

Dirty Filthy Rich Men | Dirty Filthy Rich Love

Kincaid

Dirty Games Duet (Weston King)

Dirty Sexy Player | Dirty Sexy Games

Dirty Sweet Duet (Dylan Locke)

Sweet Liar | Sweet Fate

(Nate Sinclair) Dirty Filthy Fix (a spinoff novella)

Dirty Wild Trilogy (Cade Warren)

Wild Rebel | Wild War | Wild Heart

Men in Charge

Man in Charge

Man for Me (a spinoff novella)

The Fixed Universe

Fixed Series (Hudson & Alayna)

Fixed on You | Found in You | Forever with You | Hudson | Fixed Forever

Found Duet (Gwen & JC) Free Me | Find Me

(Chandler & Genevieve) Chandler (a spinoff novel)

(Norma & Boyd) Falling Under You (a spinoff novella)

(Nate & Trish) Dirty Filthy Fix (a spinoff novella)

Slay Series (Celia & Edward)

Rivalry | Ruin | Revenge | Rising

(Gwen & JC) The Open Door (a spinoff novella)

(Camilla & Hendrix) Slash (a spinoff novella)

First and Last

First Touch | Last Kiss

Hollywood Standalones

One More Time

Close

Sex Symbol

Star Struck

———————

Written with Kayti McGee

Dating Season

Miss Match | Love Struck | MisTaken | Holiday for Hire

———————

Written with Sierra Simone

Porn Star | Hot Cop

ABOUT LAURELIN PAIGE

With millions of books sold, Laurelin Paige is the NY Times, Wall Street Journal, and USA Today Bestselling Author of the Fixed Trilogy. She's a sucker for a good romance and gets giddy anytime there's kissing, much to the embarrassment of her three daughters. Her husband doesn't seem to complain, however. When she isn't reading or writing sexy stories, she's probably singing, watching shows like Kaos or House of Dragons or dreaming of Michael Fassbender. She's also a proud member of Mensa International though she doesn't do anything with the organization except use it as material for her bio.

www.laurelinpaige.com
laurelinpaigeauthor@gmail.com

Made in the USA
Columbia, SC
27 October 2024